KOREA AT WAR

Conflicts That Shaped the World

Michael

TUTTLE Publishing

Tokyo | Rutland, Vermont | Singapore

Contents

Korea, a peaceful, isolated society, was forced into the modern world of imperialism. Defeating China and Russia for control of the strategic peninsula, Japan annexed Korea after putting down armed resistance from makeshift Korean guerillas.

The four decades of Japanese rule saw the emergence of an intense, passionate Korean nationalism and the militarization of Korean society. Korean nationalists became divided in their vision of a modern nation, a division that laid the foundations for future conflict.

At the end of World War II, the U.S. and Soviet Union partitioned Korea and fostered the creation of two separate client states. These new states North and South Korea were divided by ideology and geopolitical orientation but united in the desire to reunify the nation by force if necessary.

North and South Korea were engaged in a low-key war since their independence in 1948; a full-scale war began with the North Korean invasion of the South on June 25, 1950. North Korea's attempt at reunification by force failed when the U.S. intervened, and in turn, the U.S./UN armed forces' effort to reunify the country failed when China intervened.

After a two-year stalemate, North Korea, its ally China and the U.S. agreed to a ceasefire. However, the war did not end as both North Korea and South Korea were still determined to reunify their nation under their own regimes.

After the ceasefire of 1953, both North and South Korea worked on modernizing and industrializing their halves of the peninsula while focusing on the long-range goal of reunification. The tension between the two remained high with many, often violent incidents, mostly provoked by the North.

From the mid-1970s South Korea economically surpassed the North, democratized, and won increasing global recognition while North Korea's economy stagnated, its global influence declined and it lost its chief financial patron, the Soviet Union. Meanwhile, tensions and clashes between the two alternated with brief periods of détente.

Impoverished and isolated, the North Korean regime focused on survival while South Korea continued to economically expand and prosper. Pyongyang compensated for its weakness by focusing on weapons of mass destruction, making the unending Korean conflict more dangerous than ever.

By the third decade of the twenty-first century, the Korean conflict had lasted three generations, the longest in modern history, with no end in sight. People in both Koreas seek reunification but have only grown further apart while the North's nuclear weapons, missiles, and cyberwarfare capabilities continue to make their conflict ever more threatening to the global community.

"Books to Span the East and West"

Tuttle Publishing was founded in 1832 in the small New England town of Rutland, Vermont [USA]. Our core values remain as strong today as they were then—to publish best-in-class books which bring people together one page at a time. In 1948, we established a publishing outpost in Japan—and Tuttle is now a leader in publishing English-language books about the arts, languages and cultures of Asia. The world has become a much smaller place today and Asia's economic and cultural influence has grown. Yet the need for meaningful dialogue and information about this diverse region has never been greater. Over the past seven decades, Tuttle has published thousands of books on subjects ranging from martial arts and paper crafts to language learning and literature—and our talented authors, illustrators, designers and photographers have won many prestigious awards. We welcome you to explore the wealth of information available on Asia at **www.tuttlepublishing.com**.

Published by Tuttle Publishing, an imprint of Periplus Editions (HK) Ltd.

www.tuttlepublishing.com

Copyright © 2023 by Michael J. Seth

Unless otherwise stated, all photos and maps in the 4 color section are from Wikimedia Commons.

Library of Congress Control Number: 2022947041

ISBN 978-0-8048-5462-7

Distributed by:

North America, Latin America & Europe
Tuttle Publishing
364 Innovation Drive
North Clarendon VT 05759 9436, USA
Tel: 1(802) 773 8930
Fax: 1(802) 773 6993
info@tuttlepublishing.com
www.tuttlepublishing.com

Asia Pacific
Berkeley Books Pte Ltd
3 Kallang Sector #04-01
Singapore 349278
Tel: (65) 6741 2178
Fax: (65) 6741 2179
inquiries@periplus.com.sg
www.tuttlepublishing.com

26 25 24 23
10 9 8 7 6 5 4 3 2 1   2211TP
Printed in Singapore

Introduction

The Demilitarized Zone (DMZ) that separates North and South Korea is the most heavily fortified and dangerous border in the world. It can be visited on guided tours, but it cannot be crossed. And what bizarre and scary tours they are as soldiers from the other side stare at you through binoculars watching your every move. You must walk with nothing in your hands, visibly displaying that you are carrying no weapons. You walk when told to do so by your intimidating military escort, and stop with feet aligned when instructed to do so. It becomes quickly obvious that this is not just a border but a war zone. And indeed, the two Koreas are at war, one that formally started on June 25, 1950, when North Korean forces launched an invasion of the South but never ended. The Koreans have been at war with each other for three generations, the longest formal conflict in modern times.

The actual start of the war can be traced even earlier to the partition of this ancient, ethnically homogeneous land by the United States and the Soviet Union in 1945; and to the subsequent creation in 1948 of two rival states: North and South Korea. The division occurred in one of the world's oldest and most homogeneous societies. Unified in the seventh century, the Korean Peninsula experienced thirteen centuries of political unity with only modest changes in its borders, a continuity matched by few countries in the world. It was one of the most homogeneous lands—at the start of the twentieth century there were no significant ethnic minorities, no linguistic differences, and no major religious divides. Regional differences were minor. Although heavily influenced by China, Korea remained a distinct world apart with its own language unrelated to any other, its own unique writing system, national dress, cuisine, and customs. All Koreans considered themselves one people apart from non-Koreans.

Korea's cultural distinctiveness stems in part from its geography, inhabitants of a peninsula 600 miles (1,000km) long and averaging about 120 miles (200km) in width jutting out from the mainland. Rugged mountains reaching 9,000 feet (2,750 meters) and two rivers, the Yalu and the Tumen, separate it from the mainland of Asia where it shares an 840-mile (1352km) border with China and a tiny 14 mile (23km) border with Russia. The 185-kilometer (115-mile) Korea Strait separates the peninsula from the Japanese archipelago—just wide enough to make these very different lands. It is a mountainous country with small but fertile plains that have historically supported a dense population. It has a temperate climate with severely cold winters in the north and mild temperate ones in the extreme south; summers are everywhere hot and humid. The total area of Korea, North and South, is about the same as Great Britain. As a modest size country, it has always been surrounded by larger more powerful neighbors. In modern times these have been China, Russia, and Japan. All three countries have fought each other in wars on the peninsula. Since 1945 China, Russia and the United States have been deeply involved in the ongoing Korean War. It is the only conflict in which the three post-World War II superpowers have become militarily engaged, the only one where China and the United States have directly fought each other.

Today the Korean people are a people divided into two states: the Republic of Korea (ROK or South Korea) and the Democratic People's Republic of Korea (DPRK or North Korea). North Korea at 46,000 square miles (120,000 square km) covers about the same area as England or New York State, while South Korea at 39,000 square miles (101,010 square km) is a little smaller. The South has most of the best agricultural land and two-thirds of the population: fifty million to North Korea's twenty-five million. Despite sharing the same language, ethnicity, and heritage, they are separated by radically different political and social systems and by three generations of hostility. Both Koreas proclaim themselves the sole government of all the Korean people, but neither recognizes the other. Both Koreas are heavily armed. South Korea has the world's sixth-largest army; North Korea has an even larger one, ranked fifth in size after China, the United States, India, and Russia.

For three generations North and South Koreans have lived in a state of war. This has profoundly shaped the development of the two states but in extremely different ways. North Korea has evolved into the world's most militarized society, its most totalitarian, and most isolated. It has become a strange cult-state, with ICBMs and nuclear missiles and a population that suffers from chronic malnutrition. It is a nation where most of the population lives in darkness, literally, since electricity is available only a few hours a day at most and is figuratively cut off from the world. South Korea, while also heavily armed, has made an unprecedented leap from one of the world's poorest to one of its richest and most dynamic countries. It has also become a society with a vibrant democracy and internationally competitive firms and a global center of entertainment and pop culture.

How did this homogeneous society with more than a millennium of unity become a divided nation at war with itself? How did this society, once among the least militarized in the world, become one perpetually at war? How did one nation, arbitrarily split into halves at the end of World War II, develop into such two radically different societies within a single lifespan? These are some of the questions this history will try to answer.

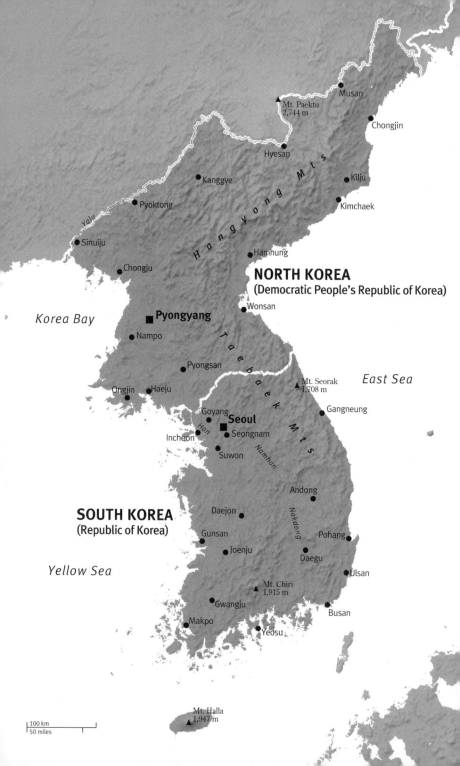

Musan

Mt. Paektu
2,744 m

Chongjin

Hyesan

Hamgyong Mts

Kilju

Kanggye

Kimchaek

Pyoktong

Yalu

Sinuiju

Hamhung

Chongju

NORTH KOREA
(Democratic People's Republic of Korea)

Wonsan

Korea Bay

Pyongyang

Nampo

Taebaek Mts

Pyongsan

East Sea

Mt. Seorak
1,708 m

Ongjin

Haeju

Gangneung

Goyang

Seoul

Han

Incheon

Seongnam

Suwon

Namhan

Andong

Daejon

Nakdong

SOUTH KOREA
(Republic of Korea)

Gunsan

Pohang

Yellow Sea

Joenju

Daegu

Ulsan

Mt. Chiri
1,915 m

Gwangju

Busan

Makpo

Yeosu

Mt. Halla
1,947 m

100 km
50 miles

CHAPTER 1

"Righteous Armies"

About an hour by car south of Seoul is one of South Korea's peculiar tourist attractions—Independence Hall. Set in extensive, attractive grounds with a small lake it is a massive fifteen-story-high structure the size of a soccer field, focused on the country's struggle for independence against Japanese rule. One can walk past one vivid, graphic illustration of the brutalization and subjugation of the Korean people after another. One wax figure scene shows jack-booted Japanese officers resting their feet on a small wooden cage containing a Korean whose head is bent almost to his feet in the confined space. As a monument to a people's sense of victimization, Independence Hall is truly impressive. But it is not unique. There is a similar museum in North Korea.

Independence Hall may be a good place to start this account of Korea's endless war, a conflict rooted in the nation's experience as a victim of modern imperialism. In the late nineteenth century, the great powers terminated Korea's isolation, shattered its ancient society, and turned the peninsula into a battleground of rival imperialist powers. Koreans responded to this and the subsequent loss of their sovereignty in varied ways. And these different responses sowed the seeds of its internal division.

Land of the Morning Calm

When the British, Russians, and other Western powers first approached Korea they found a land long at peace and uninterested in all but the most minimal engagement with the outside world. Korea was called by the Chinese "Chao Xian" which can be liberally translated as "land of the morning calm." This was a fitting description of nineteenth-century Korea. But it was not always so calm. Ancient Korea was a land of warrior-aristocrats, descendants of the hunters and nomads of the Inner Asian steppes and the Manchurian plains. After they settled in the peninsula and adopted farming, three kingdoms arose each ruled by warrior aristocracies that resembled, and most likely introduced, many of the traditions of the samurai of Japan. These kingdoms fought with each other until one of them, Silla, unified the peninsula in 676. Korea remained politically unified until 1945.

The ancient Koreans loved horses. They were mounted archers and swordsmen who competed in contests of martial skills. Their society included aristocratic women who, possessing considerable freedom of movement by the standards of pre-modern times, competed with men in polo. Buddhism was the state religion, and monks too had martial traditions and fought to defend the kingdom. They had much defending to do since Korea bordered some of the most formidable warriors of history: the Khitans, the Jurchens, and the Mongols as well as their far more populous and sometimes aggressive neighboring states—China and Japan. Fiercely independent, Koreans successfully turned back more than one invasion; in the seventh century they twice defeated armies from China, and in the thirteenth century the Koreans fought off the Mongols for nearly four decades before finally submitting.

Over the centuries this martial tradition changed under the influence of Confucianism which entered Korea from China. Confucianists promoted the ideal of rule by meritorious, scholarly officialdom not by warrior aristocrats. The increasingly Confucianized aristocracy became divided into the two hereditary groups: *munban*, who were scholars and civil officials, and *muban*, who were warriors that defended the kingdom, but the status of the latter declined. Confucianization and the decline of military culture accelerated under the Joseon dynasty that came to power in 1392. However, there was a brief awakening of the warrior spirit with the Japanese invasions of the 1590s. After being quickly overrun by the massive Japanese army in 1592 the Koreans put up a spirited resistance to the samurai warriors and under Admiral Yi Sunsin won a string of naval victories. But then Korea turned inward, towards isolationism and its military weakened.

By the 1860s Korea had not fought a war in more than two centuries and had not had a major domestic rebellion or upheaval since the fourteenth century. Once a land of warriors, it was now ill-prepared for war. Military training in Joseon did not help since it was often based on mastery of ancient texts on warfare rather than on practical training and experience. The country's army became small and by the late 1800s, much of it existed solely on paper. People simply collected salaries without serving. The handful of troops manning the country's fortresses had only the most antiquated weapons. The need for a strong military was not apparent since, as a member of the tributary system, Korea fell under the Chinese protective umbrella, which was sometimes leaky, but mostly served to insulate the country from foreign invasion. So, a combination of factors—the absence of serious external threats, popular disdain for soldiers, the fact that serving in the military was not a vehicle for advancement in society but a dead-end, and being a society dominated by scholar-bureaucrats who had little appreciation for martial skills—led to the atrophy of the country's military. There were few countries in the world in the nineteenth century less military-oriented than Korea.

Koreans lived in self-imposed isolation, engaging with the outside world as little as possible. There were no foreigners living in Korea and few Koreans ever traveled abroad. Foreigners were forbidden to enter. The only exceptions were the Chinese emissaries who followed a prescribed route through the country, entered Seoul through a special gate and while visiting stayed in a special compound. They had only limited contact with non-authorized Koreans. Then there were the Japanese who were allowed to trade as long as they stayed in their walled compound outside Busan.

Koreans traveled only to China on diplomatic missions where they engaged in trade, saw the sights in Beijing, and met with Chinese officials, merchants and scholars. There were also the occasional, actually rare, official visits to Edo, Japan. Koreans did not have relations with any other countries. Since the country was closed to Westerners, Korea became known in the West as the "Hermit Kingdom." It was an apt name, for Koreans engaged only in a modest amount of trade with its neighbors and felt little need to concern themselves with the rest of the world. But Koreans were unable to insulate themselves from the restless, and relentless, expansion of Western imperialism.

Abrupt Entry into the World of Modern Imperialism

Koreans were not entirely unaware of the West despite their isolation. In the seventeenth and eighteenth centuries, some Korean visitors to Beijing encountered the European Jesuits who had a mission there. They brought back telescopes, clocks, maps, and a few Chinese translations of Western books on math and science, which were read with interest. Koreans so liked clocks that they made pretty good replicas of them, even of cuckoo clocks. So impressed were they with the accurate Western calendar that at one point they considered inviting Jesuits to come and share their mathematical and astronomical skills. At the start of the nineteenth century one Korean scholar, Dasan, wrote a treatise on Western medicine. A small number of Koreans in the late eighteenth and early nineteenth centuries converted to Catholicism, although their grasp of Christianity was a bit shaky.

Nonetheless, Koreans, like most East Asians, were unaware of the extraordinary advancements that were transforming the West and leading it on a path of global domination: the Industrial Revolution, global capitalism, the rapid advance of science and technology, and new ideas about political and social organization. Several things did make them notice. From 1839 to 1842, the Chinese suffered a humiliating defeat at the hands of the British in the Opium War. In 1858–60 the Middle Kingdom suffered a second defeat culminating in a brief Anglo-French occupation of Beijing, while the Russians annexed a section of Chinese territory giving it a short border with Korea. In 1854, Japan was forced to open itself to trade and diplomacy with the United States and Koreans took note of the subsequent upheaval in the years that followed.

Korea rebuffed attempts by the British, French, and Russians to open their country to trade. When the boy-king Gojong came to the throne in 1864 his father, the regent Daewon'gun, took special pride in resisting any attempts to change its policy of isolation. He cracked down on Christianity and executed several thousand Korean Catholics including some French priests who had smuggled themselves into the country. When the French learned about this they launched a punitive expedition in 1866. The poorly-armed Koreans resisted the invaders so fiercely that the French withdrew without accomplishing much. For Daewon'gun it was a great victory. In the same year, a heavily-armed American merchant ship, the *General Sherman*, with a crew of Americans, British, Malays, and Chinese, sailed up the Daedong River to Pyongyang hoping to trade. They were politely told by the local official, Pak Gyusu, that foreigners were not permitted, and they had to leave. The ship got stuck on a sandbar, there was an exchange of fire, and at some point, the locals set fire to the ship killing the crew as they jumped off. There were no survivors.

When the Americans learned the fate of the missing ship several years later, they carried out their own punitive expedition. In what the American press called "the splendid little war against the heathen" five ships and 1,200 men under Admiral John Rodgers and Frederick Low, the U.S. minister to China, sailed off to Korea with a letter demanding an account of the *General Sherman*. Landing on Ganghwa island they killed hundreds of Korean defenders yet were unable to find their way to Seoul and withdrew. For Koreans, it was another victory.

The two incidents—the French and the American attacks—reveal a couple of things about Koreans. They were capable of fighting very bravely, even to death, rather than surrender. Yet they also illustrated that, despite these "victories," they were hopelessly weak militarily, in no position to defend themselves against modern invaders. Korean soldiers were armed with pikes, arrows, and ancient matchlock firearms which hadn't been used in the West since the invention of the musket in the sixteenth century. So poorly armed and manned was the Korean army that Daewon'gun had to call upon private tiger hunters to defend the fortresses. They too were only armed with ancient matchlocks.

Korea was able to resist half-hearted attempts by the French and the Americans to open the country, but not the determined effort of their modernizing neighbor Japan. In 1868, in what would be called the Meiji Restoration, a group of reform-minded samurai overthrew the Shogunate and began the revolutionary transformation of Japan into a modern industrial and military power. In one of their first foreign initiatives, they sent an envoy to Busan to announce the new government and seek to open direct diplomatic relations. The Koreans were disgusted by the Western dress of the officials, which was not only culturally offensive but reinforced the old idea that the Japanese were semi-barbarians. They also were offended by the idea of imperial restoration since that implied the Japanese "king" outranked Korea's king. The Japanese leadership who regarded Korea, the closest land bridge to Japanese islands, to be of vital concern for their country's security was frustrated by Seoul's refusal to deal with them.

In 1873, Meiji leaders seriously considered provoking an incident and invading Korea. The idea of an invasion was called off but in the spring of 1875, the newly-acquired modern warship *Unyo* sailed into Busan and demonstrated its power by firing its guns. Then, accompanied by other ships, it began surveying the coast. When it was fired upon by Korean shore batteries it returned fire and destroyed them. It then landed troops and took a small fort. The Japanese returned with more forces and demanded an apology for firing on its ships.

Faced with this demonstration of power, the Korean court decided to begin negotiations. With the support of the young king Gojong who with his father out of the way was now able to assert himself, the Koreans signed the Treaty of Ganghwa in February 1876. Its twelve articles permitted Japan to survey coastal waters, allowed Japanese to reside in treaty ports, and to have rights of extraterritoriality; that is to be immune to Korean law. A further trade agreement was signed opening the country to Japanese trade and investment.

Korea's isolation ended and its entry into the modern world began at gunpoint. It would not just be the end of isolation, but the end of peace. The Korean people entered not just the modern world but a century and a half of violent upheavals and perpetual war.

Ganghwa Island

The treaty that marked the end of Korea's isolation is named for the island of Ganghwa. Less than an hour's drive from Seoul, Ganghwa today is a popular day trip, famous among Koreans for a kind of turnip with medicinal properties that grows there, for its setting on the sea, and its history. And it has a lot of history. Ganghwa is not a big island, about 116 square miles (304 square km), about twice the size of Staten Island in New York. It is 17 miles (28km) long and 14 miles (22km) wide; the highest point is Mani Mountain about 1,500 feet (470m). Its importance stems from a strategic location in an estuary of the Han River where Seoul is situated. It is separated by the land by just less than a mile and is today connected by two bridges.

In 1232, when the Mongols were invading Korea, the rulers of the country ordered the court to retreat to the easily defended island. The entire government was transferred there, with palaces, offices, temples, arsenals, and residences. For almost four decades the Korean kingdom used it as a base for the country's remarkably stubborn resistance to the Mongols. From across the narrow strait that separates the island from the mainland, Korean soldiers would jeer at and taunt the Mongol forces. Again, in the seventeenth century, during the time of the Manchu invasions, the government fled there. The island thus became a symbol of Korea's determination to be free of outside control.

This strategic island blocking the entryway into Seoul is the spot where the French arrived in 1866 only to meet fierce resistance from its defenders, and it was where the Americans landed five years later. Then the Japanese came in 1876, captured a small fort on the island, and killed and wounded its defenders. Today Ganghwa is no longer a symbol of resistance and isolation but administratively part of the city of Incheon, a bustling port, and is not far from Incheon International Airport, one of the busiest in the world. It is also not far from Songdo, a newly created high-tech city designed as a place to welcome international businesses and organizations. Once a bastion to keep the foreigners out, it is now part of the country's main gateway to the world.

Opening to the World

In 1882, Korea opened diplomatic and trade relations with the United States and sent a mission to Washington the following year. Soon it had diplomatic ties with Russia, Britain, France, Germany, and several other countries. Foreigners arrived, diplomats from Europe, merchants from China and Japan, Russian timber cutters and tiger hunters, as well as American missionaries. The missionaries opened schools, and modern medical clinics and converted some Koreans to Presbyterianism and Methodism. Foreign businesses sought concessions for mines, railroads, streetcars, electrification projects, and telegraph and telephone lines. A steady flow of young Koreans began to go abroad for education. The largest number went to Japan; it was nearby, culturally similar, and cheaper than Western countries. Many of these came back impressed with that country's swift modernization and saw it as a model for Korea. Smaller but not insignificant numbers went to the United States where they encountered racism but were also impressed with what they saw as a wealthy, advanced, and powerful society. A handful went to Russia and Western Europe for study, and they too were impressed. Almost all came away with a sense of just how weak, vulnerable, and "backward" their country was. However, they also came with a belief that Koreans could emulate these new centers of civilization just as they had successfully emulated, and in some respects surpassed, China in the past.

This sent into motion a search for external models to restore the country's place in the hierarchy of civilized societies. The problem was there was not just one model but several. Thus, from the earliest beginnings of its modernization Koreans were united in their goal to make their homeland a prosperous autonomous society that was strong enough to defend itself and a proud member of the civilized world, but not on the methods of achieving this. Naturally, some conservatives resisted or sought to minimize innovation, to hold on to old values, but their influence waned after it became increasingly clear that the world had changed too much to maintain the old ways.

The Korean government realized it had a weak military and understood the importance of addressing this. At first, the steps it took were very modest. Gojong in 1881 created a Special Skills Force, a small group of soldiers trained in modern weapons. The following year, regular soldiers, angry over not being paid and resenting this privileged group, murdered the Japanese officer in charge. The Special Skills force was then abolished. In 1883, the court created a Special Guards Command trained by a Chinese officer Yuan Shikai. These were pathetically small efforts yet part of something more fundamental: a change in attitude toward the military by the educated elite. Many Korean officials and professionals were also quick to grasp the importance of broader reforms to strengthen the state. Some admired how the Japanese were developing an industrial state with a modern military. In 1884, a group of young Koreans who had traveled to Japan attempted a coup with plans to emulate the Japanese Meiji Restoration. The event, called the Gapsin Coup, failed when the Chinese intervened with a military force. Most of the coup's leaders fled to Japan.

A Shrimp among Whales

Koreans have a saying that their country is "a shrimp among whales," and indeed as Koreans began to grapple with the need for radical reform, they found themselves in an extraordinarily difficult geopolitical position. Korea was surrounded by three empires, each seeking to gain control over their country, each meddling in its internal affairs: Russia, China, and Japan. A declining China was desperate to protect its periphery and that meant keeping control over the Korean Peninsula. The Russians expanding in Asia needed warm water ports for their empire in the Far East. The Japanese sought to protect their periphery seeing Korea as "a dagger pointing to the heart of Japan." This meant taking control over the peninsula before other powers did, and Japanese imperial ambitions started with Korea. For all three empires, Korea also was a useful market for goods and resources. The Russians sought timber; the Chinese, ginseng; the Japanese, rice. But it was above all the strategic location of Korea that interested them.

At first, the struggle for the mastery of Korea went in China's favor. The Gapsin Coup provided Beijing with an excuse to intervene militarily. Chinese troops removed the short-lived reform government and restored the old regime to power. From 1884 to 1894 the Chinese exercised a great measure of control over Korea through their representative Yuan Shikai, a young general who would later become the ruler of China. It was a lost decade for Korea, which didn't have much time to lose if it was to modernize fast enough to survive. For ten years, the Chinese hindered efforts by Koreans to carry out reforms that might lessen their grip on the country. They made it difficult for Koreans to travel abroad, pressured the Joseon government to order students abroad to return home, and blocked efforts by Seoul to open embassies in Western countries. But the Chinese could not keep out the foreign missionaries who opened schools and hospitals and exposed young Koreans to new ideas. Nor could they keep out the Japanese and Russians who opened businesses and engaged in political intrigue.

China's period of dominance came to an end in 1894 when the Donghaks revolted. The Donghak ("Eastern Learning") movement was founded in 1864 by Choe Je-u, who mixed Korean religious practices and Confucian ethics and cosmology with ideas derived from Christianity: belief in a single divinity and the concepts of universal brotherhood and equality. A panicked government in Seoul called for Chinese assistance but before troops could arrive, Korean officials were able to negotiate with the Donghaks, promising to look into their grievances, and things quieted down. Though they were no longer needed, the Chinese forces arrived anyway and as they did, so did uninvited troops from Japan. Tokyo was not going to allow China to consolidate its hold on the peninsula. Instead of fighting the Donghaks, the Japanese and Chinese fought each other, and Japan's modernized forces carried out a crushing defeat of the Chinese forces. With the Chinese driven out and the Japanese in effective control of Seoul, Tokyo sponsored a new reform government, which included Gapsin veterans who returned from exile in Japan.

Japan's elimination of China from the Korean scene briefly gave it a dominant position in the peninsula. Japanese troops in Seoul began to intervene in the government, helping to install a pro-Japanese reform-minded cabinet. This new cabinet carried out sweeping changes, establishing equality under the law by doing away with the legal privileges of the old aristocratic *yangban* class and abolishing slavery. But as well-intentioned as these Korean reformers were, their credibility was undermined by the fact they operated under the protection of Japanese bayonets. Then the Japanese overplayed their hand when they murdered one of their formidable opponents, Queen Min.

Queen Min

One of the events that galvanized the opposition to the Japanese was the horrifically brutal murder of Queen Min. Queen Min was staunchly anti-Japanese, rightly seeing them as the chief threat to the independence of her kingdom. Born in the aristocratic Yeoheung Min clan in 1851, she was selected by Gojong's father to be the wife of the young king, fifteen at the time. She was a good choice, attractive, intelligent, and from a good family, but not one of the more powerful clans that could be a rival to the monarchy. Furthermore, she was an orphan so she had no meddlesome immediate family for the king and his clan to deal with. But Daewongun underestimated her. As the young princess entered her twenties, she formed a faction that helped engineer the ousting of the regent and put her husband in charge. Queen Min then appointed relatives and acquaintances to key positions although they never dominated the state. Too realistic to be an isolationist like her father-in-law, she supported sending military officials and officers to China for training, and she promoted the teaching of the English language.

She was deeply suspicious of the Japanese and since Gojong was increasingly reliant on her advice, she represented a threat to the Japanese effort to control Korea.

In 1895, the Japanese minister to Korea, Miura Goto, plotted her assassination. In the early hours of October 8, about fifty Japanese "ronin assassins" entered the Gyeongbok Palace with the collaboration of pro-Japanese guards who let them enter through one of the gates. As they burst in, they caused a commotion since they were not sure where in the large palace complex the queen was. Gojong unsuccessfully tried to distract them to allow her to escape. After beating some court ladies and threatening the crown prince at sword point, they found Queen Min and stabbed her to death. Then the assassins dragged the body of the dead queen and those of two court ladies they had also murdered into nearby woods, doused them with kerosene, and burned them. The incident shocked the Korean and international public. Miura was recalled, and 56 Japanese thugs were put on trial in Hiroshima. But when international attention waned all were acquitted.

In 1897, Queen Min was posthumously declared Empress Myeongseong and buried in a proper tomb in an elaborate royal ceremony. The Eulmi Incident, as it became known to Koreans, did as much as anything to instill hatred and distrust of the Japanese. Queen Min's death became a rallying cry for later Korean resistance fighters.

The Short-lived Empire

The Japanese elimination of China and the death of Queen Min served to draw Russia in. In early 1896, a pro-Russian faction at court spirited King Gojong out of the palace and past the watchful eyes of the Japanese over to the Russian legation, positioning the king to rule from a location protected by Cossacks. At this point, a group of Korean progressives formed the Independence Club, led by the American mission school-educated Yun Chiho. Later, a Gapsin Coup veteran, Seo Jaepil, who returned from the U.S. with an American education, an American wife, and an American name (Philip Jaisohn) would join the Club. The Club called for a modern representative government and an independent foreign policy. In 1897, they named their nation the Great Korean Empire, and Gojong was proclaimed emperor. This put Korea on an equal footing with its imperial neighbors. However, before the Independence Club could enact more reforms, the king, worrying about its power, shut it down; its leaders fled back into exile. But Gojong kept the imperial title.

Meanwhile, Tokyo had invested too much in Korea to let it slip under the control of Russia. In 1904, it attacked the Russians, launching the Russo-Japanese War. To the amazement of the West, Japan emerged victorious from this conflict in the following year. Russia conceded Korea and much of Manchuria as a Japanese sphere of influence. President Theodore Roosevelt, who brokered the peace settlement, tacitly gave Tokyo a free hand in Korea in return for its recognition of the American presence in the Philippines. Britain, too, as part of an alliance it made with Japan in 1902, recognized its primacy over the peninsula. In 1905, with the blessing of the great powers, Japan declared Korea a protectorate. Western states closed their embassies, and Korea became a Japanese possession in all but name.

The Militarization of Korea

While the great powers were fighting over control of Korea, the Koreans were developing a new understanding of the need for military strength if they were to safeguard their independence. Despite the elite's Confucian disdain for soldiers, Koreans were quick to understand they had to strengthen their country's military to survive. When the kingdom sent officials to China, Japan, and the West, they reported on the militaries in those countries and urged their kingdom to emulate them. Japan's martial traditions and military prowess were admired by many younger members of the elite. Since much of the Sino-Japanese War was fought in Korea, the Koreans had observed the power of a modernizing military as the Japanese forces routed the Chinese.

At first, efforts to create a modern military were small-scale, half-hearted, and woefully underfunded. After 1894, Korea created a modern-style Ministry of War that had considerable power. Gojong himself, reflecting the change in attitude, adopted the title of *Gwangmu* ("Brilliant and Martial") when he declared himself Emperor in 1897 and frequently appeared in a military uniform, something unthinkable just a short time earlier. The amount of the budget devoted to the military increased. The army, while remaining small, with the help of foreign advisors became more professional. It was, of course, too little too late but did reflect a growing appreciation of the importance of a modern military.

The new positive view of the military was reflected in the country's leading intellectuals and political thinkers. Influential writers such as Sin Chaeho and Pak Unsik began celebrating Korea's military heroes. Much of this was part of their admiration of Japan and the West, and their absorption of the glorification of military power that characterized these countries at this time.

1907 as a Turning Point

At the start of the Russo-Japanese War in 1904, the Japanese took over effective control of the country. This was a step-by-step process. Korea still had its monarch, his cabinet, and his appointed governors to administer the provinces. There was still a very small Korean army and police force, but the real decisions were made in Japan. Advisors, mostly Japanese but also a few Westerners, were appointed by Tokyo to each ministry; they wielded considerable authority. Japan stationed troops in the country that outnumbered the local military, and it created a central bank that was in fact a Japanese bank. Japan, not Korea set the tariffs and controlled customs. As they took control of the country, the Japanese found Korean officials who would cooperate, men such as Yi Wanyong, the education minister who later became notorious among Koreans as a treacherous villain. But they encountered difficulty with Gojong who never signed the protectorate treaty or accepted the subordinate status of Korea.

Desperate for foreign support against the Japanese takeover, Gojong sent the American missionary Homer Hulbert to the U.S. to ask for help; Roosevelt refused to meet with him since he regarded the Japanese takeover of Korea as a settled question. In 1907 the monarch secretly sent three representatives to the Second Hague Peace Conference with a petition requesting international assistance to recover the county's sovereignty. The major powers at the conference ignored them. In dejection, one of them committed suicide. Yet their mission was not a complete failure for it generated considerable publicity in the Western press and embarrassed the Japanese government. Tokyo decided Gojong must go, and they forced him to abdicate in July to be replaced by his mentally incompetent son who became Emperor Sunjong, the last Korean monarch.

The abdication of Gojong proved too much for many Koreans. Angry mobs in Seoul attacked and burned the homes of pro-Japanese ministers including Yi Wanyong. The prominent aristocratic reformer Pak Yeonghyo plotted a coup to remove the pro-Japanese ministers but it was discovered and he was exiled to the southern island of Jeju. More organized and sustained violence began on July 31, 1907, when the Japanese ordered the disbanding of the small 8,000-member Korean Army. Instead of surrendering their arms many soldiers and officers began an armed resistance. By this act, they inaugurated more than a century of continuous fighting of some sort. It was at this point that Korea became land-engaged in armed conflict.

The Righteous Armies

The major armed uprising began on August 1, 1907, when the Japanese authorities ordered the dissolution of the Korean Army. In a formal ceremony, Korean troops were gathered at a training ground in Seoul and each given severance pay as they surrendered their arms. It didn't go well. After it started, shots from rebellious soldiers rang out and the ceremony was quickly concluded. Before the ceremony, the commander of the First Battalion, First Regiment shot himself in protest. Immediately afterward, the soldiers he had commanded joined by troops from the Second Battalion began an insurrection. Japanese forces in the capital put it down before the day was over. Seventy Korean soldiers were killed and 100 were wounded. However, hundreds of other Korean soldiers fled to the countryside where they began an armed resistance to the Japanese. They were in turn joined by the garrisons in Ganghwa and Wonju to the east of Seoul. A major anti-Japanese resistance by "righteous armies" had begun.

The tradition of righteous armies went back to the sixteenth century. In 1592 the Japanese, under the military hegemon Hideyoshi, invaded Korea; the largest overseas invasion in history up to that time. Korean forces were quickly overwhelmed. China intervened and a devastating war between Korea, its Ming Chinese allies, and the Japanese lasted eight years before the Japanese withdrew. During this war, which is seared into the collective memory of Koreans, private individuals formed irregular military units which they called "righteous armies" (*uibyeong* in Korean). This quaint term came from the old Korean tradition that people had the right to resist unjust and unethical authority. They were not just rebelling to overthrow a government or to advance a cause but to uphold the correct moral order. Usually led by *yangban*, the aristocratic scholarly class that traditionally provided the officials that governed the state, their rank and file consisted of peasants, former officials, and Buddhist monks.

In the late nineteenth century, some Koreans revived this tradition to again fight the Japanese. The first *uibyeong* was formed in 1895, at the end of the Sino-Japanese War and following the murder of Queen Min. They became known as the Righteous Armies of Eulmi (after the name for the lunar year). Following the Protectorate Treaty in 1905, a few bands of guerillas known as the Righteous Armies of Eulsa harassed the Japanese. Despite being called "armies" they were generally small bands of a few dozen to a few hundred poorly-armed fighters, led by *yangban* with no military training or experience. Isolated with no overall coordination they were not very effective. It was only in the late summer of 1907 that the righteous armies became a widespread movement.

Unlike the few isolated rebel bands that had appeared at the time of the Sino-Japanese War and in 1905, what was different in 1907 was the sheer number and widespread appearance of these groups and the fact that instead of being created and led almost exclusively by Confucian trained *yangban*, they were often organized and led by ex-military men.

The rebels attacked police stations, telegraph lines, railway lines and stations, and any symbol of the Japanese presence in the country. They had no central leadership, no overall strategy, the various groups seldom coordinated their activities, and they were poorly armed. Many had only bamboo sticks and knives. Some were armed with ancient matchlocks, few had modern arms, and getting them was extremely difficult although some were obtained through gun runners. This was largely a leaderless, spontaneous uprising of tens of thousands of ordinary Koreans who sought to drive the foreigners out of their country and restore the country's independence. Most were loyal supporters of the dynasty. There was an exception to this lack of coordination. Yi Inyong, a *yangban* scholar, organized several thousand fighters for an assault on Seoul. He was joined by Heo Wi, also a *yangban* scholar. Heo had organized a righteous army in 1896 but after a while disbanded it. In 1907 he organized another larger group. With their combined groups, Yi Inyong and Heo Wi planned to take control of the capital and replace the Yi Wanyong-led puppet cabinet and install a patriotic one that would resist Japan. In December 1907 their forces made it within a few miles of the capital before being driven back by heavy Japanese fire. It was enough to give the Japanese a good scare. But there were no more campaigns organized on this scale again.

Righteous army attacks never posed a serious military threat to the Japanese hold on Korea, yet they were more than a mere nuisance. Many Japanese civilians, businessmen, and civil servants left the country out of fear for their security or sent then families back to Japan. Tokyo was forced to send additional troops to crush the rebellion. In 1908, the military commander General Hasegawa stated that putting down the insurrection was more difficult than the fighting in the Russo-Japanese War. There were no battle lines, fighters could blend in and be harbored by local populations. No battle was ever decisive since new bands were formed to replace the defeated ones. The Japanese resorted to scorched earth tactics creating enormous havoc and hardship in much of the countryside. They would enter a village, check the household registers, and match the number of men with the number they found in them to see if villagers were sheltering guerillas.

In some cases, whole villages that had given shelter to guerillas were burned to the ground. Some villagers placed red crosses in front of their homes thinking this international symbol of humanitarianism would deter the Japanese from destroying them. Canadian journalist Frederick MacKenzie reported that in some districts, villages were devoid of women and children since they had fled elsewhere for safety. The brutality of the Japanese campaign horrified foreign missionaries who wrote to their embassies. At one point the British government considered launching an investigation into the reports of atrocities. However, Japan was a key ally in Britain's overall geopolitical strategy, so London did not follow through.

Guerillas issued manifestos in the manner of rebels and protesters in traditional Korea charging the Japanese authorities with deceitful and immoral behavior. Some taunted them. "You thought there were no men left in Korea;" one declared, "you will see. We country people are resolved to destroy your railways and your settlements and your authorities." The fighters were mostly peasants, but also included miners, bandits, hunters, *yangban*, and discharged soldiers, the latter two groups usually led them. Tiger hunters were especially effective. Tiger hunting, a great tradition in Korea, was done by professionals who used long-barreled guns that had to be reloaded after one shot. Since they could not afford to miss or wound the tiger they only fired when they were sure of a fatal hit. People joined the righteous armies for many reasons. Yu Pyonggi, age 27, from a distinguished family told his Japanese interrogators that serving their country had been a family tradition, and he needed to do something to help the country for the sake of his family name. So, in 1908 he amassed 700 men for his band. Hwang Sa-il, 35, a farmer with no children paid a man to use his wife for what he hoped would be a fertile concubine, but the husband wanted her back and threatened to kill them both. To escape this situation, he joined a righteous army but then in 1909 turned himself in. Men's reasons for joining were varied, yet they were united in their desire to rid the country of the Japanese.

The fighting reached a peak in 1909 when there were (according to the Japanese) 83,000 Korean fighters with whom they fought 1,900 engagements. The number of dead is not known for sure, but some estimates claim up to 10,000 fighters were killed. In September of that year, the Japanese army launched the "the great southern pacification" campaign in Cholla province where the guerilla activity was most intense. The effort was largely successful. Eventually, the lack of progress discouraged the guerillas, and the righteous armies melted away. But this happened gradually with small units continuing to fight until 1911. Lacking any central leadership, unable to obtain any foreign support, lacking access to modern weapons, and facing a highly disciplined trained military that was determined to crush them, the righteous armies failed in their attempt to drive out the Japanese. After 1910, armed resistance continued and Korean resistance to the Japanese did not end until Japanese rule did. However, it mainly took place outside of Korea by exiles who fought the expanding Japanese Empire.

Some Korean opponents of the Japanese took to assassinations. When American Durham White Stevens, the Japanese-nominated advisor to the Korean government went to the United States in 1908 to promote Japanese rule in Korea, he was shot and killed in San Francisco by two Korean students, Chang In-hwan and Jeon Myeongun. The most famous of these assassinations was the shooting of Ito Hirobumi, the man sent over by Tokyo to supervise Korea's integration into Japan, by An Junggeun. Every Korean today knows the story.

An Junggeun

An Junggeun was born in Haeju, Hwanghaedo (Yellow Sea Province). His father An Taehun, an educated gentleman, provided him with a traditional education centered on the Chinese classics. In normal times the young An would have prepared for the civil examination but these were abolished in 1894. So instead of being a government official, he entered business, specifically the coal business. Along the way he met a French priest and converted to Catholicism and took the name Thomas An. Like so many Korean nationalists of the time, his exposure to Christianity helped foster an openness to the new ideas of the world and opposition to the Japanese. He was also influenced by his father who was sympathetic to the anti-Japanese cause as well.

It wasn't, however, until the 1905 Protectorate Treaty that An Junggeun became politically active, helping to establish two schools to promote modern learning. In 1907, the year when the anti-Japanese sentiment turned to armed struggle, he went to Vladivostok and joined the resistance, becoming a "general." His early activities were not very successful, so he joined others in a scheme to assassinate Ito Hirobumi, the Resident-General and the maestro of the Japanese takeover of Korea. In 1909 Ito went to the northern Manchurian city of Harbin for talks with the Russian Minister of Finance, part of an effort to promote cooperation between the two imperial powers in Northeast Asia. Ito and the Russian minister were to meet at the Harbin Railway Station. An, who had as a youth earned a reputation as a marksman, was waiting. With his pistol he opened fire as Ito was standing at the rail platform, killing the Japanese leader and wounding the Japanese Consul General, a Secretary of the Imperial Household Agency, and an executive of the Japanese owned South Manchurian Railway. As he fired, he shouted "Hurray for Korea" in Russian. An was immediately seized by Russian police who turned him over to the Japanese two days later.

In prison, An Junggeun justified his action by listing 15 crimes Ito had committed. The first was ordering the murder of Queen Min (which Ito had not done). The second was the dethroning of Emperor Gojong. The other charges represented a laundry list of grievances and outrages widely held by Korean nationalists: blocking education, preventing Koreans from going abroad, and plundering the country's forests and mines. Others included forcing Koreans to use Japanese money, forcing them to sign unequal treaties, carrying out massacres of innocent Koreans, and spreading the rumor that the Koreans wanted Japanese protection. He was executed in March 1910 after a trial. Interestingly he left behind an unfinished essay "On Peace in East Asia." Rather than an attack on Japan, it was a Pan-Asian call for Chinese, Korean and Japanese unity against the West.

Dignified, articulate, and full of moral outrage, An Junggeun became a hero to many Koreans, a symbol of their desire for independence and their grievances against the indignities and suffering brought on by foreigners. In the 1980s Japan's two most common bills, the 1,000 and the 10,000 yen notes, were graced by the portrait of Ito Hirobumi, principal architect of Japan's modern transformation, the author of its first constitution, and perhaps the country's more respected modern leader. Meanwhile, every day mail was entering the country from South Korea with postage stamps issued for the special first-class mail rate for Japan, stamps bearing the likeness of An Junggeun.

Entering the Colonial Period

In 1910 the dynastic state of Korea came to an end but the modern Korean nation was just being born. Among educated Koreans, a new sense of common identity emerged. It was a sense of being part of a "nation"; a common community of self-governing people who were part of an international order of nations. It was the hope of many of these Koreans that the independent state would not just be restored but reborn as a modern, progressive society of prosperous people bound by shared language, customs, history, and a shared vision of the future. As this concept of nationhood emerged it unified Koreans, who overcame the old barriers of inherited class and status. But it also divided Koreans as they developed different ideas of what that vision of the future should be. It was these different visions that laid the foundations for Korea's endless civil war.

CHAPTER 2

Colonial Oppression and Divided Nationalists

Introduction

On April 29, 1932, the Japanese in Shanghai celebrated the birthday of their young emperor Hirohito in the city's Hongkou Park. Gathered on a dais in the park were men who represented the growing presence and power of Japan on the Asian mainland: General Shirakawa Yoshimori, commander in chief of the Shanghai Expeditionary Army; Ueda Kenkichi, commander of the 9th Division of the Imperial Japanese Army; Vice Admiral Nomura Kichisaburo of the Imperial Japanese Navy; Kawabata Sadaji, head of the Japanese residents association; and Shigemitsu Mamoru, a diplomat. They were proud members of Japan's expanding empire which included Taiwan, Korea, much of Micronesia, parts of China, and the recently-added Manchuria. There was also a twenty-three-year-old Korean named Yun Bonggil present, who came to spoil the celebration. As the Japanese anthem was playing Yun placed a bomb hidden in a water bottle on the stage and then ran. The bomb killed Shirakawa and Kawabata. Nomura, who would later be conducting negotiations with the U.S. government in Washington when the Japanese attacked Pearl Harbor, lost an eye. Shigemitsu lost a leg. In September 1945 he would limp across the deck of the U.S.S. Missouri to sign Japan's surrender before General Douglas MacArthur.

Yun Bonggil who was captured and executed was motivated by hatred for the Japanese. He was not alone in this hatred. Koreans reacted to Japanese colonial rule by developing a strong sense of nationalism born from their resentment over the foreign occupation of the country and a desire to regain independence. But as they sought to regain control over their country Koreans became ideologically split into competing visions of what an independent Korea would look like. These ideological divisions, along with the animosity among Koreans who resisted Japanese rule toward their countrymen who accommodated it, were combined with a passionate nationalism, forming a toxic mix that made the conflict among Koreans after 1945 so intense and intractable.

A Very Peculiar Colony

Imperialism was an unhappy experience for most people who lived under colonial rule during the great age of empire. But in few places did it leave so a bitter legacy as in Korea. Today the British are generally liked in India and most of their former African colonies. One is unlikely to encounter much hatred of them in Jamaica or Malaysia. Nor is there much resentment of the French in Morocco, Senegal, and most of their other former colonies. The Americans are generally liked in the Philippines. By contrast, even the casual visitor to Korea will encounter the lingering hatred and resentment of Japan's rule of their country. In movies, the Japanese are usually depicted as cruel, villainous characters. If there is anything North and South Koreans can agree on it is that the colonial period was one of unmitigated oppression.

Yet the colonial period was rather short, just 35 years, and not all that bad. Japan's colonial administrators were great modernizers creating or strengthening some of the institutions and infrastructure of modern-day Korea. They established industries, built an extensive railroad network, modernized the cities and towns, expanded education, and created a forward-looking, efficient civil service. Korea by 1945 was more industrialized with better infrastructure than almost any colony. Many Koreans, not most, but a significant number prospered under it. So why the legacy of bitterness? It was not because Japanese rule was especially oppressive or exploitative, although like most imperialist enterprises it was both, but because

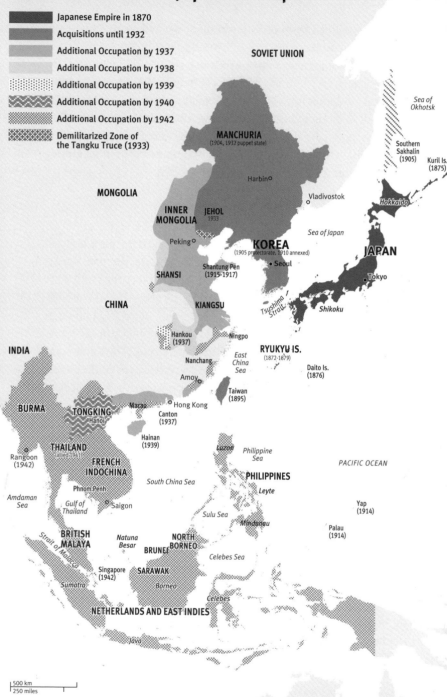

Korea as Part of the Japanese Empire

Japanese Empire in 1870
Acquisitions until 1932
Additional Occupation by 1937
Additional Occupation by 1938
Additional Occupation by 1939
Additional Occupation by 1940
Additional Occupation by 1942
Demilitarized Zone of the Tangku Truce (1933)

SOVIET UNION

Sea of Okhotsk

MANCHURIA
(1904, 1932 puppet state)

Southern Sakhalin (1905)

Kuril Is. (1875)

MONGOLIA

Harbin

Vladivostok

Hokkaido

INNER MONGOLIA

JEHOL 1933

Sea of Japan

JAPAN

Peking

KOREA
(1905 protectorate, 1910 annexed)

Seoul

SHANSI

Shantung Pen (1915-1917)

Tokyo

CHINA

KIANGSU

Tsushima Strait

Shikoku

Hankou (1937)

Ningpo

RYUKYU IS.
(1872-1879)

INDIA

Nanchang

East China Sea

Daito Is. (1876)

BURMA

Amoy

Taiwan (1895)

TONGKING

Macau

Hong Kong

Canton (1937)

Hanoi

Hainan (1939)

PACIFIC OCEAN

Rangoon (1942)

THAILAND
(allied 1941)

FRENCH INDOCHINA

Luzon

Philippine Sea

PHILIPPINES

Amdaman Sea

Phnom-Penh

South China Sea

Leyte

Yap (1914)

Saigon

Sulu Sea

Gulf of Thailand

Mindanao

Palau (1914)

BRITISH MALAYA

Natuna Besar

NORTH BORNEO

BRUNEI

Celebes Sea

Singapore (1942)

SARAWAK

Sumatra

Borneo

Celebes

NETHERLANDS AND EAST INDIES

Java

Strait of Malacca

500 km
250 miles

of the unusual nature of its rule and of Korea itself.

In many European colonies, the colonizers ruled indirectly through local chiefs, sheikhs, or rajas. Japan ruled directly and thoroughly. By the 1930s, when the colonial government was able to impose itself on the population with full force, about a quarter-million Japanese civilian, military, and police personnel were employed in Korea. This was roughly equivalent to the British presence in India which had more than fifteen times the population, and ten times greater than the number of French in Vietnam which had about the same number of people as Korea. While a Southeast Asian or African peasant might encounter a British or French colonial official only rarely, ordinary Koreans encountered them every day—the Japanese schoolteacher, the village policeman, the postal clerk. The police were particularly intrusive, with the power to judge and sentence for minor offenses, collect taxes, oversee local irrigation works, even inspect businesses and homes and see that health and other government regulations were being enforced. It was a top-down administration with all officials, police, and military directly answerable to the governor-general. Koreans served mainly in the lower ranks of the bureaucracy and were excluded from any meaningful participation in decision-making.

Furthermore, Japan's colonial rule had the feel of an occupation, with a highly centralized national gendarmerie and strategically located military garrisons throughout the country. The governors-general were all military men who wore military uniforms—even schoolteachers in the early years wore swords. The governor-general himself had far more power than any Korean king ever had; he answered only to the prime minister of Japan and was accountable to no one in the peninsula. The harsh military character of the colonial administration was partly a response to the hostility with which many Koreans greeted the Japanese and the fact that the Japanese began their rule while still carrying out military campaigns against the righteous armies. And the military occupation-like feel to colonial rule was also the result of another unusual aspect of Korea's colonial experience—it was ruled not by a distant and alien nation, but by a familiar neighbor, sharing much of its cultural heritage and with a legacy of having previously invaded the country. In short, from the Korean point of view it was a military occupation by a neighboring country.

Then there was Japan's assimilation policy. In many ways, this was the most unique and bizarre aspect of its colonial occupation, an effort not to just rule Koreans but to erase their separate identity and make them Japanese. This feature, as we will see, became particularly pronounced during the Second World War.

If Japan's rule was not typical, Korea was not a typical colony either. Most colonies were cobbled together from different ethnic groups and different pre-existing political units. There was never a state of India, it was a cultural and geographic region with many languages and ethnic groups. Nor was there ever an Indonesia, a Nigeria, a Tanzania, a Congo or a Cameroon, or an Iraq; all were entities created by colonial administrators. Korea was different. It was an ancient, ethnically homogeneous society living under its own rule for 1300 years with only modest changes in boundaries. Geographically defined by the peninsula, culturally by a people with their own language, writing system, and traditions of self-rule, it had all the ingredients for modern nationalism. Furthermore, the people had no experience of having foreigners living among them, let alone ruling them.

Oppression and the Nationalist Uprising

The colonial administration did not begin well. Terauchi Masatake, a hardened army general who came to Korea as the first governor-general, was met upon his arrival with an assassination plot. He responded by launching a sweeping crackdown, arresting seven hundred Koreans. One hundred five were convicted of being involved after being tortured and confessing. Their forced and often far-fetched confessions, a forerunner of those elicited in North Korean show trials, were often so outlandish they drew the attention of the Western press. This, along with the fact that most of those targeted were Christian, attracted too much bad publicity. An embarrassed Japanese government released many of them. But the colonial government took no further chances, and the early years of their rule were a continual reign of terror with tens of thousands of Koreans arrested, beaten, and tortured. Korean language publications were subject to strict censorship when they were permitted at all, which was seldom. Especially humiliating for a people proud of learning, public education for Koreans was restricted to just a few years of basic education. All this contributed to growing tensions that gave birth to a mass national uprising in 1919.

In Tokyo on February 8, 1919, over 600 Korean students attended a meeting where they passed a declaration calling for immediate independence. The group then sent members to Korea to agitate for independence there. At the same time within Korea, several different groups were quietly discussing independence in early 1919. They included leaders of the new religion of Cheondogyo, a group of Presbyterians based in Pyongyang, Methodists in Seoul, and a group affiliated with Chungang High School, including two of the country's most prominent businessmen. The arrival of the students and news of their call for independence helped stimulate these groups into action. Then there was the death of Gojong on January 21, 1919. Rumors circulated that he was poisoned by the Japanese or forced to commit suicide although there is no substantial evidence to support either of these claims. But the news only added to the tension in Seoul as the city prepared for his funeral on March 3. Taking advantage of the large number of people expected to gather for the occasion, representatives of these groups decided to issue a declaration of independence in Pagoda Park in Seoul on March 1. Thirty-three signed it: sixteen Christians, fifteen Cheondogyo, and two Buddhists. The plan was to send a petition to the Japanese and the U.S. governments and to the Paris peace conference.

The signatories, mostly religious leaders, were hardly revolutionaries. They were careful to emphasize the nonviolent nature of their protest. They did not intend to instigate a mass uprising. Concerned about security they decided to simply read the declaration at a restaurant on February 28. After that, they planned to send a measured petition hoping to make what would be a reasonable and just appeal to leaders in Tokyo, Washington, and Paris. Yet unintentionally they sparked a national uprising in which thousands were killed or imprisoned. This happened the next day, March 1, when a person who happened to have a copy, decided to read the declaration to an enthusiastic gathering on a peaceful Sunday afternoon. The electrified crowd began marching down the streets of Seoul shouting out for immediate independence. Within days the demonstrations calling for independence spread until they reached nearly every part of the country. In the next few weeks, they took place in every province and city and 90 percent of Korea's more than 200 counties. Estimates of the number of people who participated range from 300,000 to two million with most historians believing it was somewhere between these figures, perhaps one million. This was a truly large number. To put it in perspective, anti-imperialist demonstrations appeared throughout the non-Western world in the spring and summer of 1919—in China, Egypt, India, the Philippines, and elsewhere. But nowhere were they on the same scale as in Korea, and nowhere did they take place throughout the country and involve so many different people including students, farmers, businessmen, and women.

The March First Movement as it became to be called, turned violent. This was not caused by the demonstrators but by the reaction of the Japanese. Panicky colonial police and gendarmes fired on crowds, carried out mass arrests, and in one grim case marched the demonstrators into a church and then set fire to it. Officially 553 were killed, 1,409 injured and over 14,000 arrested. Most likely this was a gross undercount. By some estimates, 7,000 were killed. Eventually, the demonstrations were suppressed. Yet it was a milestone in Korean history. The scale and breadth of the protest movement demonstrated just how much Koreans resented being under foreign rule. It was the first great display of modern Korean nationalism. This was no longer a matter of righteous armies defending the dynasty, but the demonstrators calling for something new, a modern Korean nation. We have seen how quickly Korean intellectuals assimilated the new ideas of nation, and nation-state; with the March First Movement, Korean nationalism and its struggle to establish a modern independent Korean state moved from teahouse discussion to popular sentiment.

Koreans today look with pride at the March First Movement, yet there is something poignant about it. Koreans would rarely be as united as they were in 1919. While the aspiration to become a modern, autonomous, and progress state became near-universal, how to achieve this would soon divide them. During the next century, they could agree on this: that Koreans were a single people, a single nation and they ought to live in a single independent and progressive state. But they could not agree on the way to achieve this and just what is meant by being progressive and modern.

Yu Gwansun

The most iconic figure in the March First Movement was a young girl, Yu Gwansun, "Korea's Joan of Arc." Yu was born in 1902 in the provincial town of Cheonan about 50 miles (80km) south of Seoul. She was lucky enough to attend school as most girls still received no formal education, and she was an outstanding student who received a scholarship to attend the prestigious Ewha Hakdang, an upper-level school for girls in Seoul. The terms of the scholarship required her to be a teacher, but she never lived to become one. Founded in 1886 by an American missionary Mary Scranton, Ewha was the first modern school for girls and evolved into Ewha Women's University, the world's largest women's university, and one of the most prestigious institutions in Korea. Ewha girls knew they were part of the modern elite of Korea, and it was therefore not surprising that when the March First Movement took place in Seoul, they were among the first to participate. She and several other students were arrested by the authorities, but the school officials were able to negotiate their release.

On March 10, the Japanese authorities closed all schools and Yu returned home. There she became an eager proponent of the movement going from village to village encouraging people to participate. On April 1 she participated in a demonstration in Cheonan which she helped organize. The demonstration began at 9 am in the central market. Three thousand attended, a large number for a modest-sized provincial town, and an example of just how widespread the demonstrations were. As they shouted "Long Live Korean Independence" Japanese police opened fire on the unarmed demonstrators, killing nineteen of them including Yu's parents. As one of the organizers, she was arrested and offered a light sentence in return for a plea of guilty and information on the others. She refused and the Japanese police badly tortured her. While in prison she attempted to organize another demonstration for Korean independence among the prisoners. She was tortured again and died from the injuries sustained. She was only eighteen. Yu, both at the time and ever since, became a symbol of the resistance against Japanese rule.

Divided Nationalists

The March First Movement created a domestic and international embarrassment for the Japanese who then responded with changes in the colonial administration. Tokyo instituted some reforms that permitted Koreans to open Korean language newspapers and periodicals and to form organizations to preserve their culture. It promised them some role in the administration and generally lightened up the heavy hand of colonial rule. The hated gendarmerie was replaced with a national police force. Japanese teachers no longer wore swords to class. And Tokyo replaced the army generals that had been supervising the administration of the colony with more liberal-minded naval officers. A somewhat more open period took place from 1920 to the early 1930s that allowed some limited freedom for Koreans to meet, debate, and organize. However, any calls for independence were prohibited and thousands of Koreans were jailed and tortured for stepping beyond the narrow bounds of freedom of expression.

These modest concessions did little to stop the Korean nationalism movement from emerging as a powerful force. The term Korean nationalist movement is a bit misleading since it implies an absent unity. Korean nationalists all sought to regain the nation's independence, but they had no single organization, leader, or unifying vision of how to achieve independence or what just what that liberated state would look like. Although a varied group, Korean nationalists can be categorized in two ways. There were the moderate gradualists who were willing to work within the colonial regime and the independence fighters who refused to cooperate with the Japanese but sought to overthrow their rule. The independence fighters in turn became divided into the communists and the non-communists.

Gradualists like the influential writer Yi Gwangsu felt that Korea had to first improve itself, educate the people, and learn to become modern. Then, when the Korean people had achieved a sufficient level of maturity and "modernity," Korea could become independent. Many educated Koreans held this view. They often looked at their own country's history and culture with a degree of embarrassment, seeing it as backward. They were ashamed of its weakness, and how easily it lost its independence. They blamed this on Confucianism, the lazy and self-serving *yangban* class, and their country's subservience to China. For them, independence was a long-term project led by people like themselves who could simultaneously cooperate with the Japanese while establishing schools, newspapers, and self-improvement societies that would lead the ignorant masses into the modern world. Only then would Korea be ready to join the world of sovereign states. Thus, they were able to persuade themselves that they were forwarding the independence movement by collaborating with the colonial occupiers. It is easy to ridicule the obvious self-serving nature of these moderate, gradualist nationalists; still, most were sincere.

Moderate gradualists promoted modern schools and the effort to establish a Korean university. Some like the northern landowner Cho Mansik were influenced by Gandhi's nonviolent, noncooperation nationalist movement in India. Cho established an organization to encourage Koreans to buy locally made products and boycott Japanese imports. These more moderate forms of protest and national consciousness-raising could not survive the more repressive administration of the 1930s. During the Second World War, the Japanese insisted that all prominent Koreans actively support the war effort, which meant that most of the more moderate nationalists were pressured into giving speeches or other public displays of support. This weakened their nationalist credentials and would haunt them after liberation.

The independence fighters included underground groups within Korea, but efficient Japanese policing severely restricted their activities. Most who actively sought the overthrow of the regime operated outside the country. Colonial rule created a diaspora of exiled Koreans politically and militarily engaged in the struggle for national independence. Their efforts were undermined by geography and ideology. Most independence movements in the first half of the twentieth century had an important base of operations: London; Paris; Switzerland; New York; or another overseas location. Koreans were scattered. Tokyo with its large Korean student population was one center but they were carefully watched by Japanese police which limited their activities. Some exiles were in Siberia, Hawaii, and the U.S. mainland. A few were in Europe. Many were in China, but even here they were dispersed: some in Shanghai, some in the Chinese interior, and some in Manchuria. The most important center, until taken over by the Japanese in the late 1930s, was Shanghai. Exiles from different groups gathered there in 1919 to form the Korean Provisional Government. Syngman Rhee served as its first president but wielded little actual control over it. Later many different nationalist leaders rotated as president and other officers, but overall, the Korean Provisional Government was ignored by the international community and had little real control over the various exile groups.

Geography wasn't the only factor working against them; so were their ideological divisions. In the 1920s the independence fighters became split into the communists and non-communists. The non-communists were a diverse group. A few in the 1930s were attracted to fascism. Most looked to the liberal democratic societies of the West, especially the United States as a model for their own society. Many such as Syngman Rhee were not radically different from the gradualists in their vision of a modern Korean society led by members of the educated elite. They differed in their opposition to any compromise with the Japanese authorities. Other Korean independence fighters, turned to radical explanations and radical solutions for the country's plight. A small number looked to anarchism; many more to communism.

Few Koreans were aware of communism until after the Bolshevik Revolution of 1917. Lenin's denunciation of imperialism and his offer to help victims of colonial oppression excited young Koreans. When Lenin called an international conference of the Toilers of the East in Moscow in 1922, Koreans were the largest group to attend. Considering their poverty, and the geographical and political obstacles they faced in reaching Moscow, it is surprising how many participated. They returned with a new vision for society. Marxism was especially attractive since it provided an explanation for the country's weakness, its poverty, and its victimization at the hands of the Japanese. It was an all-embracing philosophy that, like Confucianism, offered a blueprint for a virtuous harmonious society. Communist converts were deeply suspicious of the moderates who they saw as elitists. What they wanted was not just independence, but a social revolution led by the masses of peasants and workers. The first communist groups were organized in Siberia and became affiliated with the Bolshevik Party in Russia. These groups, however, played only a marginal role in the independence movement.

In 1925, a group of young Koreans organized a secret Korean Communist Party in Seoul but within months this was discovered by the Japanese police, and they were arrested. A second Korean Communist Party was organized the following year, its members were arrested within a few months. Not easily discouraged, young radicals organized a third and then a fourth party which suffered the same fate. There were four communist parties within three years. Eventually, an underground party managed to barely survive but it was so restricted and secretive that it remained isolated from the larger international communist movement and the members from each other. Nonetheless, some Korean communists managed to organize labor unions and in the northern part of the country "red" peasant unions. More active were the communists in China. Thousands of Korean independence fighters joined the Chinese Communists. But they became divided into two groups that had little contact with each other. From 1935 one group was based in Yenan in the northwestern part of the country and another in the 1930s fought the Japanese along the Manchurian borderlands.

Korea's World War II

Westerners generally regard the Second World War as beginning with the German invasion of Poland in 1939. In Asia, it began the Japanese military expansion into China. After 1930 Japan came under the domination of ultra-nationalist military and political circles, turned away from international cooperation to growing hostility toward the West, and pursued imperial expansion in Asia. In 1931 the Japanese Kwantung Army took control of all of Manchuria. In 1932 Japan set up a puppet state of Manchukuo. Manchukuo, in turn, became the base for further expansion into China. This profoundly affected Korea in two ways. First, it changed Korea's role from the periphery of the Japanese Empire to closer to its center and made it a strategic staging post for this further expansion. Secondly, it resulted in the Japanese tightening their grip on the peninsula. The first spelled opportunities for Koreans, and the second was a setback for Korean nationalists.

Full-scale war broke out when in 1937 Japan began its invasion of proper China. Tokyo's plan was for a short campaign that replace the increasingly nationalist and hostile government of the Guomindang in Nanjing with a more pliant one. Since the Republic of China was considered militarily weak, no match for the more modern, disciplined, well equipped, and highly efficient Japanese Imperial forces, a quick victory seemed assured. But the war went on much longer than expected. Nanjing, the Chinese capital fell, but the Guomindang government of the Republic of China retreated into the deep interior of China establishing its new headquarters at Chongqing, and carried on the resistance. In 1938 it was becoming increasingly clear to the Japanese that bringing China under its control was going to be a major long-term effort. Japan went into full-scale wartime mobilization while moving in an increasingly totalitarian direction.

With the outbreak of the China war, the colonial administration of Korea transformed itself from an increasingly repressive one to a totalitarian one. No longer content just to prevent Korean nationalist sentiment and to suppress opposition to the colonial regime, it tried to coerce the entire population into actively supporting the Japanese imperial cause. In 1937 the colonial government formed a Korean League for the General Mobilization of the National Spirit with branches in every county and township. This was to spread knowledge and support for the expansion of the empire into China. As the Japanese incursion into China turned into a major conflict the colonial regime created state-sponsored organizations of all types designed to control the activities of the Korean people and direct them toward the war effort. In 1938 it formed the Korean Federation of Youth Organizations as an umbrella organization to control and utilize all the country's youth groups. The authorities ran Local Youth Leadership Seminars and Training Institutes for Children's Organizations. Writers were organized into the All-Korean Writers Federation and there were similar nationwide associations for laborers, tenant farmers, and fishermen. The colonial authorities also created another all-embracing organization, the Korean Anti-communist Association, which also had branches in every province.

Few Koreans could escape becoming involved in some mass organizations and participating in mass rallies and campaigns. Beginning in September 1939, the first day of each month was Rising Asia Service Day, on which people were required to perform tasks for the sake of developing the new Asia. In 1940, the entire colony was organized into 350,000 Neighborhood Patriotic Associations, each with ten households. These became the basic units for the collection of contributions to the war effort, imposition of labor service, maintenance of local security, and rationing. Education became highly militarized and regimented. Compulsory military drills were introduced at all middle and higher-level schools. Political rallies became part of schooling, as were mass mobilizations of Korean youth for the war effort. In incremental stages, the colonial government brought students into the war. In October 1940, all student organizations automatically became branches of the Citizen's

Total Mobilization League. Students found their time increasingly occupied by extracurricular activities such as collecting metal for the war effort and attending patriotic rallies. College students were sent to the countryside to explain the war effort to farmers and rural folk. In the early 1940s, the school term was shortened, and secondary school students were required to work on military construction projects. Student labor groups were formed to do "voluntary" work such as building airstrips and defense works. By the spring of 1945, virtually all classroom instruction above the elementary level was suspended and students were involved in labor and military service.

After 1940 hundreds of thousands of Koreans were drafted and sent to Japan to work in the factories and mines, relieving a labor shortage. So many Koreans were shipped off to Japan that by 1945, they made up one-quarter of Japan's entire workforce. Labor conditions in Japan were harsh, workers were often put up in crowded dormitories, and their movements were restricted. Conditions were hardly better at home with rationing and mobilization of men and women for "voluntary" work.

As bad as these mass mobilization campaigns and the large-scale forced labor were, no legacy of wartime Korea left a greater scar on the national psyche than the policy of forced assimilation. Under the slogan "Japan and Korea, One Body" the Koreans were to become a kind of Japanese. This was based on a historically false contention that in ancient times Japan had ruled Korea and that the two peoples were united under Japan's divine imperial family. When they separated, Japan went on to progress, but Korea remained backward. Now it was Japan's duty to lift the Korean people (their cousins) and reunite them with the people on the home islands. For this reason, in official bureaucratese Koreans were called the "peninsular people" to distinguish them from the "homeland people," that is ethnic Japanese of the archipelago; the term "Korean" was often avoided. This theory, largely without historical basis, was around during the onset of colonial rule but with the war, it was now official doctrine—Koreans were Japanese if a kind of inferior branch. All Koreans were required to register at Shinto shrines which were constructed everywhere. This, of course, was an alien cult, that almost no Korean took seriously, but now they were to become Shintoists. Buddhists had long been able to accommodate other spiritual practices but for the small but growing Christian minority, this was sacrilege. For almost all Koreans, being forced to register and worship at these shrines was offensive.

Then in late 1939, the government issued the Name Order which set in motion a process by which all Koreans were to change their names to Japanese ones. From 1940 almost all employed by the state or its agencies and their families were pressured to adopt Japanese names. Eventually over four-fifths of the population did. For a culture that revered ancestors and for whom names represented lineages that could be traced back centuries, this was especially painful. Some Koreans simply adopted the Japanese pronunciation for the Chinese characters with which they wrote their names. Others adopted entirely new ones. At the same time, the Japanese sought to erase the Korean language. In 1940, all instruction in schools switched to Japanese, Korean language newspapers, and other publications were shuttered, and Koreans in public offices and schools could be punished for speaking their own language. This last measure met with limited success since most Korean could hardly carry on a simple conversation in Japanese and many, probably a majority, could not speak it at all.

Above all, the Second World War was a time of mass uprooting. Besides the many who were simply conscripted and carted off to Japan or some labor site, millions of Koreans left voluntarily to seek work in the expanding empire. The largest number went to Manchuria to work in the factories, on the railroads, and wherever needed. Smaller numbers were in far-flung parts of the Japanese Empire—in China, Southeast Asia, and the Pacific. Even within Korea, there was a huge migration from the agricultural south to the industrializing north. By 1944 one in eight Koreans was living outside of Korea, and one in five in Korea were living outside their home province. Put another way more than a third of the adult population was living away from home. Virtually every Korean found his or her normal routine disrupted by the endless mass mobilization campaigns.

So, this was Korea at the end of the Second World War: a mobilized, uprooted, bullied population, subject to constant indoctrination and denied their own identity. It was a population filled with discontent. In the countryside, millions of peasants during the colonial rule had lost their land. More than three-quarters of them were tenants giving up to half their crop to their landlords. And they were the luckier ones. Many thousands of Koreans were forced into the mountains, clearing land, and seeking to stave off starvation by planting crops and then moving on. As a result, the forests, of this once green land disappeared and the barren mountainsides symbolized the rape and exploitation of the country under colonial rule. In the cities and towns, laborers worked for half or less of the wage of their Japanese fellow employees and served under Japanese supervisors. Efforts to organize labor unions were suppressed. Even those middle-class professionals who benefitted economically from colonial rule resented being treated as second-class citizens in their own country.

Comfort Women Camp

Of the many tragedies brought upon the Korean people by the Japanese during the Second World War, few have lingered more as an emotional issue than the "comfort women." An estimated 200,000 women, mostly from Korea but also from China and the Philippines, "served" in the Japanese military in China, Burma, Thailand, Vietnam, Malaya, Manchukuo, Taiwan, the Dutch East Indies, Portuguese Timor, New Guinea, Hong Kong, Macau, and French Indochina. "Comfort women," as they were euphemistically called, may have started as volunteers lured by the promise of money. But later most were either tricked into service or conscripted.

The practice grew out of Japanese authorities' concern about their soldiers committing rape, and concerns about the spread of venereal disease. They were also concerned about officers accidentally leaking secrets. The first "comfort station" was established in Shanghai in 1932 but it became common only after the war started. Women in the comfort camps were virtual prisoners. They serviced up to thirty men a day, typically working from nine or ten in the morning to the late evening, certain hours of the day were reserved for officers. Usually, they were given one day a month off. In theory, they were paid, not directly but to the manager of the camp who was supposed to share the money with them. Yet, in many cases, the women received no pay at all, and could not quit or even leave the camps except when escorted. The appalling conditions come through in memoirs. One Korean woman was recruited when she was eighteen, she thought it was to work in restaurants. She was shipped off with sixteen other young ladies to a camp in Burma. Suffering from despair, several in her group committed suicide.

The end of the war brought an end to their ordeal, but it did not bring an end to their suffering. Not only did the women have to find a way to get home, but when they returned, they had to deal with the shame their experience brought. Some were shunned by their own families and never married. Some who never made it home were abandoned and forgotten in China or Southeast Asia. Only in the 1980s did some of the surviving women speak out, scholars began probing into their history and the general public took notice of them. The rape and abuse these women underwent symbolized the rape and abuse the Korean people felt toward the Japanese, they were all victims. The refusal of the Japanese government to at first acknowledge their existence and later to pay them compensation contributed to the lingering resentment of Koreans toward Japan.

Forgotten Victims of Nuclear War

On a Sunday morning in August 1945, Mr. Shin was working in a plant on the outskirts of Hiroshima. Still, in his teens, he had been conscripted and sent to Japan from his hometown in the southeast of the country where he was attending high school. Since it was Sunday, he had the morning off and went fishing. He heard air raid sirens, but he was used to these, many were false alarms about imaginary American planes. He had been in an air raid and had seen U.S. aircraft up close spraying gunfire. He took cover as trained but thought, "I am Korean, American bullets and bombs won't harm me, just the Japanese." Secretly he was thrilled by the air raids, their increasing frequency probably meant that contrary to what he was hearing on the radio, reading in the press, and being told by his superiors, Japan was losing. Maybe the Americans will liberate us, he thought.

He heard no bombs that morning, but while fishing there was a flash of light in the stream. Moments later he felt a wave of heat come over him. A hill blocked the view of the city, but it was clear something had happened. He decided to keep fishing but soon heard commotion and cries and screams. Hundreds of badly burned people were fleeing the city. The factory personnel set up a first aid station, and many of the people they treated died. He gradually realized that an enormous explosion had obliterated the central city and caused incredible casualties. Mr. Shin was lucky; he survived without serious illness and lived into old age. Many Koreans were not so lucky. Somewhere between 5,000 and 8,000 Koreans perished when the atomic bomb was dropped on Hiroshima. Another 1,500 to 2,000 died in Nagasaki. Most, like Mr. Shin, were conscripts sent to Japan to work in the factories. After the war the Japanese government compensated the victims of the atomic bombs, that is, Japanese victims. Koreans were denied the benefits given to Japanese survivors even though the Japanese government was responsible for putting them in what proved to be harm's way. Not until 2008 did Japan finally address the issue. It was one more thorn in the side of Korean-Japanese relations, reinforcing the Korean sense of victimhood. It was yet one more sad chapter in Korea's century of conflict.

Divided Koreans at War

The common oppression of wartime Korea did not unite Koreans. Instead, it made the divisions among them worse. The Japanese no longer simply tolerated passive acceptance of their rule but demanded active support. Koreans who were moderate, gradualist nationalists willing to work within the colonial system to create the basis for a future independent Korea had to compromise their nationalist goals to a far greater extent than before. Businessmen, intellectuals, and social leaders were required to make public statements praising the Emperor, the Empire, and the Imperial cause. And of course, they had to change their names to Japanese ones and perform ceremonies at Shinto shrines. Many prominent Koreans read speeches on the radio written for them, urging their countrymen to dedicate themselves to the Japanese Empire. Some refused, but most went along. They complied since independence seemed far away as the Japanese Empire was only growing stronger and they felt they had to postpone the struggle for independence. For many moderates, cheerleading for the Empire was just one further practical compromise they had to make. A few might have genuinely embraced the imperial cause, or they were simply opportunistic, but for many, it was a painful decision. As a result, the nationalist credentials of most moderates were undermined. When the Japanese Empire came to a sudden and unexpected end, they were in a weaker position to lead the post-liberation nation. The radicals, on the other hand, were less compromised, they went underground, were imprisoned, or fled the country. When they returned or emerged from prison after the war, they were filled with anger and contempt for those who had cooperated with the colonial regime.

Fighting against the Japanese

Korean nationalists in China fought the Japanese but they did not do so in a unified way. During World War II many of the more conservative anti-communists served with Chiang Kai-shek and the Guomindang government in its fight with the Japanese, while the communists fought with Mao Zedong and the Chinese Communist People's Liberation Army. Although all Koreans in China were focused on resisting the Japanese and liberating their country, most found themselves fighting each other after the war. In a way, the anti-Japanese struggle was a training ground producing combat hardened veterans that formed part of the core of the North Korean, and to a lesser extent, the South Korean armies.

In the wartime Chinese capital of Chongjing, the Korean Provisional Government established an armed wing—the Korean Liberation Army. As with almost all the resistance movements it was a small group of armed fighters, hardly an army still it played an outsize role in both the nationalist mythology and post-liberation politics. Created in September 1940 it started humbly with only 30 members in 1942 and never reached beyond 300. However, many of its members later served as high-ranking officers in the South Korean army. It was headed by Ji Cheongcheon with Lee Beomseok as the Chief of Staff. The Korean Liberation Army was placed under the authority of the Chinese army but was given independent authority in 1944. Some of its fighters fought with the British in India, participating in the Battle of Imphal. In 1945 it began working with the OSS (Office of Strategic Services), the forerunner of the CIA. A group under Lee Beomseok was to land in Korea ahead of the allies and begin operations there. The date for the secret landing was August 20. Lee Beomseok was an interesting figure. Son of an official who claimed distant descent from the royal family he studied at the Sinheung Military Academy. But he never got his moment of glory, the Japanese surrendered five days before his group was to land in Korea rendering the operation unnecessary. Lee went on to become an important player in the early days of Korea's civil war he cofounded the Korean National Youth Corps, an organization of right-wing anti-communist thugs.

The non-communist Korean resistance fighters were far outnumbered by the communists. Many of the latter served with the Chinese Communist Party. Even before the Japanese invaded China in 1937, thousands of Koreans had become members of the Chinese Communist Party, and some had accompanied Mao Zedong on his famous Long March to the remote Yenan region of northwest China from 1934 to 1935. These "Yenan Koreans" were joined by thousands of others in the late 1930s who fought in the communist People's Liberation Army. The Yenan Koreans included many of the best-known independence leaders such as Kim Dubong, a distinguished linguist and scholar, and the military leader Mu Jeong. During the war, a special unit, the Korean Voluntary Army consisting of Korean communists under the leadership of Mu

Jeong, fought the Japanese in separate units alongside the People's Liberation Army. Eventually, tens of thousands of Koreans served with Mao's People's Liberation Army, making up what was by far the largest group of anti-imperialist Korean fighters.

Manchurian Borderlands

Still another group of Korean independence fighters operated little bands of guerillas in the remote mountains of Manchuria. These Manchurian-based independence fighters, although communists were only loosely connected with other Korean communists. It was from them that the leadership of North Korea later emerged.

Manchuria is mostly a flat plain, with some mountainous areas near the Korean border reaching their highest point at Baekdusan (Changbaishan in Chinese), a dormant volcano about 9,004 feet (2744 m) in elevation. Baekdusan's summit is shared by China and Korea. It was the source of two rivers: the Tumen which flows north and the Yalu (Amnok) 840 miles (1350km) which flows south. The two rivers form the Sino-Korean boundary. While Manchuria is noted for its brutally-cold winters, its soil is fertile enough to support agriculture. During most of Korea's long history it was not part of China but a wild, frontier region home to nomadic and semi-nomadic people, and short-lived states. It was the stamping grounds of some of the most formidable warrior folk in history: the Khitans; the Jurchens; the Mongols; and the Manchus who lent their name to the region. In the second half of the nineteenth century, as the Russians annexed a remote piece of outer Manchuria, the Qing government promoted settlement.

Qing encouraged the Chinese to settle but the Koreans, uninvited, came as well. Koreans began emigrating to Manchuria in the 1860s; by 1910 there were 260,000 mainly in the borderlands. Most simply sought opportunity and an escape from poverty but after 1910 many left for political reasons as well. By 1931, 900,000 Koreans were living in Manchuria; about two-thirds in the border areas. One area Kando (Jiandao), became majority Korean. For many Koreans Manchuria was a new land of opportunity; a new home. They made the most of it by being resourceful farmers and even managing to grow rice in an area that was previously considered too cold for the crop. But, for others, it was a temporary refuge until conditions in Korea enabled them to return home. Most never returned and became part of China's ethnic minority population. However, some did after the liberation in 1945, mostly to North Korea.

The rugged terrain, the weakness of the local government to establish order, and the anti-Japanese sentiments that motivated many Koreans to settle there, made the Manchurian borderlands an ideal base for guerillas. A turning point came with the Japanese takeover of Manchuria from 1931 to 1932. Koreans who thought they had escaped Japanese rule now found themselves in the middle of its empire. Many resisted. When the Chinese Communist Party organized the Northeast Anti-Japanese United Army (NEAJUA) under Yang Jingyu, Koreans joined by the thousands. The NEAJUA's First Army Second Corps consisted mostly of Koreans including Kim Il Sung and most of the later leadership of North Korea. Korean fighters set up small People's Revolutionary Governments where about 20,000 peasants lived under their authority. As small as they were, the People's Revolutionary Governments offered models for the socialist utopia they hoped to create when Korea was liberated.

Koreans Fighting for the Japanese

While some Koreans were fighting against the Japanese in China, others were fighting for the Japanese. Thousands of Koreans volunteered to serve in the Imperial armed forces. Since many of the Koreans who were recruited to fight for Japan fought in counterinsurgency operations it sometimes meant Koreans fighting for independence were fighting Koreans upholding the colonial system. This was not an unusual or unique situation among colonial peoples, but it did leave a complicated and bitter legacy. North Korean leaders would later find themselves in combat with some of the very South Koreans who fought them during this time.

Many young Koreans were willing to serve in the Japanese Imperial Army as it was an opportunity to improve their status in life, to have excitement, and to travel. The Japanese glorified military service, making it more attractive. The Japanese government, on the other hand, was uneasy about relying on Koreans for their national defense so the number that entered military service was very small. This began to change in 1938 when the Korean Special Volunteer Soldier System was launched. It began after the China War started, but it had been discussed and planned earlier so it was not initially a response to the war, which the Japanese assumed would end soon. The number of applicants greatly exceeded the small numbers that were accepted. The Japanese kept the numbers small because in addition to the fact that they were not entirely comfortable with having Koreans in their military, few Koreans were proficient in Japanese, and it was generally believed they lacked sufficient patriotism. To this was added Japanese prejudices against Koreans who they regarded as intellectually dull, dirty, selfish, and in general, incapable of being good soldiers.

As it became clear that the war was not going to end soon, the number of Koreans accepted increased to 17,000. In addition to these volunteers, high school and college students joined as part of the Korean Student Volunteer Soldier System. After 1942, as the manpower shortage became serious the military was opened up to more Koreans and finally, when they were not getting enough volunteers, they began conscripting Koreans. However, the Japanese military command continued to distrust the loyalty and capability of Koreans and they were often assigned to rear echelon tasks, especially prison guard duty rather than combat duty. Over two hundred thousand Koreans served in the Japanese military during the Second World War. More than three-quarters of them were drafted during the last year of the conflict.

Serving the Japanese often meant alienating family and friends as well as earning the scorn of later generations. In the case of Ji Cheongcheon and Hong Sa-ik, it led to a strange friendship. Ji was born Ji Seok-gyu in 1888. He was among the handful of Koreans who attended the Japanese Military Academy. Commissioned as a second lieutenant in the Japanese army in 1919 he defected to the Korean resistance in China. There he adopted the name Ji

Cheongcheon literally "Earth and Blue Sky." His classmate was Hong Sa-ik. Hong, a year younger, was from a *yangban* family in Gyeonggi-do near Seoul. In 1905 he entered the military academy of the Korean Empire. When it was abolished, he transferred to Japan's Central Military Preparatory School, as a government-financed student along with the Crown Prince Yi Eun. He went on to attend the Japanese Army Academy and was a classmate of Ji. The two were among the small handful of Koreans to become officers in the Japanese army.

But then their paths diverged. While Ji went to China to fight the Japanese, Hong went on to attend the Japanese Army War College. Eventually, Hong rose to Major General. He too fought in China but with Imperial Japan's Chinese Expeditionary Army during World War II. He became a lieutenant general, the highest-ranking Korean in the Japanese military. In 1944 he was placed in command of the Philippine prisoner-of-war camps. That same year Ji was given an independent command over the Korean Liberation Army, which had previously been under the control of the Republic of China's military. Hong and Ji remained friends and, at considerable risk to himself, Hong financially supported Ji's family. He also stubbornly refused to adopt a Japanese name at a time when all Koreans were being pressured to do so, but simply gave his Korean name a Japanese pronunciation. It is surprising that somehow, he was able to do this and still have a successful career in the Imperial Army. Ji Cheongcheon tried to secretly persuade him to defect and join the resistance where his rank, experience, and knowledge of the Japanese military would be a coup for the Korean Liberation Army. But Hong remained loyal to Japan.

After the war, Ji returned to Korea as a nationalist hero. He entered South Korean politics by serving as a member of the National Assembly in the 1950s. Hong never returned. He was tried for the mistreatment of prisoners at the Manila Tribunal and hanged as a war criminal in 1946. His son and his wife lived in South Korea but suffered harassment for being family members of a traitor and war criminal. They emigrated to the United States.

A Legacy of Division

Japan's colonial legacy, especially in the last wartime decade left the Korean people deeply divided. The colonial experience of another pair of men illustrates this: Kim Il Sung who would lead North Korea and Park Chung Hee who would lead South Korea.

Few people in history so shaped a nation as Kim Il Sung molded North Korea. Kim Il Sung was born Kim Seongju on April 15, 1912, the day the Titanic sank, in the village of Mangyeongdae outside of Pyongyang. He was the eldest of three sons of Kim Hyeongjik, an elementary school teacher who could trace his family back twelve generations to Cholla Pukto in the southern part of the country. Kim Hyeongjik, a Christian, attended Sungshil School established by American missionaries in Pyongyang. (It is fascinating just how many Korean nationalists of all stripes came out of American mission schools.) Kim Il Sung's mother, Kang Banseok was also a Christian, and her father Kang Donuk was a Presbyterian elder. The young Kim grew up just outside rapidly-modernizing Pyongyang. It was a provincial city since any Korean city that was not Seoul was a provincial city, but it was a large, prosperous urban hub. A major center of Christianity, Pyongyang was called the "Jerusalem of the East." It was also a center of Korean nationalism and opposition to Japanese rule. Kim Hyeonjik was arrested by the Japanese in 1917 for taking part in nationalist activities. He was released the following year. He was lucky; his brother was also arrested for nationalist activities and died in prison.

In 1919 Kim Hyongjik took his family to Manchuria, where he worked not along the border but as a Chinese herbal medicine doctor in Changchun in central Manchuria. The young Kim Il Sung was seven. Kim Il Sung attended two Chinese schools. When he was seventeen, he joined the South Manchurian Chinese Communist Youth Organization which resulted in him being expelled from school before he completed the eighth grade. As the eldest son, he worked to support his family. When both his parents died, he was free to pursue his own life which was to become a revolutionary and independence fighter. Moving to the frontier he joined the Chinese Communist Party and became part of the mostly Korean ethnic

Second Corps First Route Army of the Northeast Anti-Japanese United Army. In 1934, Kim Il Sung was arrested during a massive purge of Korean members. Koreans, working as Japanese informants, penetrated the army and the Chinese began to purge them. But Kim survived the purge and at 25 he became the commander of a unit that at one point numbered 200 to 300 men. The young guerilla fighter gained prominence when, leading a band of about 80 guerillas, he captured the small border town of Bocheonbo on June 4, 1937. After killing a few Japanese policemen, destroying some Japanese buildings, and giving some speeches, he and his band left. It was a small incident but an embarrassing one, for the Japanese generally maintained tight control of the border. Newspapers in Korea widely reported the incident, giving the young Kim a measure of fame. In late 1937 the Japanese created a special unit to hunt him down, but it was unsuccessful. Kim Il Sung briefly captured another border town, Musan, in May 1939. Subsequently, his first wife Kim Hyosun was captured by the Japanese in 1940. He later married Kim Jeongsuk, a fellow partisan and daughter of a farmer. His brother, Kim Cheolsu, was also killed fighting the Japanese. In 1940, following a massive Japanese campaign to stamp out guerilla activity in the region, Kim fled to Khabarovsk in Siberia. There he led a battalion of guerilla fighters in the 88th Special Reconnaissance Brigade of the Soviet 25th Army, but he saw no further action during World War II.

While Kim Il Sung was fighting the Japanese, Park Chung Hee, the man who would become his most formidable opponent in the long Korean War, was fighting for the Japanese. The wartime paths of these two future leaders could hardly have been different. Park was born on November 14, 1917, five and a half years later than Kim Il Sung, in Kumi in the southeast province of Gyeongsang Bukdo. The youngest of five brothers and two sisters of a poor *yangban* family, he excelled as an elementary student. He was admitted to Daegu Normal High School which trained teachers. There he did not excel as a student but at least passed and was assigned to an elementary school in a mining town not far from home, where he taught for three years.

The one area of high school where Park performed well was at the military drills in which all students were required to participate. His hero was Napoleon, and his dream was not to be a teacher but a soldier. This he managed to achieve by entering the Military Academy of the Manchukuo Imperial Army. He was a bit older than the other students, yet had the advantage of speaking better Japanese than most Korean students there. Manchukuo Military Academy was established in 1939, modeled after the Japanese Military Academy but less prestigious. Nonetheless, it was a great opportunity for a young Korean. Park, who took the Japanese name Takagi Masao, must have impressed his Japanese instructors because they recommended him for the Japanese Military Academy, an honor bestowed on few Koreans. At graduation, he was given a gold watch by the Manchukuo puppet emperor Puyi. The war and the empire ended before he could attend the school in Tokyo.

When Park enrolled in the Manchukuo Military Academy in April 1942 the Japanese Empire was expanding, with one great victory after another. Park could look forward to many opportunities to win military glory for the Empire. However, when he graduated in April 1944, the situation changed. He was sent to a remote post near the border of Inner Mongolia, and a year later Japan surrendered. After the war, he returned to Korea and enrolled in the Korea Military Academy created by the Americans during the occupation. He was arrested in 1948 and accused of organizing a secret Communist cell within South Korea but this was never confirmed. Nevertheless, he was sentenced to death, saved from execution when at the urging of senior officers his sentence was commuted, and he consequently left the army. When the Korean War started, he returned as a lieutenant colonel and fought against the army of former Manchurian guerilla, Kim Il Sung.

Korea was a restless, discontented society when the Japanese surrendered in 1945. It was a society mostly united in its resentment of Japanese rule and desire for independence. However, it was ideologically divided, and then suddenly, in the late summer of 1945, it was politically divided into two separate zones of occupation.

CHAPTER 3

The Emerging Civil War, 1945–1950

The Division of Korea

On the night of August 10 1945, two men met in a room to draw a line on a map. The State-War-Navy Coordinating Committee assigned Colonel Dean Rusk and Colonel Charles Bonesteel to determine where to divide Korea into two occupation zones: Soviet and American. The matter was urgent. On August 6, the United States dropped a nuclear bomb on Hiroshima, and on August 8, the Soviet Union, three months after promising to do so, declared war on Japan. Immediately the Soviets began an offensive along Japan's northern frontier with Sakhalin, Manchuria, and the extreme northeast corner of Korea. The Americans were now concerned about the advance of Soviet forces into Korea since their control of the peninsula could pose a threat to a planned American occupation of Japan. They were right to be concerned, the Japanese forces along the border with the Soviets had been hollowed out and were no match for the Soviets with their tanks, planes, and artillery. All of Korea could easily be occupied by the Red Army before the distant Americans, whose closest forces were 600 miles away, could arrive. The Americans hoped Moscow might agree to a divided occupation on the model of Germany and Austria.

During the meeting, which lasted until the early morning hours of the next day, Rusk and Bonesteel looked at the map they had available: a National Geographic map of Asia. They noted that the thirty-eighth parallel divided Korea into two roughly equal sized halves but left Seoul in the southern portion nearest Japan.

That was where they decided to draw the line. This proposal was passed along, signed off by President Truman on August 13, and sent to Moscow where, to the surprise of many, Stalin immediately approved. It was indeed surprising since Moscow could have easily accomplished what it had failed to do at the start of the century: gain control of the entire Korean Peninsula. Perhaps Stalin hoped agreeing to this would open the door to a joint occupation of Japan, or perhaps he just wanted to avoid a potential conflict with the United States in Korea.

It is not likely that the participants in this agreement understood the consequences of their actions. Nor did they realize they were permanently dividing one of the oldest, most homogeneous nations in the world and setting the groundwork for modern history's longest conflict. The participants knew little about Korea. The line they drew was drawn out of convenience; a spur-of-the-moment decision made in the contingencies of war. It was an arbitrary line that had no basis in geography or history. It divided provinces, valleys, villages, and families. No Korean was consulted in this decision or even knew of it until later. Nor is it likely that any Korean would have approved of their country being sliced in half even if only temporarily. Koreans had been divided ideologically, divided in the response to colonial rule, divided on their vision of a future but united in the sense of being one people.

In addition to agreeing to partition the country, the Allies agreed not to give it independence, at least not right away. During the war, Franklin Roosevelt had proposed a thirty-year trusteeship during which time Koreans could be trained to govern themselves. Of course, this ignored the fact that Koreans had 1300 years of governing themselves, but it is doubtful that Roosevelt was aware of this. Stalin thought this too long and it was reduced to twenty years. Koreans knew nothing of this. Japan's surrender to them meant liberation and the restoration of their independence.

Liberation: A Brief Moment of Joy

One of the most important moments in modern Korean history took place on Sunday, August 15, 1945. Koreans were told by the Japanese authorities to gather around the nearest radio to hear an announcement from the emperor. This was most extraordinary since the remote, godlike Japanese emperor never addressed his subjects; the general public had not even heard his voice. As they listened, few could make out his words since most Koreans could not understand Japanese well and those who could, did not comprehend the archaic form of the language the imperial family used. But the message got through: Japan was surrendering. To people isolated by strict censorship and accustomed to receiving only reports of victories, the news came as a shock. They may have known the war was not going well, but they had not expected this. Almost immediately, Koreans broke out into spontaneous celebrations—singing, weeping, and dancing in the streets. Symbols of Japanese authority were destroyed, and the families brought out hidden copies of the *taegukki*, the Korean national flag, or a hastily made one and proudly displayed it. At night the landscape was lit by Shinto shrines set on fire by Koreans.

Koreans wasted no time in organizing the skeleton of a government. People of all political views met to plan for independence which everyone assumed was imminent. They organized people's committees (*inmin wiwonhoe*) to deal with practical issues such as securing food supplies, imposing order, and preventing clashes with the Japanese authorities that mostly avoided interfering. Within two weeks, people's committees were organized throughout the country, in all thirteen provinces as well as in cities and countries. On September 6, several hundred delegates from the various committees gathered in Seoul and proclaimed the Korean People's Republic (KPR). Syngman Rhee was named chair, and other prominent Koreans of various political views, including a left-leaning intellectual, Yeo Unhyeong, and a conservative businessman, Kim Seongsu, were given important positions. Six days later, delegates of the KPR drew up a program calling for the confiscation of land owned by Japanese and national traitors. They also called for the limiting of rents to 30 percent, the establishment of an eight-hour workday, a minimum wage, and other reforms. There has been some controversy over the people's committees and the KPR. Both their names and some of the radical reforms suggested a possible communist influence but there is no clear evidence of this. They do seem to have been unplanned, spontaneous groups that included prominent and respected members of the local communities doing their best to prepare the way for independence.

Tragically this act of cooperation among almost all Koreans, this optimism and this unity was very short-lived. It is sad to think that this brief moment of euphoria would be followed by years of tragedy, and that this burst of national unity would be followed by decades of division and bitter conflict. In the days after Japan's surrender most Koreans wanted independence, peace, and unity. They got instead another foreign occupation, more conflict, and greater division.

Untrustworthy Trusteeship: The Creation of Two Koreas

The original plan among the Allies was to create a UN trusteeship, but there was no trust on any side. The Americans didn't trust the Soviets, the Soviets didn't trust the Americans, and the Koreans, at least in the South, didn't trust either of them. In December 1945, the U.S., the Soviet Union, China, and Britain met in Moscow to discuss setting up the trusteeship. It was to last four to five years, realistically reduced from the previous plan of twenty years. An American-Soviet Joint Commission was created to work out details. Up to that point, Koreans had known nothing of the secret wartime plan for a UN Trusteeship, and they reacted to the news with spontaneous outrage. On both sides of the parallel, massive demonstrations took place. At first, these included members of the Korean Communist Party but when Moscow told them to support the plan, they fell in line. The Soviets then used the opposition to the trusteeship as an excuse to clamp down on non-communist political groups in their sector. In the South, demonstrations continued adding to the sense of disorder there and making it hard for the Americans to govern.

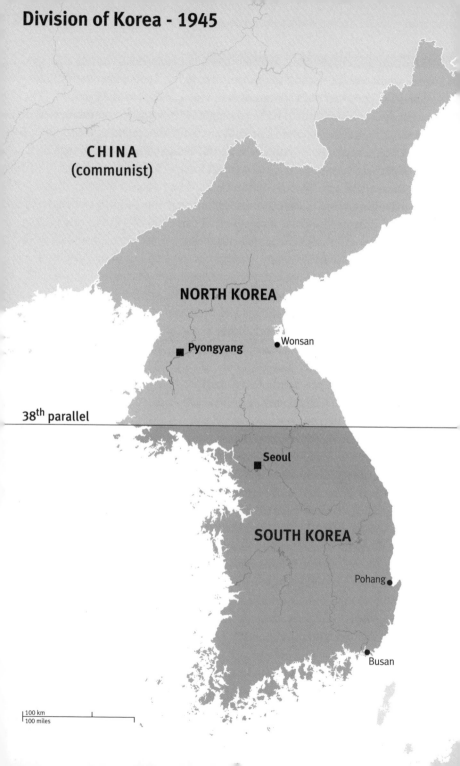

Division of Korea - 1945

CHINA
(communist)

NORTH KOREA

● Wonsan

■ Pyongyang

38th parallel

■ Seoul

SOUTH KOREA

Pohang ●

Busan ●

100 km
100 miles

The Occupations: the Soviets Get there First

On August 11, 1945, the Red Army crossed the short (14-mile wide) border into northeast Korea. After advancing into the industrial northeast of the country, it took out time to loot and cart back much of the industrial equipment to the Soviet Union. Two weeks later the Soviet forces entered Pyongyang. What they found was a local people's committee in charge headed by Cho Mansik. Unlike the Americans who ignored them the Soviets at first worked with the people's committees in the North, gradually setting up their administration. What they needed were reliable partners. Cho, who was Christian, didn't qualify, and the local communists were largely unknown and not trusted by Moscow. Nor did the Soviets fully trust Kim Dubong and the Yenan communists who were returning to Korea.

Then on September 19, a group of Manchurian guerillas arrived at the port of Wonsan from Siberia—an unauthorized return they had arranged themselves. This group of about sixty prominent guerillas chose Kim Il Sung as their spokesman. Wearing the uniform of the Red Army, with his reputation as a guerilla fighter, speaking some Russian, and possessing personal charisma, the Soviets after interviews with him decided they found their man. From October they began to promote him as the communist leader in their zone. He was not alone in the communist leadership, Kim and his guerilla comrades shared positions of responsibility with the returning Yenan communists and the Soviet Koreans. The latter group was from the Korean minority in Russia, brought in for their language skills and their knowledge of the Soviet-style system that Moscow was constructing in its sector. After the autumn of 1946, there was a fourth group of communists that Kim had to share power with— southern communists such as Pak Heonyeong who fled North in the wake of a crackdown on leftists in the American zone.

The Soviets, in partnership with their Korean communist allies, were quick to construct a nascent state. In early 1946 they supervised the election of a Provisional People's Committee acting as a quasi-government under Soviet guidance. It carried out sweeping reforms. The industry was nationalized—an easy step since most of it belonged to the now-departed Japanese. More radical was land reform. The state confiscated large estates, without compensation to their owners, divided the land into small parcels and gave them to the former tenants. Farmers got their land. The landowners fled south and the *yangban* class that dominated Korea for centuries was gone in the North. A series of laws established an eight-hour day and a minimum wage, promoted equal rights for women, and made divorce easy. The old hierarchal class and the patriarchal system were abolished (at least on paper), and everyone was to address each other as "comrade," avoiding the honorifics that marked social status among Koreans.

A new people's committee was elected in 1947 with the name "provisional" dropped, indicating a measure of permanence to the emerging state. The Soviets also created an army in the North. In 1946 they established national police and railway defense units. The police force headed by the Soviet Korean Pang Hakse was modeled after that of Stalinist Russia, but without political prisons. Those convicted of political crimes were simply sent to the Soviet Gulag. Meanwhile, with Soviet approval, the Manchurian guerilla leader Kim Chaek founded a Pyongyang Institute to train military officers and political cadres. The Soviets established a Central Security Training School which was a de facto military academy. Its first class graduated in the fall of 1947. In February 1948, the Soviets officially organized the Korean People's Army. It was under close Soviet supervision with three Soviet advisors attached to each regiment. By that summer it had 40,000 troops. In short, by 1948 the Soviets had established a communist state.

The consolidation of the new communist order was not accompanied by violent class warfare. This was in contrast to the civil conflict and mass executions that took place with the establishment of the Bolshevik regime in Russia and the People's Republic of China. Partly this was because most of the landlord and business class had fled to the South. Yet there was opposition, and it was dealt with ruthlessly. In November 1945, there were mass protests against the communists in the city of Sinuiju which were violently repressed. Student protests in the northeast industrial city of Hamheung, calling for the withdrawal of Soviet forces, were also brutally crushed. On March 1, 1946, the date commemorating the great national uprising against the Japanese in 1919, citizens carried out public protests directed at the occupation forces and their Korean communist allies; these too were met with harsh measures. After 1946 what remained of any opposition had been either exiled to Siberia or had fled to the South.

The Chaotic U.S. Occupation in the South

In contrast to the orderly, swift creation of a Soviet-style state in the North, the U.S. occupation was characterized by a lack of preparation, lack of purpose, and general chaos. The American forces didn't arrive until September 6th. When they did set foot in Seoul, the U.S. soldiers were greeted by the Koreans as liberating heroes. Unfortunately, the occupation leaders almost immediately squandered some of their goodwill with two blunders. First, they ignored the representatives of the Korean People's Republic, refusing to even acknowledge them, and disregarded the local people's committees. Second, the head of the newly formed United States Military Government in Korea (USAMGIK), General John Hodge ordered Koreans to continue obeying the Japanese colonial authorities in the country. This latter was an expedient move to keep the colonial administration going while the U.S. military set up its own. After ignoring the people's committees which had been successfully managing things, it is hard to imagine any move more likely to alienate the Koreans than to ask for their obedience to the hated Japanese.

While the Americans, realizing their mistake, quickly sent the Japanese home, they struggled to find Koreans they could work with to build a stable order. They were distrustful of the communists and other leftists and gravitated toward the old landowning elite. The landowners tended to be more educated, more familiar with Westerners, and sometimes spoke English. They largely dominated the Representative Democratic Council (the USAMGIK) created in 1946. But as a leadership group they had two shortcomings. The first was that they had served and prospered under Japanese rule so had tarnished reputations; they were considered traitors and collaborators by many Koreans. The second was that they were major landowners at a time the peasant majority in the countryside was clamoring for land reform. The most effective leader was Syngman Rhee who returned to Seoul in the fall of 1945. He seemed the perfect fit for leadership, possessing sterling nationalist credentials, fiercely anti-Communist, and American educated. But Rhee used resentment over the trusteeship to rally support around himself which only made life difficult for the USAMGIK, and in general, the Americans found him too authoritarian, too nationalistic, and too stubborn to deal with.

Looking for an alternative for leadership the moderate and charismatic leftist Yeo Unhyeong seemed promising, but he was assassinated in the summer of 1947. Desperate, the Americans sought out Seo Jaepil. Returning from a successful career as a physician in the U.S., the octogenarian Seo was dying of cancer. He took a look at the home he hadn't seen in half a century and returned to America. In the end the search for a moderate leader of some stature, untainted by collaboration with the Japanese, or by association with the communists, who could preside over the internal divisions of Korea and unite them, failed. Instead, the South Koreans got Rhee, who aligned himself with the conservatives and outmaneuvered his opponents. Meanwhile the American authorities struggled to maintain a sense of order amidst labor strikes, student unrest, and violent incidents caused by right-wing youth groups, many of them refugees fleeing from the North.

Meanwhile, the USAMGIK began constructing a state. It had not been the intention of the Americans to create a separate state in the South, at least during the first two years when they continued to hope that somehow a deal could be brokered with Moscow and both countries could withdraw and leave behind a unified nation. Yet, the Americans were already building their own Korean state. The USAMGIK constructed a security apparatus. It started with the Korean National Police headed by Chang Taeksang. Chang had served under the Japanese as many of the officers of the force. This was unfortunate since Chang and the National Police were unable to shake their reputation as collaborators who served the hated colonial security forces. In January 1946 the USAMGIK created a 25,000-member constabulary force, a paramilitary force that became the nucleus of the South Korean army. To train officers, the Americans established a Korean Military Academy. For the first class, they selected twenty veterans of the Japanese army, another twenty who had served in the Japanese-controlled Manchurian army, and twenty from the Liberation Army. However, the Liberation Army refused to work with Japanese collaborators, so ultimately the first officer class consisted entirely of those who had served the Japanese Empire. Although these officers included competent people, they, in contrast to the North Korean security forces, had little in the way of nationalist credentials. The three-year military occupation was not without some successes. It passed sweeping educational reform that prepared the way for what would be South Korea's extraordinary effective school system, it laid the basis of a functional state, but it failed to give what most rural people in the South wanted most—land reform.

American occupation forces, and their right-wing South Korean allies increasingly manning the security forces, cracked down on those who opposed the emerging political and social order much as the Soviets and their Korean communist allies had done in the North. The Korean Communist Party was headquartered in Seoul and the vast majority of its members lived there. They helped organized labor strikes and student protests. Many public protests were directed at the Korean "collaborators" the US occupation appeared to have placed in positions of power. In September 1946, the occupation authorities closed Communist newspapers. This led the Korean Communist Party to switch to new confrontational tactics in its opposition to the occupation authority. Later that month, the Korean Communist Party helped organize a general strike. It began on September 23 with a railway strike in Busan involving more than 40,000 railroad workers from throughout the country. They were joined by workers in other industries including chemical and metal workers. By the end of the month between 250,000 to 300,000 workers were on strike. The most violent incident occurred in the southeastern city of Daegu on October 1, while strikers were demonstrating, police fired on them, killing one. The next day protesters and students paraded the body in the streets, calling for higher wages, the right to organize, better working conditions, and the release of political prisoners. Losing control of the situation and fearing that the violent situation which was concentrated in Daegu and the southeast would spread to other parts of the country, the USAMGIK used tanks and heavily armed vehicles to restore order accompanied by Korean police, and right-wing groups. Two hundred and seventy-four were killed in Daegu.

This was a key turning point. Suspecting a communist conspiracy possibly directed from Moscow (which it was not) the USAMGIK outlawed the Korean Communist Party. At this point, most of the communist leaders, joined by many sympathetic artists and left-learning intellectuals, fled to the North. What was happening in the peninsula was that although the two halves of Korea did not correspond to any ethnic or other differences, the pre-existing ideological divide among Koreans was becoming a geographical divide as conservatives fled to the South and leftists fled to the North.

Kim Gu

One ambitious Korean neither trusted nor supported by the Americans despite his anti-communism was Kim Gu. Among the resistance fighters, few are more admired today in South Korea. He was born Kim Changsu in 1876, the year Korea was forced open to the world, in a rural village in Hwanghae Province in what became North Korea. His family were poor peasants who claimed to be able to trace their ancestry back thirty-one generations to an illustrious lineage. The young Kim Gu studied Chinese classics with the hope of rising above his humble status. After failing a local civil service exam, he joined other discontented commoners and took part in the Donghak uprising of 1894. Its easy defeat by the government and Japanese forces discouraged him and he left the movement. In 1896, outraged by the murder of Queen Min, he developed a deep hostility to the Japanese and murdered a Japanese tourist while in Manchuria. Kim insisted the Japanese man was an officer in disguise, noting that he was carrying a sword, although the evidence suggests he was simply an employee of a trading company on a sightseeing tour. Kim was sentenced to death, but his term was commuted to a lighter sentence by King Gojong.

Kim escaped prison, became a Buddhist monk, then converted to Christianity and helped found two modern schools. In 1908 he joined the New People's Organization, an underground nationalist group. In 1911 he was arrested by the Japanese for being connected to the plot by An Myeonggeun to assassinate the Governor-General, but was released in 1915. In prison, he took the pen name Kim Gu. In 1919 he joined the Korean Provisional Government in Shanghai where he served as minister of police; from 1927 he served on and off as its president.

Kim Gu's claim to fame came with his decision to organize a series of terrorist acts against the Japanese. In 1931 he created the Korean Patriotic Corps that carried out two noted terrorist acts the following year: One of these was the Sakurada Gate Incident in which one of his agents tossed a bomb at the Japanese emperor's carriage, narrowly missing the imperial ruler. The most famous terrorist attack was the Hongkou Park Incident in Shanghai which killed and injured high-ranking Japanese officials. After the outbreak of the war between Japan and China, he followed the government of Chiang Kai-shek to Chongqing. There, in 1940, he organized the Korean Liberation Army, in which Ji Cheongcheon served. His units took part in warfare in China and Southeast Asia. He worked with the OSS (the forerunner of the American CIA) and planned to land in Korea.

After 1945, when he returned to South Korea, he was one of the best-known independence fighters. His nickname was "The Assassin" and he was well known for traveling with an entourage of bodyguards and concubines. Yet, despite his fame, he found himself politically marginalized. Strongly objecting to the Trusteeship, at one point he planned a coup against the U.S. Military Government. Kim Gu was also adamantly opposed to the creation of two Koreas and went to Pyongyang in April and May of 1948 for the South-North Joint Conference in a desperate last attempt at reconciliation between the two emerging regimes. Despite his inability to capitalize on his fame, he was seen by Rhee as a rival and was assassinated in the summer of 1949. His assassin, An Duhui, an army second lieutenant, was sentenced to life but was released after less than a year, reinstated, promoted, and had a successful career doing business with the army. Later he made statements suggesting, as had been suspected, that Rhee was behind the assassination. In 1996 the aged An was himself assassinated by a bus driver seeking revenge for the murder of his hero Kim Gu.

Yeo Unhyeong

Another would-be leader of Korea was Yeo Unhyeong. While it is easy to see Korea as polarized between left and right, Yeo defies easy classification. Much of his early life was typical of Korean nationalists. He was born in 1888 in the country town of Yangpyeong in Gyeonggi province, which surrounds Seoul, into a *yangban* family. He attended the pioneering Christian Baejae School at the age of fifteen, and transferred to another school, but quit before graduating. After leaving school he began studying the Bible and befriended the American missionary, Charles Allen Clark. He helped Clark found a Christian school before enrolling in the Pyongyang Presbyterian Theological Seminary. Restless, he left shortly after and went to China where he studied English literature at a university in Nanjing. Then in 1917, he moved to Shanghai, the location of so many Korean nationalists. He assisted in organizing the Mindan, the Korean Residents' Association there, which became a basis for independence activities.

Inspired by the Bolshevik Revolution he joined the Communist Party, and in 1922 attended the First Congress of the Toilers of the East in Moscow. While in Moscow he met Lenin, Trotsky, and Sun Yat-sen. Returning to Korea he became the editor of the *Chungang Daily News*. It was while he was editor that a famous incident occurred. At the Berlin Olympics in 1936, the Korean athlete Sohn Kee-chung won the gold medal in the marathon race. A rare Olympic gold medal for an Asian and the first for a Korean. But since

Korea was no longer an official country he participated as a member of the Japanese team. When the photo was published in the paper it was doctored to replace the flag of Japan on his jersey with the forbidden flag of Korea. The outraged Japanese shut the paper down.

During the Second World War, Yeo lived a rather unusual life. The Soviet Union was, until the very end of the war, a neutral party in the Pacific theater and maintained an embassy in Seoul. Yeo was seen as having connections with Moscow, so he was useful as a go-between, and the Japanese left him alone despite his leftist and nationalist leanings. When the Japanese surrendered on August 15, the colonial authorities turned to him as an intermediary to help in the decolonization process. At the same time, he helped organize the Korean People's Republic and became its vice-premier.

Handsome, charming, experienced, and with good relations with both conservatives and communists, Yeo seemed to be a natural leader for a post-liberation Korea. But he was a man of moderation in an environment of extreme passions. Forced to step down from the Korean People's Republic by the U.S. military government, outmaneuvered and brushed aside by the communists and the rightists, he failed to play a key role in post-1945 politics. Worried about the growing emergence of two separate regimes, the left-leaning Yeo formed the Coalition Committee with the right-leaning but also moderate Kim Gyusik to bring all sides together. It is doubtful they would have succeeded but it is impossible to know because in July 1947 he was assassinated by Han Chigeun, a recent refugee from North Korea and an active member of a right-wing group.

Two Koreas Are Born

The Joint Commission was supposed to work out the plans for the preparation of a unified, independent Korea but nothing was accomplished when it met in 1946. A stumbling block was Moscow's stipulation that any political groups that opposed the trusteeship be barred from participating in the self-governing process. Since all political groups except the Soviets' communist allies were adamantly against the idea of trusteeship, this was an obvious non-starter.

By the spring of 1946, it was probably already too late to create a unified governing entity. The border between the two zones was being treated as a permanent one and the outlines of a separate state in the North were already being established when the Joint Committee met. The body's second meeting the following year also yielded no results, after which the U.S., seeing no progress and wishing to extricate itself from the peninsula, turned the question of independence over to the United Nations. The UN formed a Temporary Committee on Korea which decided elections would be held in the spring of 1948. When it was clear the Soviets would not cooperate, the UN held elections anyway in the areas that were accessible to them, that is, in the South. This meant there was to be a separate election in the South, which would, in all likelihood, mean a separate government.

Some South Koreans were appalled by the possibility that the division would become permanent. Kim Gyusik and others made a desperate last-minute attempt to work out some form of agreement with the North. Kim Gyusik was the ultimate moderate. Born in 1881 at the dawn of Korea's opening to the modern world, the orphan received an education at a missionary school run by the famed American "millionaire missionary" Horace G Underwood, Kim went on to graduate from Roanoke College and obtain a master's degree. Returning to Korea in 1905, Kim became involved as an educator and reformer. In 1913 he left China and joined the anti-Japanese nationalists there. After 1919 he served in the Korean Provisional Government as foreign minister, education minister, and vice president. Returning to Korea, Kim opposed the right-wing extremists and their ally Syngman Rhee, while also being strongly opposed to communism. For a time, USAMGIK commander John Hodge saw in Kim a fluent English speaker, an admirer of the West, and a moderate conservative: a person he could work with as a possible leader of Korea. Following Yeo's assassination, Kim Gyusik worked hard to avoid the creation of two states. However, his desperate mission to the North accomplished nothing. After this failure, he retired from politics. Two years later he was kidnapped by the North Koreans and died in North Korea in December 1950, perhaps executed or perhaps as a result of brutal treatment. It was a sad end for a person who had devoted his life to the independence and unity of his country.

The UN went ahead with its supervised elections in May and a National assembly was elected in the South. Three hundred political parties participated, but of course, the Communist Party was absent. In July, the Assembly elected Rhee as president, and with the UN's blessings, the Republic of Korea (ROK) was declared in Seoul on August 15. Separate preparations for independence took place north of the parallel. A constitution was drawn up for the new state, modeled on the 1936 Soviet Union constitution. It was drawn up in Moscow by Soviet officials who had it translated from Russian into Korean and then presented it to their Korean clients. The North then carried out its elections, which it claimed were secretly conducted in the South as well. An assembly met; two-thirds of the delegates were supposedly southerners and approved by the new government. They then proclaimed the Democratic People's Republic of Korea (DPRK) on September 9. What is important to bear in mind is that both these Koreas claimed to be the only legitimate ones. The ROK considered its control of only the southern half of the country a temporary situation. The leaders of the DRPK regarded their control over the northern half also a temporary situation. The constitution of the DPRK specified Seoul as the capital (Seoul means "capital" in Korean). Pyongyang was only intended to be the temporary government headquarters.

The Pre-War Korean War

The Korean War proper began with the North Korean invasion of the South on June, 25 1950, but a low-grade civil war had already begun with the birth of the two new Korean states in the late summer of 1948. Both the ROK and the DPRK assumed the division was temporary. They each took actions to prepare for reunification on their terms: occupying strategic points along the border; building their military forces; and crushing any possible internal support for the other regime.

The newly created armies of the two Koreas fought many skirmishes along their border. Most were very small. Some were not. One of the larger clashes took place from May 4 to May 7 1949, at Kaesong, a city just south of the thirty-eighth parallel. Twenty-two South Korean soldiers and as many as 100 civilians were killed, while North Korean casualties remain unknown. More serious fighting took place at the strategic Ongjin Peninsula in June 1949. The same month, the South sent 150 Horim (forest tiger) guerillas northeast of Kaesong. They roamed the area carrying out sabotage until they were killed by the KPA (Korean People's Army). This was one of many incidents provoked by the South. ROK commanders were so eager to attack the North whenever they could that the U.S. more than once threatened to cut off military aid if they provoked a conflict. The North too probed and sought to get hold of strategic points along its border and it was not always clear who started a particular clash. While some were very minor skirmishes, others were more on the order of battles. For instance, in August 1949 fighting took place over control of Song'ak Mountain outside Kaesong. North Korea claimed the ROK commander Kim Seokwon started it by attacking the North. Kim Seokwon, the former Japanese officer who led the hunt for Kim Il Sung in 1938, had a reputation for aggression, and was hated by the Northern regime. The battle raged for several days. Hundreds of ROK soldiers were killed and the KPA took control of the mountain.

That the conflict between North and South Korea was not based on regional differences but on ideological and political ones is illustrated by the leaders involved. Some of the leaders of the North, including Pak Heonyeong, the number two figure in the DPRK in the late 1940s, were from the South. Many ROK leaders were from the North. This was especially true of the military, which was dominated by northern-born generals. The ROK army was divided into two factions—the Northwest faction and the Northeast faction, each named for the region of the North they were from. The Northwest faction was led by the two Paek brothers, Seonyeop and Inyeop, who were from Pyongyang. Jeong Ilgwon, who like the Paek brothers had served as an officer in the Japanese Imperial Army, hailed from

Hamgyong Province and led the Northeast Faction.

Closely aligned with the ROK military were rightwing youth organizations often dominated by northerners. The most important was the Northwest Youth Organization—an anti-communist civilian group led by Kim Seokbeom, an ally of the Paek brothers. It was founded in late 1946 by refugees from the North. The Northwest Youth Organization was part of the sorting-out process of leftists from the South heading north of the parallel, and conservatives from the North heading south of it. The organization was run along semi-fascist lines; under its motto of "Nation-First," members marched in the streets and assaulted suspected communist sympathizers. It was not the only such group but it was the largest, most prominent one. The Northwest Youth Organization carried out vigilante justice and acted as a para-military force in suppressing uprisings in Cheju and elsewhere, although it had no legal authority. It became aligned with Syngman Rhee who found it useful in intimidating his opponents.

Insurgency in the South

Korea is a mountainous country without large broad plains. No place in the country is out of sight of the mountains. Here, mountains have special meaning. They are sacred places whose spirits are sought for help. They are also places of refuge, the home of most of the country's Buddhist temples. Buddhism and nature worship converge with Sansin the mountain spirit, whose shrine is found in almost every temple. After 1948 the mountains were also a refuge for those who opposed the Rhee regime in Seoul. As a result, independent South Korea was plagued by guerilla insurgencies. Some of these were encouraged and supported by North Korea. The Kangdong Institute in the North, under the direction of Pak Heonyeong and his southern communist comrades, trained insurgents. Some 600 graduates were sent to the South, along with hundreds of others. They included two important and experienced communist leaders: Kim Samyeong and Yi Juha. Most of these insurgents slipped across the border into the Odae Mountain and

Taebaek Mountain regions not far below the thirty-eight parallel.

Much of the guerilla fighting in the South, however, was more homegrown and was led and fought by locals. This was especially true in the rich rice-growing region of Cholla. Tenancy rates were high and discontent with the landlord-dominated ROK government was strong, so it didn't take much effort to recruit resistance to the regime. The CIA in early 1949 estimated that there were up to 6,000 guerillas operating in the mountains. The guerillas were often supported by local villagers who provided them with sacks of rice and other necessities. They were poorly armed, often with only bamboo sticks, but the rugged terrain and the lack of trained ROK troops worked to their advantage. Yet it was not enough of an advantage to sustain a serious internal threat. In the spring of 1949, the ROK army under Colonel Jeong Ilgwon conducted a major counter-insurgency campaign. He created a pass system; people were issued identity cards and watchtowers were set up outside of villages. He insisted that the troops avoid looting or molesting women. The campaign was largely successful. From November 1949 to March 1950 another campaign resulted in as many as 6,000 guerillas or suspected guerillas killed, including Kim Samyeong and Yi Juha. The loss of these two veteran commanders was a particularly hard blow to the North. By the spring of 1950, there was still some guerilla activity in some of the mountains; however, it was waning.

South Korea's successes in dealing with the guerillas were in part due to the small corps of professional Japanese trained officers in the ROK army and the advice and assistance from the Americans. Among the former was Jeong Ilgwon who led the country's insurgency efforts. Jeong was born in Siberia in 1917 where his father worked as an interpreter for the Russian Imperial Army. After the Bolshevik Revolution, he moved with his family back to Korea, where he grew up in the northeastern province of North Hamgyong. Later they moved to Manchuria and the young Jeong entered the Manchukuo Imperial Army Academy. He was captured by the Soviets at the end of the war, was released and afterwards went to the American occupation zone. He graduated from the first class of what became South Korea's military academy in 1946 at which time he assumed the leadership of the Northeast faction of the ROK army. His campaign against the guerillas was carried out with the assistance of American advisors. When the U.S. military withdrew from Korea in the months after independence it left behind a small 500-man advisory group to assist with training and logistics; a group dominated by the legendary James Hausman. The talented and energetic Hausman played an outsize role in training, advising, and shaping the ROK army, even though he worked with a shoestring budget. The two, Jeong and Hausman, worked closely together in developing effective counter-insurgency strategies.

The bloodiest insurgency in the South, also homegrown, took place as far from the North as possible. About 60 miles (100km) south of the Korean mainland in the beautiful subtropical island of Jeju (also spelled Cheju). It is a 705 square mile (1,826 square km) lush island province with fine beaches and picturesque villages. The 6,400 ft. (1950 m) Mount Halla in the center is almost always in view. It is a popular vacation spot for South Koreans as well as Chinese and Japanese; Korea's Hawaii. Nothing about this friendly, laid-back tourist area hints at its horrifically violent past. Separated from the rest of Korea, Jeju people speak a dialect that is nearly incomprehensible to other Koreans and have many customs and traditions that set them apart from mainland Koreans. But by the twentieth century, they were no longer isolated. They were actively involved in the nationalist movement.

At the end of World War II, the Jeju People's Committee governed the island with little outside interference until 1947 when anti-government demonstrations began. During the Second World War, many of the men of Jeju had left for Japan and elsewhere for work. While away they became radicalized and sympathetic to the communists. When these islanders returned, they brought their leftist leanings with them; some became affiliated with or at least sympathetic to the Korean Workers' Party, as the Korean Communist Party was officially called. Jeju islanders were strongly opposed to the May 10 separate elections and began a general strike in protest. The strike morphed into a violent uprising. The newly emerging South Korean state sent 3,000 National Constabulary to the island but hundreds of these joined the rebels and Seoul lost control of the situation.

By the fall of 1948, there were about 4,000 rebels on the island refusing to acknowledge the legitimacy of the Republic of Korea. Although poorly armed (some had only sharpened bamboo sticks) they won some engagements with ROK security forces. When Seoul sent in the new ROK army to put down the resistance, the troops mutinied at the port of Yeosu before getting on ships to the island. Eventually, the Rhee government used a combination of troops, national police, and armed rightwing thugs to impose a reign of terror over the island. Thousands of the islanders perished. Most died in what can only be termed massacres rather than battles. For example, on November 13, 1948, soldiers attacked the village of Haga, setting fire to houses and killing people as they tried to escape. They burned the bodies to destroy the evidence. In the village of Tosan, government forces marched in on the night of December 15 and 16, lined up all the men between 18 and 40, and shot them, leaving 150 dead. Most of these incidents were covered up by the South Korean government for two generations.

Fighting and killings continued through 1949 and into 1950. In August 1950 an order was given by the ROK government to round up thousands and then sort them into A, B, C, and D groups in order of their degree of disloyalty. In the following month, the most untrustworthy A and B groups were executed. There is no agreement on how many of the island's 280,000 inhabitants perished. The best estimates are between 25,000 and 30,000 killed or wounded. A specially formed Jeju Commission in March 2011 identified 10,729 killed and 3,920 missing, many of them women and children. Most who have examined the uprising believe the real number was higher. Of those killed, 84 percent died at the hands of the police, the military, or rightist groups, and 12 percent of the deaths were caused by insurgents.

No part of Korea was spared the violence, the hatred, the turmoil of the years after liberation, not even the relatively remote island of Jeju.

Planning for an Invasion

While the guerilla campaigns in the South were not making much progress, the conditions for a reunification of the country under the North Korean leadership seemed favorable. The instability and restlessness in the South continued and Kim Il Sung and Pak Heon-yeong believed that the guerilla activity could be easily rekindled. Furthermore, geopolitical factors favored the North.

Washington's commitment to the defense of South Korea seemed uncertain. The Americans supported the ROK and, of course, wanted to check the expansion of communism but were at best ambiguous about the strategic importance of the country. American forces began withdrawing from the peninsula in September 1948, the last troops leaving the following year. By then only the 500-member Korean Military Advisory Group remained to assist the South Korean army. In 1949 the U.S. Congress severely reduced what had been generous aid to South Korea and also reduced the funding for its army. Concerned about Rhee provoking war, the U.S. limited its supplies to its ROK army to small arms, supplying only a few aircraft, limited artillery, and no tanks. It even restricted the sales of small arms so that the ROK forces had only a fifteen-day supply of ammunition. Congress cut funds for the U.S. military and, dealing with a reduced budget, the Defense Department began looking for places to save money; it decided Korea, a low priority for the Pentagon, was one of those. The U.S. military found that it had "little strategic interest" in maintaining troops on the peninsula.

The uncertainty of the U.S. commitment to South Korea was highlighted on January 12, 1950, when Secretary of State Dean Acheson gave a press conference in which he excluded South Korea from the USA's "defensive perimeter." This was and has been since interpreted as meaning the Americans were willing to write off South Korea and focus their efforts to contain communism elsewhere. Historians still debate over how crucial this press conference was in convincing Stalin and Kim Il Sung that the U.S. would not intervene to save the South. Scholars examining the Russian archives could find little evidence that the speech had much impact on either since America's lack of commitment was already apparent.

Whether or not it had much influence on the decision to invade the South, it indicated how low a priority Korea was for policymakers in Washington. Meanwhile, the winds of change were blowing in an advantageous direction for Pyongyang. The end of the civil war in China only made the geopolitical landscape more favorable for North Korea. The People's Liberation Army was scoring one victory after another in 1948 and 1949, and on October 1, 1949, Mao Zedong proclaimed the People's Republic of China in Beijing. So momentous a development must have been persuasive evidence to the leadership in Pyongyang that history was on their side. They must also have been encouraged by the U.S. decision to abandon its Guomindang allies—a move that demonstrated the reluctance of Washington to get involved in a conflict in Asia. The communist victory in China also freed up tens of thousands of veteran Korean troops who had been serving in the Chinese Communist People's Liberation Army.

At one time Americans assumed that the plan to invade South Korea was part of the Kremlin's grand strategy for global dominance. However, in the 1990s, when the Russian archives became open to scholars, the evidence clearly showed that the initiative came from Pyongyang. Since the North Koreans were so passionate about reunification this should be no surprise. In 1948, Kim Il Sung and Pak Heonyeong sought Moscow's permission and support for an invasion. In March 1949, Kim Il Sung met with Stalin to ask for assistance with the two-year economic plan Pyongyang had launched. While he had the old dictator's attention, he made a pitch for an attack on the South. He argued that the South would never agree to peaceful reunification and if they waited too long it would grow stronger and attack the North. The time to help the people below the parallel shake off the yoke of the southern reactionaries and their American masters was now. Stalin showed no interest. Kim and Pak brought up the subject again when they attended Stalin's seventieth birthday party. The American troops were gone, the civil war in China was resolved and the situation seemed more favorable. But Stalin was still reluctant. Then on January 30, he changed his mind. What caused him to do so? Was it Acheson's

Korean Yangban (Aristocrats) Playing Baduk (Go) Wearing their characteristic white clothes and black horsehair hats, the *yangban* dominated Korean politics and society until the early twentieth century. Note the distinctive style of Korean interior architecture, all part of the country's unique cultural heritage.

Gojong – the Last Monarch of Independent Korea Dressed and posing in the style of a European monarch, King (Emperor after 1897) Gojong was forced to abdicate by the Japanese in 1907 after refusing to cooperate with them. He was an indecisive and inconsistent ruler sometimes supporting and sometimes opposing modernization reforms. In the end he became a symbol of Korea's lost sovereignty.

Japanese and Chinese Forces Fight at the Battle of Pyongyang Depicted in this Japanese painting, Tokyo's modernized armed forces inflicted a severe defeat on the Chinese at the Battle of Pyongyang in 1894. This led to Japan's victory in the Sino-Japanese War, a conflict fought over influence in Korea. *(Saint Louis Art Museum)*

Queen Min This intelligent woman, while promoting the opening of her country to the outside world, remained strongly anti-Japanese. Her brutal murder by Japanese agents in 1896 became a rallying point for those who resisted Tokyo's effort to take control of Korea.

Righteous Armies Made up of ordinary Koreans, Righteous Armies were mostly small guerilla bands often led by local aristocrats and former soldiers after the army was disbanded in 1907. They fought the Japanese until finally suppressed in 1911. Isolation and lack of coordination reduced their effectiveness.

An Junggeun An is famous for having assassinated Ito Hirobumi, the principal architect of Japan's takeover of Korea. After the 1909 assassination in Harbin, China, he was arrested and executed. An remains a national hero in Korea.

Japanese Officers in Korea Japanese officers with their Western-style uniforms stand in contrast to the Koreans in traditional dress, mostly *yangban*, in this photo. Japanese rule of Korea operated along the lines of a military occupation.

Japanese Suppression of Korean Resistance During Korea's occupation, resistance to Japanese rule was met with brutal repression. In this photo from 1905, three Korean resistance fighters are prepared to be executed by firing squad.

Yu Gwansun During the March First Movement of 1919, a nationwide mostly peaceful mass demonstration calling for independence, young student Yu Gwansun was arrested, imprisoned and died after being tortured. She became a national symbol of resistance to Japanese rule.

Comfort Women In this photo, Korean "comfort women" are shown with their American liberators. These women were forced into military brothels to serve Japanese troops during the Second World War. For decades after the war the government in Tokyo denied their existence.

Hong Sa-ik in Japanese Uniform Hong Sa-ik was one of many Koreans who voluntarily joined the Japanese military. He became a general and the highest-ranking Korean in the Japanese army. He was executed after the war for war crimes committed during the Japanese occupation of the Philippines.

大韓民國三年一月一日
臨時政府及臨時議政院新年祝賀式紀念撮影

The Korean Provisional Government in Shanghai Formed by nationalist exiles in 1919, the Korean Provisional Government was divided between many factions ranging from radicals to conservatives and was not very effective. Nonetheless, many of its officers became political leaders in South Korea after 1945.

Kim Gu launched a number of terrorist attacks on the Japanese from his exile headquarters in China. One narrowly missed assassinating Japanese Emperor Hirohito. He is still considered a nationalist hero by many Koreans.

American Troops Arriving in Korea 1945 When U.S. forces arrived in Seoul in September 1945, they were enthusiastically welcomed by Koreans as liberators. However, that goodwill quickly dissipated when it became clear that rather than granting immediate independence, the Americans intended to impose a military occupation.

Soviet Liberation of Northern Korea Like the Americans, the Soviets arrived in Korea with little preparation, little understanding of the country and no clear plan. They, nonetheless, were also initially greeted as liberators.

Stalin and Mao Although they initially resisted Kim Il Sung's plan to invade the South and reunite Korea, Stalin and Mao eventually supported it.

Syngman Rhee on the Cover of Time The South Korean nationalist leader and first president of the Republic of Korea was hailed as an anti-communist, pro-Western hero by *Time* magazine and many other Americans. Most U.S. officials found him to be a stubborn authoritarian and difficult to work with.

Yeo Unhyeong A moderate leftist, Yeo Unhyeong was seen by many Koreans and Americans as an alternative to Syngman Rhee as a leader for South Korea as well as a unified Korea. His assassination ended that possibility.

General Paek Seonyeop The young general was one of South Korea's most effective military commanders. Like many of the ROK's officers he was from what would become North Korea. After the Korean War he retired, still in his forties, and lived to be one hundred-years-old.

North Korean POWs in Seoul North Korea captured Seoul just three days after invading but soon after, things would take a downturn for the North. Here UN troops round up captured North Korean soldiers during the Second Battle of Seoul.

UN Vehicles Crossing the 38th Parallel during the Korean War UN forces crossed into North Korea in early October 1950 following the successful Incheon landing despite warnings from the Chinese that they would intervene if Americans and South Koreans did so.

The Battle of Incheon The Incheon landing, which began on September 15, 1950, was a turning point in the war. It meant an end to Kim Il Sung's attempt at reuniting the country by force.

North Korean Refugees Millions of North Koreans fled the fighting during the war with the largest number arriving in Busan, the temporary wartime capital of the ROK. When UN forces withdrew from the North in late 1950, hundreds of thousands of civilians left with them.

Syngman Rhee and Douglas MacArthur The two men, both in their 70s, were charismatic anti-communist leaders whose determination to retake North Korea expanded and prolonged the Korean War.

The Invasion of North Korea UN and ROK forces take the war to North Korea as they pass a destroyed North Korean T-34. The invasion of the North proceeded swiftly until Chinese intervention turned the tide.

Mu Jeong One of North Korea's most charismatic leaders and a fine public speaker, Mu Jeong was a rival to Kim Il Sung. Entrusted with the defense of Pyongyang, he was blamed for its capture by UN and ROK forces.

General Matthew Ridgway General Ridgway took over as commander of UN forces after President Truman fired General Douglas MacArthur in April 1951. Soon after assuming command the war became a stalemate.

Chinese POWs The Chinese army in North Korea was renamed Chinese People's Volunteers to avoid the appearance of a direct U.S.-China conflict. Poorly equipped and with unreliable supply lines and a lack of air cover, they suffered a high rate of casualties.

Pak Heonyeong Leader of the Korean Communist Party before 1945 and head of the domestic faction of the North Korean leadership, Pak Heonyeong was blamed for North Korean failures during the war and was executed in 1955.

press conference? It is not known, but even then he was emphatic that it be done with minimal risk. In April 1950, he invited Kim and Pak to Moscow where they laid out their plans. The two North Koreans argued that it would be a swift campaign, over in three days. The ROK army would collapse, the South Korean people would rise up and unification would take place immediately.

Stalin insisted that the North Koreans get Mao's approval before final preparations were made, and Mao, over the objections of some of his Chinese comrades, granted it in May. The timing was not ideal for Mao who had unfinished business to attend to. The remnants of the Guomindang regime were still holding out in the island province of Taiwan. Mao didn't have much of a navy but a lot of men on small crafts were all he needed to take the island and conclude the civil war. Men on boats and rafts took the island of Hainan in the spring of 1950. However, the invasion of Taiwan was delayed when the troops training for it on the coastal mudflats were infected with flukes. The delay was costly. Before they could begin the assault, Kim Il Sung invaded South Korea and the U.S. put warships in the Taiwan straits blocking the Chinese communist invasion. Taiwan was saved by Kim Il Sung's war, or one could say, literally by a fluke. With Mao on board, Soviet officers drew up a "Preemptive Strike Operational Plan." Soviets helped with the planning and supplied equipment—T-34 tanks, artillery, and other weapons while making it clear no Soviet troops could be involved. The name "Preemptive" sounds cynical, but the North had real concerns that Southerners would attack if, and when, they could. The timing was for late June, just before the rainy season created logistical problems.

Every factor appeared to support a quick victory. The North was militarily stronger, better armed, and better prepared. It had 150,000 men under arms versus 100,000 for the South. A large portion of these experienced combat veterans had returned after fighting in the Chinese Civil War and World War II. The North had hundreds of tanks, the South none; it had scores of aircraft, the South hardly any; it had far more artillery. The army was more unified, and less faction-ridden than the ROK. Moreover, the North had a more reliable patron to back it up. North Korea's leaders had far more credibility as nationalist leaders than the southern regime dominated by those who had served or collaborated with the Japanese and prospered under their rule. Another key factor was that the North Korean regime, or so it believed, enjoyed enormous support among the southerners, especially as the North promised the land redistribution and the labor reforms that most Southerners wanted. Pak Heonyeong seems to have genuinely believed and convinced the other DPRK leaders that the people of the South would rise against their hated regime and welcome their northern liberators. It is easy, therefore, to understand why Kim Il Sung invaded the South in June 1950: he was convinced, and he had convinced both Stalin and Mao, that it would an easy victory.

Had things gone as planned Korea would have been swiftly reunified. The war would have been short and not very bloody. The long conflict among Koreans over different visions and strategies for achieving a modern progressive society would be over. Koreans would no longer be at war, no longer divided. But the war did not go as planned. It didn't end in three days or three years but continues seven decades later.

CHAPTER 4

Failed Attempts at Reunification

The War Begins

On June 20 the ROK 17th Regiment stationed on the Ongjin Peninsula began noticing suspicious movements on the North Korean side of the parallel. The small peninsula was strategically important. Jutting out below the thirty-eighth parallel it was the only part of North Korea's Hwanghae Province in South Korea. It was hard to defend since it was connected to the rest of the ROK only by sea. Yet it was a good place to keep watch on North Korea because the mountains in the center offered a vantage point over the main road between Seoul and Pyongyang. This is what the regiment's commander Paek Inyeop was doing when he noticed North Korean bases across the divide were filled with high-ranking officers, but there was a strange lack of civilians. Paek put his troops on alert. He was ordered by his superiors in Seoul to call the alert off so as not to cause an incident. Instead, Paek simply lowered the alert. But when the United Nations inspectors arrived, he canceled it at their request. Unlike the South Korean commander, the UN inspectors who were conducting a regular United Nations mandated tour of the parallel saw no sign of any trouble coming from the North.

Paek remained concerned and ordered his men to be battle-ready. His suspicions that the North might be up to something proved correct. At 4 am on the morning of June 25, KPA forces began a thirty-minute bombardment of his forces. This was followed by an attack. After hand-to-hand combat, some of his troops were forced to retreat. North Korean shelling resumed and continued to 5:30 a.m. Paek, to his frustration, was unable to return artillery fire since his 105mm artillery was under the control of U.S. advisors. Korean People's Army (KPA) tanks then moved in and the ROK troops were forced to evacuate from the Ongjin Peninsula in boats, which they managed to do in a somewhat orderly fashion. This was the start of North Korea's effort to retake the South by force. It was an effort that almost succeeded.

On the eve of the Korean War, the North had a population of about ten million and the South about 20 million. Despite the South being much bigger in population, the North had most of the advantages. It had most of the industry, a highly organized and disciplined government, and the backing of the Soviet Union and China. South Korea lacked even the North's modest industrial base. It was politically less stable. There was unrest in the countryside, and its government was not fully accepted as legitimate by many of its people. Importantly it had a more reluctantly engaged patron. In strictly military terms North Korea was much stronger. Its forces numbered something over 150,000 troops organized into ten divisions. Another 30,000 were in reserve. Many, perhaps a majority, were experienced veterans of the fighting in China. They had several hundred tanks, mostly T-34—the dependable World War II Soviet ones, 200 heavy artillery, 110 attack bombers, 150 Yak fighter planes, and 35 reconnaissance aircraft. In contrast, South Korea had only 98,000 men under arms, no tanks or heavy artillery, and just 22 planes. It had some experienced and well-trained officers but few combat veterans.

Both Brigadier General William Roberts, who headed the Korean Military Advisory Group, and the U.S. Ambassador to Seoul, John Muccio expressed confidence that the ROK army was developing into a competent fighting force that could handle a North Korean attack. But Washington refused to supply the heavy artillery, tanks, or planes that Rhee pleaded for as necessary to defend the country. Officials in Washington simply distrusted Rhee, fearing who would use them to launch an attack on the North. And that was precisely what Rhee, at least ultimately, wished to do. Just one day before the invasion two UN observers and officers in the Australian Air Force filed a report after a two-week inspection tour of the 38th Parallel. They characterized the ROK Army as nothing more than a lightly armed constabulary force, incapable of a major invasion of the North. But it was maintaining a "vigilant defense." This was just what the Americans wanted, a military only strong enough to deter or stop a major offensive from the North but incapable of launching one of its own. Unfortunately, Washington had overestimated the ROK's ability to stop a surprise invasion from its rival.

Both North Korea and South Korea wanted reunification, but the North was in a much better position to achieve it. It had a well-prepared plan to do so; the South only wishful thinking. And initially, the North had the element of surprise. The North took steps to keep the invasion plans a secret. In the days before just before the attack, Pyongyang broadcasted radio instructions to the guerillas in the South suggesting that they were planning a major operation later in the summer knowing these would be picked up by the ROK. At the same time, they refrained from border incursions, so the threat seemed to be coming from the guerillas. This worked, despite Colonel Paek's concerns. Neither the ROK government nor the U.S. expected a major invasion, nor did either detect any moves toward an offensive. This was reinforced by the UN inspectors who reported that things along the dividing line were rather quiet. As a result, the ROK was not in a very good position to defend itself. It had only a single division between the North and Seoul along the Kaesong corridor—a stretch of relatively flat terrain that made a perfect path to take to the southern capital. Further, the attack began on Sunday and half the forces and the majority of the high-ranking officers were on leave. North Korea's invasion could not have been better timed.

The First Days

News arrived at the U.S. embassy of an incursion by the North early in the morning. But it was not cause for concern; just another border provocation. Only at 9:30 did the staff inform Ambassador John Muccio. He waited an hour for more information before cabling the news to Washington. There, it was late at night. When the Chairman of the Joint Chiefs of Staff, General Omar Bradley, received the news he ordered that General MacArthur in Tokyo handle it, and went to bed. The problem is that Seoul had been warning of an attack so often, and there had been so many small clashes, that the early reports were not taken too seriously. Rhee, after all, was trying everything to get the Americans to supply him with more weapons and support. And the UN inspectors had just visited and found nothing unusual. John Foster Dulles, the prominent Republican foreign policy expert, had just been there too, posing for a picture on the Parallel but also not taking Rhee's pleas for assistance with much concern.

By the time South Korea's military commanders fully understood what was happening, Kaesong had already fallen and the way was open for a thrust toward Seoul. The ROK soldiers did not immediately panic but fought rather bravely, yet bravery could not stop T-34 tanks. Their inability to do so eventually caused the soldiers to panic with "T-34 fear." When it was finally realized in Washington that this was a major offensive, President Truman requested an emergency meeting of the UN Security Council which unanimously called for an immediate ceasefire. At the U.S. embassy Ambassador Muccio, who had earlier informed Washington that the South Korean troops were taking defensive positions and there was no cause for alarm, was now himself alarmed and spent the next two days urgently calling for ammunition for the beleaguered ROK forces.

Two days after the offensive was launched, on Tuesday, June 27, KPA forces were approaching Seoul. That morning the US embassy ordered the evacuation of all Americans in the capital. About 700 Americans crammed onto a Norwegian freighter at the port of Incheon. The US embassy departed staff for Suwon, south of the city. In his radio address, President Rhee called for the citizens to resist the invaders and then, with the rest of his government, fled to the southeastern city of Daegu. By evening, panic gripped

Seoul. Tens of thousands of residents, whole families grabbing and taking what they could carry on their backs including babies and small children, formed rivers of humanity fleeing the city. Heavy rain was coming down adding to the chaos, confusion, and misery. There was only one bridge crossing the formidable Han River that formed the southern border of the city. Many fled in boats and ferries, but the main crossing was on that bridge, and the ROK decided to blow it up. While this might have made good strategic sense, they did so while it was jammed with desperate men, women, and children. The explosion was so powerful that Americans near the bridge were thrown out of their jeep. Hundreds died in the explosion or drowned in the river. Worst from a military view, it was done prematurely, leaving 30,000 ROK forces trapped on the other side. But it only slowed down the advancing KPA a little. The offensive continued.

On that same day as the gravity of the situation emerged Truman authorized the use of air and sea forces in defense of Korea. That evening the UN Security Council passed Resolution 83 which authorized the use of force to halt North Korean aggression. This passed since the Soviet Union which would be expected to veto it was boycotting the UN to protest the failure of the United Nations to allow the government of the People's Republic of China to take the seat still occupied by the defeated Guomindang regime. Historians still ponder why the Soviets did not try to stop the UN from approving the use of forces. If they had done so they would have complicated Truman's decision to intervene, perhaps delayed it long enough to assure North Korea's victory. Whatever the reason, this enabled the United States to label its intervention as a United Nations policing action. It was the first time the UN principle of collective security to ensure international peace was tested.

Using this UN authorization, Truman at a news conference on June 29th made it clear that the U.S. was not at war but that this was a "police action." Meanwhile, on that day General MacArthur flew to Korea and traveled to the south side of the Han River. Seeing the ROK forces in disarray he informed Washington of the need for U.S. ground forces to prevent the total collapse of the ROK. On

June 30 Truman made what was probably even a tougher decision, he decided to authorize the immediate use of ground forces. At the time American public opinion strongly backed the decision to intervene. But the intervention was not as easy as it would seem. The nearest American forces were in Japan, and these were occupation forces, there to help administer the country, not combat-ready or battle-tested soldiers, and there were of course the logistical problems of getting them and their equipment to the peninsula.

An International War

The Korean War was an international conflict. On the one side were the North Koreans who, in the fall of 1950, were joined by the Chinese. The Soviets supplied some military advisors, and some airplane pilots but mainly weapons and supplies. On the Southern side, it was a truly global effort under the UN. Fifty-eight countries aided South Korea in some way. Twenty-two countries provided troops for the United Nations. The U.K., the Philippines, Australia, Turkey, Thailand, the Netherlands, France, Greece, New Zealand, Belgium, Luxembourg, Ethiopia, and Columbia sent combat troops. Sweden, India, Denmark, Italy, and Norway sent medical units. By the end of the conflict in July 1953, there were 39,000 serving in the UN in some capacity who were neither Americans nor Koreans.

All served under the UN military commander who was an American; first General MacArthur, later General Matthew Ridgway, and finally General Mark Clark. American forces far outnumbered all other UN members combined and it was primarily an American military operation. At its peak in July 1953, the total UN forces consisted of 300,000 Americans, 590,000 South Koreans plus those from other countries. Integrating these forces was always a challenge. There were problems communicating with troops from UN countries that did not speak English or Korean. Other problems included accommodating the diets of Turkish forces that needed their food to be halal, or those of Filipino or Thai who needed rice. Integrating Korean and American forces was difficult. Every

American division had KATUSA (Korean Augmentations to the United States Army) attached. American advisors were attached to Korean units. A Korean Service Corps of civilian laborers under the supervision of ROK army officers provided support to the UN units.

North Korea's Drive South

One week after capturing Seoul, the KPA made the push south to capture Daejeon. The North Korean forces were following the natural pathway through the mountainous country that would take them south and southwest until they reached Busan, South Korea's second city, and would have the entire country under their control. All seemed to be going as intended. Kim Il Sung, Pak Heonyeong, and their Soviet and Chinese allies must have been pleased. But after the initial rout of the ROK army and the quick capture of Seoul, things began to proceed less smoothly. First, the ROK army did not collapse as predicted, but units of it managed to regroup and put up more resistance than expected. As the North Koreans headed south, they sometimes found it difficult to keep up supply lines. They also found that moving tanks and heavy artillery through the mountainous terrain was a challenge. But perhaps the biggest disappointment was the failure of the South Korean people to rise up in support. The spontaneous guerilla support groups did not materialize. Therefore, the going was slower than expected, giving the U.N. troops time to arrive and reinforce the ROK units.

Taking longer than planned, the KPA arrived at the strategically located city of Daejeon on July 20. American forces under General William Dean were told to assist the ROK forces and hold the city but they were soon surrounded. General Dean escaped by fleeing into the mountains. After thirty-six days of barely surviving, he was captured and spent the rest of the war as the highest-ranking UN prisoner-of-war. The defeat at Daejeon was demoralizing for the Americans and disconcerting for the South Koreans. U.S. troops entered into battle with enormous self-confidence believing they could easily take on the North Koreans. Many thought that just the presence of Americans on the battlefield would intimidate the

North Koreans and blunt their offensive. Instead, they suffered a severe setback. The North Koreans were not intimidated at all. Their defeat of the hastily assembled American forces was a great morale booster for them and removed whatever doubts they had about achieving victory.

With Daejeon's fall, the way was open to Busan where the South Korean government had fled. This port city, at the extreme southeast corner of the peninsula across the Korea Straits from Japan, became the wartime capital of the ROK. By late summer it was the last major toehold of the ROK on the mainland. Its defense was vital if there was any chance for the South Korean state to survive. It was, therefore, the prime target of the North Koreans. The sooner they could capture Busan, the sooner they could bring the war to a victorious end. To achieve this, General Pang Hosan, commanding KPA's Sixth Division, moved south into the rich rice-growing provinces of North and South Cholla where he met only light resistance, and from there made a sharp turn to the east toward Busan. It was a well-executed maneuver, but Pang had to delay his final offensive while waiting for the arrival of artillery and supplies.

Meanwhile, the ROK's Sixth Division had managed to pull off a minor miracle. From the disparate remnants of fleeing soldiers, they regrouped into a coherent force and at the northeast city of Chuncheon they fought a stubborn resistance against the KPA. Driven out, they counter-attacked, retook the city and held it for five days, withdrawing only after they were ordered to do so. It was a critical delay for the second arm of the North Korean forces who were swooping down on Busan from the north. Soviet advisor Mayveyev Zahkorov, head of a special mission to oversee operations, credited the "unexpectedly courageous defense of the ROK's Sixth Division" for creating a key setback in carrying out the invasion.

The stand at Chuncheon further gave the Americans and the South Koreans time to establish the Naktong Perimeter around Busan—so-called since much of it ran along the Naktong River of South Gyeongsang Province. The United States Eighth Army was responsible for the seventy miles of the western flank, and the

ROK for the fifty-five miles of the northern flank. By early August this was the last stand of the UN and ROK forces, and it held. By August, the North Koreans had overrun the vast majority of the Republic of Korea which had been reduced to a small southeast corner about fifteen percent of its previous size, the part closest to Japan. As the UN and ROK generals peered on the maps they could see at a glance just how precarious the position of the South Korean/UN forces was.

The war saw a vast flood of refugees heading southward. By late July, a half-million refugees had fled to UN/ROK-controlled areas in the southeast, with 25,000 entering every day. ROK and UN officials saw this flood as evidence of the lack of support for the communists. This was true in part. Many South Koreans had no desire to live under communist rule. But it was more complicated than that. People fled because they did not want to be conscripted by the North Korean military or were afraid their sons would be. They fled because supply chains had been disrupted and they were hungry and heard rumors that the Americans had vast amounts of food and supplies. They fled the chaos of war. They fled out of sheer general panic. Busan soon swelled with refugees. However, all these refugees created problems for the ROK, which had to somehow find shelters and food for them. It also caused problems for the Americans fighting the war. UN forces found the roads often clogged with refugees making it difficult to move their troops and supplies. They also faced the problem of not knowing when a refugee would become an enemy. Some were pro-communist guerillas disguised as refugees who, at a signal, would throw down their bundles and snatch out guns, opening fire on the UN troops. These included women and sometimes children too. Others posing as refugees would block roads and prepare ambushes.

KPA forces reached the Pusan Perimeter on August 5. In mid-August, they attempted a breakthrough simultaneously at different points resulting in the Battle of Masan, the Battle of Battle Mountain, the First Battle of Naktong Bridge, and the Battle of Daegu. UN forces were able to repel these attacks. The KPA advance was stalled. At the same time, the ROK was regaining its earlier troop strength and UN forces were increasing in number. By the end of August, the KPA, already dealing with long supply lines, was having difficulty replenishing many of its units. Nonetheless, into September, morale among the KPA was fairly high, and Kim Il Sung still appeared confident that he would prevail. The KPA, after being stalled, began making some progress. Pang Hosan succeeded in capturing a position across the Naktong, inching toward Busan, while other North Korean forces attacked the northern flank and took the port of Pohang. Some prominent Koreans began leaving Busan for Cheju and the nearby Japanese island of Tsushima. It looked a bit like the last days of the Republic of China when the Guomindang leadership fled to the island of Taiwan. However, this new offensive failed.

No Gun Ri

No Gun Ri was a little farming village along a small river. It was a typical community of rice and vegetable farmers which suffered a horrible tragedy. In early July 1950, North Korean forces seized the town of Yongdon, about 7 miles (11km) west of No Gun Ri. U.S. troops evacuated hundreds of residents from nearby villages. About 800 refugees spent the night on a riverbank. Seven were killed by American troops when they strayed from the encampment. When dawn came the refugees continued down the road as they fled from the advancing KPA. At No Gun Ri, they were stopped by U.S soldiers and told to follow the parallel railway embankment since the Americans did not want them to obstruct the road they were using.

The Americans were always worried about North Korean and pro-North Koreans disguising themselves as refugees and attacking them. It happened often enough to be a real concern. American soldiers had gotten into the habit of nervously regarding all refugees as possible threats. They searched the group for knives and other weapons. Then as the refugees rested, they were strafed and bombed by American military aircraft. According to the testimony of survivors, the planes returned repeatedly and bombed them. Panicking, they ran for any shelter they could find. Some reported

Korean War Pusan Perimeter

CHINA
(Manchuria)

Yalu River

Oct. 26, 1950

Farthest U.N. advance,
Nov. 24, 1950

Chosin
Reservoir

● Hungnam

NORTH
KOREA

■ **Pyongyang**

Truce Line,
July, 1953

- - - 38ᵗʰ parallel

■ **Seoul**

Incheon Landing,
Sep. 15, 1950

SOUTH
KOREA

Sea of
Japan

Busan Perimeter,
Fastest North Korean
advance,
Sep., 1950

● Busan

Yellow Sea

JAPAN

.00 km
.00 miles

that the Americans shot at them, killing and wounding those who were on the railroad tracks. The survivors ran to a tunnel beneath a concrete railroad bridge. Soldiers from the Seventh Cavalry opened machine-gun fire into the tunnel. Children were screaming and helpless adults were praying. Some protected themselves by piling the bodies of the dead as barricades. Some managed to get away that night. The remaining refugees were trapped, as soldiers shot at them if they tried to leave. They drank the bloody water from a tiny stream that flowed under the bridge. Eventually, the North Korean forces advanced toward No Gun Ri and the Seventh Cavalry withdrew. Those still alive were rescued by the North Koreans.

The story of No Gun Ri was largely unknown, one of many incidents that occurred during the Korean War. In 1997 the survivors filed a compensation claim. The U.S. military investigated but found no evidence. However, journalists for the Associated Press conducted their own investigation and found the evidence the military had missed, including that the American soldiers were not acting on their own but were given orders to fire on civilians. The story won a Pulitzer Prize for the AP. It is now estimated that 250 to 300 civilians, many of them women and children, died at No Gun Ri. Of these, 163 have been identified. What is so tragic is that it was far from an isolated incident. Massacres and atrocities were committed on all sides during the Korean War.

The Incheon Landing

After the fall of Seoul, General MacArthur believed that a landing on the west coast and the recapture of the ROK capital would be necessary. However, initially, all available American troops were needed to defend Busan. With the Perimeter holding and more forces available, he devised a plan for an amphibious landing at Incheon. This was the traditional pathway into Seoul, the same general area where the French in 1866, the Americans in 1871, and the Japanese in 1876 had landed forces. The plan he conceived was bold. Operation Chromite called for sending 75,000 marines and 260 ships to Incheon, negotiating the dangerous tides (among the highest in the world) and the numerous sandbars. It had to be done swiftly and unexpectedly. The military brass in Washington found it too risky, and some thought it would be better to land further south near Kunsan. MacArthur insisted Incheon was where he needed to land to retake the capital.

Overall, it went amazingly well and as intended; it caught Kim Il Sung and his forces by surprise. Perhaps the North Koreans shouldn't have been so surprised though. Both the Soviets and the Chinese had considered the idea that Americans might land on the west coast and outflank the North Koreans, and warned Kim Il Sung of that possibility. A pro-North Korean-Japanese spy ring arrested in Japan days before had a copy of the plan, but there is no evidence that it found its way to Pyongyang. In any case, Kim was focused on breaking through the Naktong Perimeter and seizing Busan before the opportunity to do so ran out; all North Korean energy was placed on this. He had no other plan than to move forward as quickly as possible.

At high tide, early on September 15, marines seized the small island of Wolmido which controlled the access to Incheon. The Marine First Division, the main force, waited until the next high tide in the afternoon and landed on the mainland. The Incheon area was defended by only 2,000 North Koreans who were quickly overwhelmed. Within three days 70,000 men had landed. While the initial landings resulted in swift victories, the march into Seoul was slower. Heavy fighting on the outskirts of Seoul started on September 19; fighting took place house-to-house with KPA forces taking heavy casualties. On September 25, UN forces had retaken much of Seoul and MacArthur declared the city his, but it was not until three days later, on September 28, that the city was completely cleared of KPA soldiers. What remained of KPA forces fled. Soon the KPA forces throughout the South were in full retreat and victory was at hand.

A panicky Kim Il-sung wrote to Stalin about the situation. Addressing him as "the liberator of the Korean people and the leader of the working peoples of the entire world," he explained the situation. The KPA had been achieving great victories until the USA, determined to carry out its plan to conquer all of Korea, launched an attack on Incheon. The military situation had become "extremely grave" and Korea was in danger of becoming a colony again. Only direct assistance from the Soviet Union or China could prevent this. But Moscow was reluctant to intervene. When Stalin did reply, he suggested Kim retreat to China, the Soviet leader appeared to be willing to write off his client.

A Second Attempt at Reunification: Taking the War to the North

One wonders what would have happened if the ROK and UN forces had stopped their pursuit of the KPA at the thirty-eight parallel. The North Korean invasion had failed utterly. Both Stalin and Mao seemed to have realized this and were willing to accept a stalemate with the peninsula divided roughly where it had been. China's one concern was to keep the U.S. and its allies away from its border. Moscow's was to avoid conflict with the U.S. and keep the Americans and their allies from its short border. The conflict might have come to an end then. If it had, the war for the South would have been brief but still bloody. One estimate is that over a hundred thousand South Korean soldiers and civilians had been killed in the fighting or executed by the North Koreans. Almost 57,000 South Koreans were missing. Many of these were young men and others who had been taken to the North by the retreating KPA. Over 300,000 homes and structures had been destroyed. The Americans losses were about 3,000 killed and almost 4,000 missing. North Korea's losses are less well known. Tens of thousands of their soldiers were killed, although there were few civilian casualties. For a little over three months of fighting this altogether amounted to a high toll. But was only a small fraction of the death and destruction that would take place over the next two and a half years.

However, both MacArthur and Rhee were determined to carry the conflict to the North. MacArthur wanted to "roll back" communism, and Rhee, even more passionately, wanted to reunify his country. The prospect of doing so seemed tantalizingly close. Overconfident after the spectacular victory at Incheon, Washington on October 7 permitted MacArthur to pursue the KPA north of the parallel and destroy it. The UN passed a vaguely worded resolution that did not explicitly call for UN forces to cross the parallel but called for the establishment of "conditions of stability" throughout Korea with a unified government followed by "a prompt withdrawal of troops." This permitted UN troops to enter the North. It explicitly stated, however, that UN forces should not stay in any part of Korea longer than it was necessary to do so to achieve "stability and a unified democratic Korea." On October 9, UN forces moved across the border.

Rhee didn't bother to wait for anyone's permission. On September 30, with Seoul barely cleared of the KPA, South Korean units entered the DPRK. ROK forces were under UN authority, but this hardly mattered to Rhee and his eager generals. When they were officially authorized to begin the offensive in the North their troops were already approaching the important east coast port of Wonsan which fell on October 10. Over the following days, UN and ROK forces swept through the North with little effective resistance. In late June, as the KPA closed in on Seoul, President Rhee had made a radio speech urging his citizens to resist and then he fled. Now, less than four months later it was Kim Il Sung's turn to do the same. As the enemy moved into the country Kim Il Sung gave a radio broadcast urging his people to "fight to the last drop of blood," and then left for Kanggye, a town in a rugged mountain valley only a short sprint from China. There he set up his temporary headquarters. Meanwhile, the allies continued the drive north. ROK forces captured the industrial cities of Hamhung and Hungnam on October 17 and the UN forces reached the Yalu on October 26. On October 20, a triumphant Syngman Rhee entered Pyongyang. By mid-November, 90 percent of North Korea was occupied by UN and ROK forces.

The Chinese Intervention

Mao Zedong was becoming increasingly concerned about UN and ROK forces reaching his border. As early as late September he tried to make the Americans aware that the UN occupation of all of North Korea was not acceptable to China, and that his forces would enter if necessary to prevent it. Since there were no diplomatic relations between Beijing and Washington this message was sent via India's ambassador to China. General Nie, the acting chief of the staff of the People's Liberation Army, told ambassador K.M. Panikkar that China would intervene. The U.S. government did not take the warnings seriously. When the Americans crossed into the North, heading for the border, it caused a crisis in Beijing. The Chinese leadership was divided over whether to enter the war. Mao and one of his key military commanders, Peng Dehuai, felt it had to, but most of the leadership was concerned that a direct conflict with the United States was too risky. After internal debate, Mao came down strongly in support of intervention and the rest of the Politburo went along with their great leader. Peng was appointed the field commander. China began massing troops on the border.

On October 8, the day after the United Nations Resolution empowering UN forces to reunify Korea, Mao cabled Kim Il Sung that he would send volunteers to help the DPRK fight "the aggressors." Mao temporarily suspended the order to intervene when he learned that Stalin would not provide air support to protect the Chinese forces, making it clear that Moscow wished to avoid direct conflict with the Americans. As UN troops advanced into North Korea, Mao decided to intervene anyway, even without Soviet support. On October 19 Chinese troops began to cross the Yalu. Within two weeks Beijing had sent 200,000 soldiers into the DPRK. They came as the Chinese People's Volunteers (CPV), not as the official People's Liberation Army. Despite the label, they were regular troops, not private volunteers.

There were concerns about China in Washington. Truman had approved of invading the North but was so worried the Chinese might enter the conflict that he flew to Guam to meet with MacArthur on October 25. There the old general reassured the president that the Chinese would not intervene and, even if they did, they would be easily defeated. "I can handle it" was his message. On that very day, the Chinese attacked the ROK 2nd Corps. Peng Dehuai had begun his First Phase Offensive which struck at weaker ROK units. The 3rd Battalion, 2nd Regiment of the ROK 6th Division was largely destroyed. Its U.S. advisor died in a POW camp. The first clash between U.S. and Chinese forces was at Unsan, the site of a gold mine once owned by Americans. U.S. forces suffered a bloody setback, with many troops abandoning their vehicles and fleeing on foot. In November the Chinese engaged the ROK X Corps near Changjin Reservoir in the east but after a short, bloody battle, withdrew. They also engaged in fighting with some UN troops but on a small scale.

The Americans misinterpreted the modest nature of these attacks and the speed by which the CPV pulled back to mean that the Chinese forces were not present in Korea in very formidable strength and were not a serious threat to the UN operations. Although some South Korean reports stated that the Chinese were entering in very large numbers, most Americans simply did not believe this. The commander of the ROK 1st division, Paek Seonyeop, for example, reported that there were very large numbers of Chinese troops. He was not taken any more seriously than his brother Paek Inyeop had been when he reported suspicious activity on the eve of North Korea's invasion. Ignoring South Korean reports to the contrary, the Americans were convinced the Chinese forces were far smaller. The Chairman of the Joint Chiefs of Staff, General J Lawton Collins, pondered that the Chinese might be "saving face" with these small-scale attacks since Zhou Enlai had publicly stated that his government would not stand idly by if the Americans and the ROK pushed to the border. Like MacArthur, he and some of the other Americans who "understood the Oriental mind" knew how Asians were preoccupied with saving face. MacArthur's chief of intelligence, Major General Charles A Willoughby, did not believe these attacks by the Chinese were part of a major invasion. He estimated that only between 16,500 and 34,000 Chinese had crossed into Korea. It was even thought by American intelligence that these Chinese might be North Korean reinforcements taken from China.

In hindsight, it is difficult to understand how the UN forces could have been so confident that the war was wrapping up and so unconcerned about the Chinese. How could American intelligence have been so wrong? How, despite the bloody engagements, could MacArthur be so confident that Chinese forces posed no threat? Whatever the reason, their extreme underestimation of Chinese forces in the country and lack of understanding of Beijing's determination to prevent American forces on their border was one of the great failures of American military intelligence. MacArthur did call for the bombing of the bridges over the Yalu. But the order was countermanded by the Pentagon, fearing it could lead to a wider conflict with China. Gradually the U.S. command began to accept that substantial Chinese forces were in Korea, but MacArthur did not think they posed a serious threat as long as he had air support.

In mid-November McArthur started making plans for the complete occupation of North Korea. Promising his men that they would be "home by Christmas" he began a final "mop-up" operation on November 24. The war, the Americans believed, was almost over. The UN command was unaware that 400,000 Chinese troops were planning an attack.

On the night of November 27, Peng Dehuai began the Second Offensive. While the first was as much a probe of the enemy as an offensive, this one was a major and successful effort to drive the UN and the ROK out of the North. The Chinese People's Volunteers attacked the widely dispersed UN forces in the east, initiating the Battle of Chosin (Changjin) Reservoir. The Americans were caught completely by surprise. The next day MacArthur told the Joint Chiefs of staff, "We face an entirely new war." The UN defensive position was hindered by the fact that MacArthur had divided his forces, with the Eighth Army on the west side of the mountainous spine of North Korea and the Marine X Corps on the east. The two had difficulty communicating with each other and fought largely separate battles. The Marines put up stiff resistance at the Chosin Reservoir while suffering from the bitter cold that fell to minus 25 degrees Fahrenheit (–31 Celsius) until they were forced to evacuate by sea with heavy losses.

On the west side, the U.S. Eighth Army was in full retreat by the first of December. On December 5, Pyongyang was evacuated.

As the forces continued their retreat southward, the Eighth Army commander, General Walker, was killed in a jeep accident, dying oddly enough in the same way his mentor George Patton had. He was replaced by Matthew Ridgway. At first a rout, the UN forces began to put together a more orderly retreat as the Chinese advance slowed. Then on December 31, New Year's Eve, Peng launched the Third Offensive. Despite clear weather for bombing the Chinese forces from the air, the UN command could not stop the advance of the CPV as it crossed into South Korea. On January 4, Seoul fell to the Chinese. Peng's forces continued their advance until they reached the 37th parallel on January 7, then they halted. The UN troops retreated so fast that Peng worried it might be a trap to lure him too far south and then execute an Incheon-like landing and cut him off. It wasn't a trap; the American and ROK forces were just in full retreat.

The offensive by the Chinese People's Volunteers and the KPA and the hasty retreat of the UN troops was a shock and a humiliation to the Americans. The UN troops, faced with large numbers of Chinese attackers, reported that "human waves" were moving toward them. This became one of the great myths of the Korean War. They reported that vastly exaggerated hordes of Chinese with little regard for their own lives had descended upon them. It rationalized defeat and dehumanized the enemy. In truth, the Chinese forces attacked in large forces but not in the wildly disproportional numbers as was later believed. In most cases, the attacks were successful because they took the UN forces by surprise, and sowed panic among them. The myth of the human wave, however, helped the Americans save face.

By January, the Americans were privately considering a truce, as were the Soviets. But not Mao, who felt there was an opportunity to push the Americans out of the peninsula, or at least tire them so they would withdraw. Neither did the North Koreans want the fighting to stop. Kim Il Sung wanted the offensive to continue until the South was liberated, much as the Rhee had pushed for the liberation of the North. Pak Heonyeong was particularly insistent that they take advantage of this second chance at reunification. Nor did the South Koreans want the war to stop. Rhee did not want a truce. He was still focused on reunification.

In early February 1, the US-ROK forces, under Operation Thunderbolt, pushed the frontline back to the suburbs of Seoul. A fourth Chinese offensive on February 11 initially made progress on the east coast, pushing back ROK forces, but quickly failed. The DPRK and Chinese concerns were to hold on to Seoul since its fall would be demoralizing. Seoul, it should be recalled, was the titular capital of the DPRK, holding it gave the North Koreans the sense they had the upper hand in the struggle for reunification. But they did not hold on to it for long. In March, a UN offensive retook the city and by the end of that month the Chinese-KPA forces had been driven out of most of the South Korean territory they had gained.

The Truman administration, having pushed the communist forces back to roughly the thirty-eighth parallel, was willing to negotiate a truce. Efforts in this direction were undermined by MacArthur. In a letter to U.S. Congressman Joseph Martin, an old friend, he was critical of a truce, suggesting among other things, the deployment of Chinese Nationalists troops from Taiwan to Korea. This was a move that would possibly widen the war and one the administration very much opposed. Martin read the letter on the House floor and its conclusion, "There is no substitute for victory," was an open challenge to Truman. On April 11, Truman dismissed MacArthur as commander, replacing him with the head of the Eighth Army, General Matthew Ridgway, a competent and more obedient commander. This dismissal of MacArthur, a much-admired national hero, led to much criticism of Truman. But the policy to contain the war and not to try to widen it or attempt to bring it to the North again, gradually won general acceptance in the United States. It did not win general acceptance in South Korea where Rhee and many of his people had not given up the hope of reunification.

Not long after the replacement of MacArthur, the Chinese launched a new offensive. UN forces were forced to retreat along with parts of the front. Ridgway, while willing to retreat until the offensive lost momentum, was adamant about defending Seoul. He felt the capital falling a third time would be demoralizing to the

South Koreans. After the Battle of the Imjin River and the Battle of Kapyong north of the city, the offensive was halted. The Chinese planned a new offensive for late May but were caught off-guard when the UN forces launched their own counter-offensive in May that continued into June, regaining most of the ground previously lost and bringing them close to the thirty-eighth parallel. This was the last significant change of territory. After June of 1951 the war became a stalemate.

Paek Seonyeop

Most of the military histories in English focus on the American commanders in Korea, but the Korean generals deserve more attention. One of these was the ROK's Paek Seonyeop. Few more fervent anti-communists came from the North. Paek was born in what is now the North Korean port of Nampo, in South Pyeongan Province, the same province Kim Il Sung was born in. He was the second child of three, raised by a widowed mother. She moved to Pyongyang and the family lived in a one-room apartment. They were so poor that they often did not have enough to eat. At one point out of despair, his mother attempted to commit suicide with her children by jumping off a bridge but was dissuaded by her sister. Later his mother and her sister worked in a rubber factory, earning enough to pay for the young Paek's school tuition at Pyongyang Normal School. Despite training to be a teacher, he instead entered the Mukden Military Academy established in the Japanese puppet state of Manchukuo. Like Park Chung Hee, Paek became an officer in the Manchukuo Imperial Army and served in, among other roles, guerilla repression. His unit, the Gando Special Force Battalion, had a reputation for brutality. He participated in the Japanese campaign against the Chinese in northern China during the last year of the war.

In December 1945 Paek Seonyeop and his brother Paek Inyeop fled the communist-dominated North and became lieutenants in the constabulary. There he participated in the suppression of communist guerillas with enthusiasm. His aggressive attacks on the communists created incidents along the border. Later some critics accused both him and his brother of helping to provoke the North Korean invasion, a charge the evidence does not support. On June 25 he was assigned to defend Seoul as the commander of the First Infantry Division. He was soon forced to retreat but later contributed to the defense of the Busan Perimeter, earning some fame for his victory at the village of Dabubong.

After the collapse of the KPA following the Incheon landing, Paek was eager to pursue the war with the North and his division was the first to enter Pyongyang on October 19. After the UN Forces were pushed out of the North, he became the commander of the ROK 1st Corps tasked with defending eastern Korea. In July of 1951, he represented the ROK military at the Kaesong Truce Talks. He was then given a new assignment—to wipe out the last major guerilla stronghold in the South at Jirisan, a rugged mountainous area, now a popular national park. This is what he did best and he succeeded in early 1952. He became chief of staff and in 1953, he also became South Korea's first four-star general. He retired in 1960, still only forty years old. He lived another sixty years. It was a long life but not long enough to see the end of the Korean War.

CHAPTER 5

Stalemate and Ceasefire

The Stalemate

Kang Hunyeol and his family were forced to flee their home near Seoul in June 1950. At great peril, they made it to Busan at the opposite end of the country. He and his family returned to his home that fall after it was retaken by the UN and ROK forces, only to flee again less than three months after he arrived. Eleven weeks later he was again able to go back after his town was retaken by ROK forces for the second time. This time Kang returned alone; his family, still uncertain whether it was safe to go back home, stayed as refugees near Busan. He discovered there was no home to return to, it was in ruins. There was some hope for Kang that life could return to normal that summer when after a horrible year of fighting, the combatants began discussing a halt to the conflict. But it would be two more years before a truce was arranged and his family felt safe enough to come back to rebuild their home.

Kang and his family's experiences reflected the first year of the Korean War; one of wildly fluctuating battle lines, rapid shifts of fortune, and unpredictable turns. For the next two years, there was much less drama. Armistice negotiations began near Kaesong on July 10, 1951, and continued for two years until July 27, 1953, while the two sides fought mostly along a narrow strip of land separating the two Koreas for modest strategic advantage. Each side waited for the other to tire of the conflict. The goal of the UN forces was to recapture and secure all the territory the ROK had held before the start of the conflict. The Chinese and North Korean forces had very much the same goal—to prevent the UN and ROK from retaking any territory in the North. There were some major battles such as the Battle of the Punchbowl from August to September 1951, the Battle of Heartbreak Ridge from September to October 1951, the Battle of Old Baldy from June to August 1952, and the Battle of Pork Chop Hill from March to July 1953. They were bloody affairs but they did little to alter the course of the war.

While the ground war was fought along the border between the two Koreas, there was some fighting within the Republic of Korea. There was an uptick in the insurgency in the South reinforced by remnants of the KPA. It is difficult to determine how many partisans were active. Their numbers were small but just enough to be of concern to the U.S. military who, in the autumn of 1951, ordered the ROK military to focus more on eliminating them. Paek Seonyeop took charge of crushing these scattered guerilla groups. In a major anti-insurgency campaign from December 1951 to March 1952, ROK forces claimed to have killed 11,000 guerillas and their sympathizers and captured 9,000 more. The problem with this figure was the term "sympathizers." It is not clear how many of those killed or captured were actual fighters and how many of these were ordinary villagers who may have given shelter and support or simply had not reported their presence. Whatever the case, the local insurgencies were mostly eliminated.

The war had become a "limited" conflict between the United States and China. North and South Korea were sidelined in decision-making but still did much of the fighting. Although not an official belligerent, the Soviet Union, besides supplying material and medical service, also covertly flew aircraft labeled as Chinese or North Korean. Soviet pilots wore Chinese uniforms, and they were ordered to avoid the coast or front lines where they might be shot down or captured. Flying their new MiG-15 aircraft the Soviet pilots achieved some success in hindering American bombers and providing air cover for supply lines. The Yalu River valley along the Chinese border became known to the UN forces as "MiG Alley." So effective was the MiG-15 that the U.S. offered $100,000 to any pilot that would defect with one. Shortly after the war a North Korean pilot, No Kumsok, did defect, providing the U.S. with an example to test. The Soviets denied sending pilots; an official denial they maintained for decades.

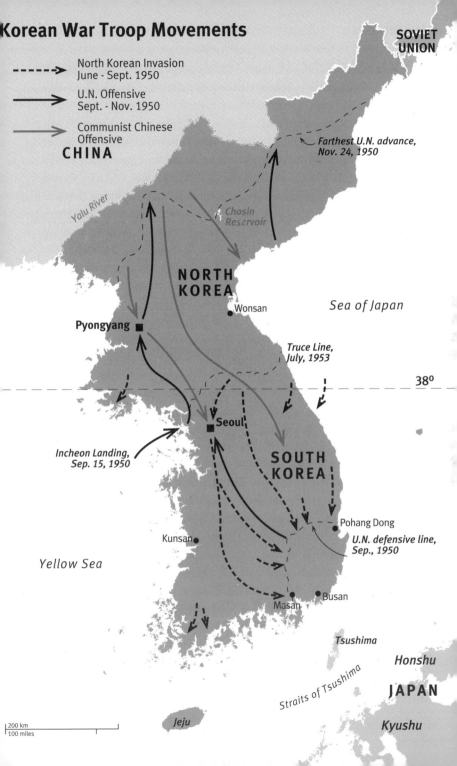

Korean War Troop Movements

- ╍╍➤ North Korean Invasion June - Sept. 1950
- ──➤ U.N. Offensive Sept. - Nov. 1950
- ──➤ Communist Chinese Offensive

SOVIET UNION

CHINA

Yalu River

Chosin Reservoir

NORTH KOREA

Farthest U.N. advance, Nov. 24, 1950

● Wonsan

Sea of Japan

Pyongyang ■

Truce Line, July, 1953

38°

■ **Seoul**

Incheon Landing, Sep. 15, 1950

SOUTH KOREA

● Pohang Dong

U.N. defensive line, Sep., 1950

● Kunsan

Yellow Sea

Masan ● Busan

● **JAPAN**

Tsushima

Honshu

Straits of Tsushima

Jeju

Kyushu

200 km
100 miles

A Miserable War

For all combatants, the last two years of the war involved hardships and suffering with little sign of any strategic gain. UN forces had to contend with the humid tropical summers and the bitter cold winters of Korea. There were the recent memories of the Chinese People's Volunteers' effective use of surprise that kept them on edge always waiting for another unexpected offensive. And morale was not helped by the growing unpopularity of the war in the U.S. Yet, the UN forces were well equipped, well-fed, and had increasingly effective medical support. This was not the case for the North Koreans and the Chinese.

The Chinese People's Volunteers underwent enormous hardships. Logistics, hindered by U.S. air attacks, were always precarious. The CPV suffered from equipment shortages and overextended communication and supply lines. The Chinese tried to deal with this by improving rail and road connections and air defense to protect their supply lines. But the underequipped Chinese soldiers, lacking air cover, suffered heavy casualties. They simply could not match the UN's firepower. Sometimes Chinese forces struck at weaker, less well-equipped ROK forces and achieved some gains, but the speedy intervention of the UN forces limited or reversed them. Besides suffering from munition shortages, soldiers were often sick from lack of clean drinking water, inadequate food supplies, and inadequate clothing. They were often forced to spend long periods in underground bunkers and tunnels, excellent places for illnesses to spread, and they were often sick. Death and debilitation from sickness added to the heavy casualty toll brought about by the UN bombing and artillery barrages.

In November 1951 Zhou Enlai convened a conference in Shenyang, Manchuria, to discuss ways of dealing with the logistical problems. At the conference, it was agreed to place more emphasis on improving rail connections and supplying more trucks and communication equipment. These measures, however, did not change the fundamental reality of the stalemate. After another meeting in February 1952 again called by Zhou Enlai, it was decided to divide the CPV into rotating shifts so that soldiers did not have to spend too long on the front and to accelerate the improvements in logistics. Beijing made efforts to supply more anti-aircraft guns, accelerate pilot training for the Chinese, and secure more material from the Soviet Union. It made some progress in providing more food and better clothing. Yet the situation for Chinese troops and their North Korean allies remained miserable.

"Very Cruel Weapons"

China and North Korea blamed much of the illnesses its forces suffered on the American use of biological weapons. The concept of biological and chemical warfare was fresh in the minds of Chinese and Koreans after their experience with the Japanese. At the Khabarovsk War Crime Trials in 1949, the Soviets accused the Japanese of operating a covert biological and chemical war research and development center that turned thousands of Chinese men, women, and children into guinea pigs in fiendishly cruel and often fatal experiments. These allegations were initially rejected by the West as mere propaganda, but they were true. Unit 731 was established in 1936 by the Japanese in the city of Harbin, where An Junggeun assassinated Ito Hirobumi. All during the China War, from 1937 to 1945 it injected, sprayed, and gassed tens of thousands of civilians with ghastly microbes and chemicals resulting in an unknown number of horrific deaths and suffering. Victims were given bubonic plague, cholera, smallpox, and botulism among other diseases. Researchers developed bacilli bombs and flea bombs. Many of these weapons were dropped on farm fields or in cities and towns in China.

How many died in these experiments is unknown, but the Chinese claimed as many as half a million. While this is probably an exaggeration it remains the largest use of involuntary human lab rats in history. And Unit 731 was not alone, other biological and chemical research units were established in occupied Chinese cities, sometimes labeled "Epidemic Prevention and Water Supply Units." Although the targets were primarily Chinese, Koreans were sometimes victims of these sinister research centers. The U.S. government knew of these experiments and the use of bio-weapons, but the general public did not. In fact, after the war, the U.S. was more interested in obtaining the information learned from those involved rather than in punishing them.

Soon after the Korean War the U.S. expanded its biological weapons program at Fort Detrick Maryland and opened up a new one at Pine Bluff, Arkansas. While the U.S. was developing biological weapons for defensive and offensive purposes it did not use them. However, the Chinese and North Koreans 1951 accused them of doing so. It is even possible that because of the high rate of soldiers becoming sick in their bunkers, they may have believed or suspected the Americans were infecting their troops. When in January 1952 Chinese and North Korean soldiers in several parts of the DPRK contracted smallpox, Beijing and Pyongyang thought the U.S. might be dropping infected insects on them, as the Japanese had done a few years earlier. In February 1952, North Korean Foreign Minister Bak Hon Yon openly charged Washington with doing so, also charging that the Americans were working with Japanese germ warfare experts including those who had worked at Unit 731. In June the United States requested that the International Red Cross investigate the charges. The Red Cross and World Health Organization ruled out the use of biological warfare, but the Soviet-affiliated World Peace Council set up its own investigation which included distinguished scientists from Western countries such as the famed British biochemist and sinologist Joseph Needham. It issued a report in September 1952 that the U.S. indeed was experimenting with biological weapons in Korea. Their report was corroborated by POWs, including several American pilots who confessed to dropping biological agents from their B-29 bombers. However, historians have questioned these findings. The outbreak of smallpox, bubonic plague, and cholera was easily accounted for by chaotic, unsanitary conditions in North Korea at the time, and there is no direct evidence of U.S. use of biological weapons. Still, some historians think the U.S. might have done so. North Koreans continued to maintain this was true and it has been one more weapon in that country's propaganda war against not just the U.S. but their South Korean collaborators (or puppets), one more way to instill the kind of hatred that has made peace on the peninsula so elusive.

Despite the willingness, and at times urging, of MacArthur, nuclear weapons were not employed in the Korean War. But other horrible innovations were. The U.S. used napalm for the first time. Developed at Harvard University during World War II and tested at a football field there, napalm is a compound made from a gelling agent and a petro-chemical such as gasoline and diesel fuel. The Americans made frequent use of napalm, dumping millions of gallons of liquid on North Korean and Chinese troops. It caused horrible burning, so horrible that many allies including Winston Churchill criticized it calling it "very cruel." Most of the casualties from napalm were probably North Korean civilians.

Operation Pressure Pump

As the war stalemated in the summer of 1951, the U.S. sought to use its superior air power to cut off supply lines and launched Operation Strangle. The U.S. Air Force flew thousands of sorties, bombing railroad lines, destroying locomotive and rail cars, vehicles, and bridges. But this had little substantive effect. Chinese and North Koreans learned to repair rail lines in hours, bridges in days, and kept supply lines in operation. On July 11, 1952, the Americans launched Operation Pressure Pump in which U.S. planes undertook a massive bombing campaign of Pyongyang and 30 other cities. Seong Hyerang, a member of the North Korean elite, recalls that up to 1952 there was at least a semblance of normality in the capital. The streets were filled with people going about their work. The new mass bombing campaign ended this. Much of North Korea moved underground, including factories, offices, and schools, and people spent considerable time in shelters. It was becoming a "bunker state." Working and living in dark, dreary underground shelters and facilities was bad for health and morale. And it left a sense of victimization among the North Koreans that made it easier for the North Korean regime to instill hatred for the United States.

American bombing of North Korea was on a scale unprecedented in warfare up to that time. Cities and large towns were leveled by bombing. According to official estimates, 75 percent of Pyongyang and 80 percent of Hamheung and Heungnam, the two biggest industrial cities, were destroyed, as were between 50 and 90 percent of the 15 other largest cities and towns. This compares with the 43 percent destruction of Japanese cities in World War II. Even with the firebombing and the two A-bombs, Japanese cities sustained much less damage than North Korean ones. And the range of targets kept expanding after the Americans ran out of factories and military installations to bomb. In May 1953, the U.S. began targeting dams. North Korea's rice crop was based on wet paddy cultivation which depended on numerous dams to control the water level in fields; these were now destroyed and the rice crop with them. By the time the fighting ended, the Americans had dropped 635,000 tons of bombs on the DPRK, more than on Germany or the entire Pacific theater of World War II. Additionally, Americans dropped 32,000 tons of napalm on North Korea. All this in a country the area of Pennsylvania and with only 10 million people.

Rhee and Kim Consolidate Power

Despite the setbacks both sides suffered in the Korean War, Kim Il Sung and Syngman Rhee each strengthened their grip on power. Rhee was not universally popular; not only was his administration filled with former Japanese collaborators, it was riddled with corruption. For example, he created the National Defense Corps to mobilize all available men for the war effort, but the organization proved a vehicle for its officers to line their pockets with military aid funds that were flowing in. His popular support was limited. Rhee used his war powers to consolidate power. His government was also ruthless toward anyone suspected of disloyalty. At the start of the conflict, he had 30,000 suspected Pyongyang sympathizers rounded up and nearly 3,000 of them executed as a preventative measure. Throughout the war, the government in Busan had carried out extra-judicial killings of those accused of supporting the enemy. Unable to find enough allies in the National Assembly to re-elect him, he declared martial law, had many of the legislators arrested, and intimidated others in sufficient numbers to have them pass a constitutional amendment that allowed for direct election of the president, which of course he won. He also created his own Liberal Party which soon gained a well-deserved reputation for corruption.

Kim Il Sung also consolidated power. This may be surprising since his invasion plan went disastrously wrong, yet the war had the effect of strengthening rather than weakening Kim's hold over his people. When the Chinese intervened, it lessened Soviet influence over North Korea. Since the Chinese, who had operational control over the war, largely kept out of domestic affairs, Kim was free to act against political rivals. He was quick to shift blame for defeats on others. As early as December 1950 he began to purge the party of rivals, holding them responsible for the early failures. Communist leaders from the South were assigned blame for the failure of the great guerilla uprising that they had promised. One of the first top leaders to be purged was Heo Kai, a Soviet-Korean who was blamed for the general populace's lack of resistance to the invaders and for not recruiting enough loyal Party members.

One of the most prominent victims of Kim Il Sung's purges was Mu Jeong. Today he is honored in North Korea and China and can be seen as a symbol of the common struggles of the two peoples. He, like so many Korean communist leaders, was born in the frontier province of North Hamgyeong; the coldest, most sparsely populated in Korea, and the one furthest from Seoul. His name was Kim Jeong but he later took the name Mu Jeong, "Mu" means "martial or military." As a young man, he joined the Chinese Communists. From 1934 to 1935 he made the Long March with Mao Zedong and became one of the leaders of the "Yenan Koreans" as those who fought with Mao were labeled. He established a military unit with the People's Liberation Army and then in 1942 with Pak Ilu formed the Korean Volunteer army, the military wing of the Korean Independence League. These fighters fought the Japanese in China alongside the PLA. He was highly regarded among Chinese military commanders,

After 1945 Mu Chong returned to North Korea. His prestige and experience as a soldier and anti-imperialist, nationalist fighter combined with the fact that he was an eloquent speaker made him a natural leader for the emerging regime. But he had two strikes against him. First, he was not well known to the Soviets, who in any case distrusted Koreans who fought with the Chinese but had little connection with Moscow. Second, he was seen as a rival to Kim Il Sung by outshining his military reputation and the Soviets had already decided to promote Kim as a leader. Added to these disadvantages was Kim Il Sung's skill at outmaneuvering anyone who challenged his leadership. So, Mu was shut out of the top circles of the leadership although he was a member of the Supreme People's Assembly.

Nonetheless, when the Korean War started, Mu's military experience was too valuable to ignore, and he was made one of the military commanders. In October 1950 he was put in charge of defending Pyongyang while Kim and most of the rest of the leadership fled to the mountain town of Kanggye near the Chinese border. With what was left of the KPA in disarray it was a hopeless task. When the city quickly fell to the South Korean and UN forces, Mu provided Kim with a convenient scapegoat for the setbacks of the early conflict. In December he was blamed for the failure to defend the country and purged from the party and dismissed as a commander. Later he left for China and died in 1952 at a Beijing hospital from stomach cancer. Unlike most victims of Kim Il Sung's purges, Mu was posthumously rehabilitated after the Korean War. His remains were interred in a tomb in his honor. While he never re-entered the top pantheon of heroes he is at least honored.

Pak Heonyeong

Another potential rival to Kim Il Sung was Pak Heonyeong. Few people were more instrumental in bringing about the Korean War. Pak was born in a *yangban* family in the south but as the illegitimate offspring of a concubine. In traditional Korea, it was common for aristocrats to take on a concubine, a younger attractive woman. But it created problems for any sons they may have had since the sons of a *yangban* and a concubine had at best an ambiguous status and found the normal career paths closed to them. They were the perpetual outsiders, too educated and refined to be commoners but shunned by aristocratic outsiders. More than a few became rebels. But in the changing world of early twentieth-century Korea, there were new opportunities and Pak took advantage of them by entering an elite modern high school in Seoul.

In 1919 he participated in the March First Movement. When it failed, he went to Shanghai and joined the Communist Party of Korea, the Irkutsk branch affiliated with the Bolshevik Party. In 1922, at only twenty-two years old, he participated in a Comintern meeting in Moscow. Upon returning to Korea he was arrested as a communist, was released, became a newspaper reporter, and in 1925 was one of the founders of the underground Korean Communist Party. The party organization was secret, but not for long, and the efficient Japanese police arrested its members. While on trial in 1926 Pak feigned insanity, eating his own feces. It worked; he was released but confined to his home. He escaped to Manchuria, then to Russia, finally returning to Korea to assume a leadership role in the underground party. At liberation in 1945, he was the chief of the Korean Communist Party which was based in Seoul. When the U.S. Military government began its suppression of communists, Pak and many others fled to the North. There he quickly emerged as the leader of the "domestic faction" of the communists in the North. Most of the communist leadership in North Korea were former exiles who had spent little of their adult life in Korea, or in some cases like Kim Il Sung, none of it. Pak was the only major leader who worked in Korea during colonial times.

Pak led a group of southerners in the North who had mostly spent their lives in Korea either in prison or underground. They created the Kangdong Institute to train agents to foment rebellion in the North. He emerged as the number two in the regime in 1948 after Kim Il Sung. The two were often photographed side-by-side and they traveled together when they met with Stalin. Despite the failure of most of the guerilla uprisings in the South, Pak became convinced, and managed to convince Kim Il-sung and the Soviets, that a DPRK invasion would be favorably received and supported in

the South. He had reason to believe this since he was well acquaint-
ed with the peasant and labor unrest in the South. And while some
villagers and students and intellectuals welcomed the KPA as liberators, the great groundswell of support for them failed to materialize.

Kim Il Sung made Pak Heonyeong and his Southerners scape-
goats for the failure to reunify the country. They were easy targets
since they had few roots or networks of support in North Korea.
While Pak could be blamed for overselling the revolutionary potential in the South, the charges against him and his colleagues
were fantastic. He was accused of being an American agent who
was deliberating seeking the defeat and destruction of the DPRK.
Arrested in 1953, he was quietly executed in December of 1955.

Wartime Occupations

North Korea attempted to bring its revolution to the areas of the
South that came under its control. Kim Il Sung in his June 26 1950
radio speech announced that South Korea was being liberated from
Japanese and U.S. imperialism and called for the reinstatement of
the people's committees that had sprung up in the days after liberation, calling them the "real organs of the people." During its two
to three-month occupation of most of South Korea, the DPRK sent
officials to these reconstituted committees to carry out the revolutionary changes that had been implemented in the North. DPRK
confiscated the property of the ROK government, its officials, and
"monopoly capitalists." They implemented the same labor laws
that guaranteed maximum hours and minimum wages as in the
North. Since the South was now part of the DPRK its laws and
policies automatically applied to it. The most sweeping measure
was land reform. Farmland was confiscated without compensation
to landowners and redistributed to each farm family. Villagers were
organized into committees to work this out.

A major task was to recruit volunteers to fight. In Seoul on
July 3, just several days after taking control of the city, the North
Koreans assembled 16,000 students and had them march through
the streets with banners saying, "Let's Volunteer for the Front."

When large numbers of youth failed to volunteer the communists gave each county and city quotas of volunteers among men eighteen or over. Thousands of young men were simply conscripted by the KPA. To what must have been the great disappointment of the North Korean leaders, few South Korean were eager to embrace their liberators. Instead of embracing the communists, hundreds of thousands fled to Busan, the wartime capital of the ROK, and other southern cities which swelled with refugees. Some moderates joined the committees, and the new North Korean liberators enjoyed some support from students and labor activists, but overall, most South Koreas were wary of the new regime at best.

The occupation was in fact, a violent affair. North Koreans released political prisoners from jails, many of whom sought the opportunity to take revenge on the police and others who had persecuted them. Many former officials and those known to be strongly anti-communist who had not managed to flee were executed. Prominent Southerners who were not automatically labeled enemies were pressed into service as propagandists for the regime. An example was Kim Gyusik, the respected moderate conservative who had tried to prevent the creation of two separate states. Since he was known to be opposed to the Rhee regime, he was encouraged to make pro-Pyongyang speeches on the radio. These speeches, with intemperate denunciations of the Republic of Korea, were likely written for him. The worst atrocities were committed by the North Koreans during their hasty retreat. Many "traitors" were executed, and others were taken with them as the North Korean forces withdrew northward. It was a brief and bloody occupation that left behind bitterness and hatred toward the DPRK among many in the South.

The occupation of the North was just as violent. Although nominally under the command of General MacArthur, ROK forces and intelligence officials often acted without much supervision. South Korea was never authorized to govern any part of the North which was administered by the United Nations. Although reminded of this, ROK officials largely ignored it and the Americans, focused on the war effort, did little to restrain them. As banners in Pyongyang announced, "The Republic of Korea is our Government," and

"Our Leader is President Yi Sungman." Rhee's officials carried out bloody reprisals backed by a law passed in the National Assembly that called for punishing collaborators. Rhee himself helped set the tone. In a speech on October 27, 1950, before a crowd of fifty thousand in the former DPRK capital he denounced the communists as "vicious animals with human faces" who were out to enslave them.

The ROK under Rhee could have hardly done a better job at alienating their "liberated" compatriots in the North. Any member of the Korean Workers' Party was subject to arrest or abuse. Since this was a mass party that included a sizeable proportion of the entire North Korean population, these punishments were unrealistic. ROK military and civilian officials executed thousands of civilians, carrying out a reign of terror in the areas under their control. Yet as bad as this was, no measure did less to endear the population to the South than the order that farmers return the land to their former landlords. When the ROK forces later retreated they took tens of thousands of North Korean with them, most of whom were young men that had been forcibly conscripted. In this way, they acted much the same as the KPA did when it retreated. Nonetheless, for all their heavy-handed methods few ordinary North Koreans put up much resistance to their southern "liberators" and their UN allies, and many seemed to have willingly cooperated with them. Their failure to actively resist was alarming to Kim Il Sung and his government. His response to this after the war was to make every effort to indoctrinate his people in the goals of the revolution and instill in them unquestioning loyalty to the regime.

As with most civil wars, this was a vicious, tragic conflict. For millions of Koreans caught up in it, such as Lee Young Ho, it was a confusing nightmare. Lee was a seventeen-year-old high school student in Seoul when the North Koreans occupied the city. His frightened family attempted to keep him home but Lee, venturing on the street, was taken into custody by the occupiers. Without his family knowing his whereabouts, he was forced into the North Korean Army, only to desert during the hasty retreat in the fall of 1950. He wound up fighting in the South Korean Army. He and his family survived, and therefore can be counted as among the fortunate.

Another survivor was Lee Hyun Sook a twenty-four-year-old who was a housewife when the North Koreans invaded. She and her husband, and their two-year-old daughter crossed the Han River by boat with her sister's family. They walked for fifteen days until they arrived in the town of Hongseong where her husband's family lived. However, their escape was a brief one. Two days later the KPA arrived in town. Since her husband belonged to a patriotic association, one of the many anti-communist groups in the South, she feared his arrest or even execution. He hid in his brother's basement, then another basement. After hiding in cellars for weeks he came out to breathe some fresh air only to be arrested. At the police station, he was beaten so badly that he almost died. Fortunately, his brother had a friend, a policeman, who managed to get him out of jail. When the ROK-UN forces regained control of the area her husband joined the ROK Army, but the injuries he had sustained from the beating prevented him from going to the front line. He was passionately anti-communist and anti-DPRK after the war.

Neither the ROK nor the DPRK did much to win over support from the other side. Rather they left legacies of fear and bitterness on both sides of the 38th parallel. The governments of South Korea and North Korea for decades dwelled on the horrors of the brief occupations, promoting mutual hatred and distrust, and contributing to the endless nature of the Korean War.

Armistice Talks

When armistice talks began in July 1951 the UN sought the following: the establishment of a truce line, the exchange of prisoners-of-war; and an agreed method of enforcing the armistice. The communists added one more—the withdrawal of all foreign troops from Korea. With these objectives in mind, the two sides began negotiations that went on and off for two years.

The Americans were becoming wary of what had become at home a very unpopular war which contributed to Dwight Eisenhower's resounding victory in the presidential elections of 1952. Eisenhower had promised to end the war, and shortly after the election, the President-elect visited Korea making it clear that this would be a key priority. The Chinese were increasingly ready to end the conflict. Already in late 1951, Peng Dehuai came to believe the war would be a protracted one and, concerned by the losses, went several times to Beijing to brief Mao on the state of things. He made it clear that he did not see any way that either side could achieve a victory. But Mao sought to continue fighting. However, by 1953, he too was ready to end the conflict. Mao had achieved his original aim of keeping the Americans and their allies away from his border, his regime had gained prestige by fighting the U.S. to a standstill. Continuing conflict served no real purpose for him. The Soviets may not have minded the war as long as they were careful not to become directly involved. With Stalin's death in March 1953, however, the new Soviet leadership was less interested in a war that did not cost them much but did not bring many benefits either.

North Korea's leadership was ready to end the conflict which was only bringing a continual rain of destruction on their country from the U.S. bombing. The only party that was not ready for a truce in early 1953 was South Korea's President Rhee. He could not accept a stalemate, and would not let go of his dream of reuniting the country that he still saw as possible if only the Americans were committed to victory. His country was also in a very different position than the North. After the summer of 1951, the fighting was confined to a narrow strip of land along the border. South Korea was free of the massive bombing raids northerners had to endure, there were no longer significant civilian casualties.

When Eisenhower visited Seoul, Rhee tried his best to persuade him to resume the offensive. The president-elect was warned before the meeting by his soon-to-be secretary of state John Foster Dulles that Rhee had three obsessions-to reunite Korea, to maintain himself in power, and to seek revenge on the Japanese. This was a fairly accurate summary of his priorities in that order. But his passion to reunify the country could not be dismissed as a personal quirk, it was shared by almost all Koreans. The difference was most, including the leadership in the North, accepted that this was no longer the time for that to happen.

Rhee was so frustrated and angry with the refusal of the Americans to launch another offensive into the North that in 1952 he threatened to pull all the ROK troops out of the UN command. This, of course, would make them freely available for Rhee to launch his own attacks. General Mark Clark who replaced Matthew Ridgway as UN Commander was instructed by the Joint Chiefs of Staff in mid-1952 to develop a contingency plan should Rhee attempt to do this. Clark came up with a plan to declare martial law in South Korea and to "secure custody of the dissident civilian and military leaders: proclaim military government in the name of the U.N." Under the code name Operation Everready, Rhee would be invited to Seoul to get him out of Busan and then detained. The UN Commander would move into Busan and seize the top ROK leaders. The UN command would then take control of the government through the ROK chief of staff. According to the plan Rhee would be ordered to accept this and cease governing in an autocratic way. If he did not, he would be held in protective custody, incommunicado and another officer would be put in charge.

In the spring and summer of 1953, serious consideration was given by the U.S. government to this plan. Some suggested the South Korean ambassador to the United States John Chang (Chang Myeon), well-liked and trusted, could be installed in Rhee's place. The plan was not implemented due to worries that Rhee, who was still popular among the South Korean people, could rally support that would undermine the effort. Alternative plans were also considered including signing a bilateral treaty with South Korea that would reassure the U.S. commitment to its defense. Still another option was signing a truce and then pulling out. In the end, it was decided that since there was no other anti-Communist, charismatic leader more effective at rallying the people than Rhee, the U.S. would just work around him.

Yet some in Washington must have regretted not trying to remove Rhee when he came close to sabotaging the armistice. During the truce talks, the issue of POWs was one of the most contentious ones. Many of the Chinese and North Koreans held by the UN did not want to go home, but Beijing and Pyongyang insisted that all be returned. Two years of protracted negotiations over the issue were finally being resolved by June 1953 reflecting Moscow's and Beijing's desire to end the war. Rhee became infuriated at the thought that the major powers were soon going to end the conflict with the nation divided. On June 18 he secretly released 27,000 North Korean prisoners who had indicated they did not wish to go back to the DPRK. The Americans were shocked and angry that the old South Korean patriot had deliberately undermined their long-sought agreement on repatriation. Rhee had some domestic support. South Koreans were tired of the conflict yet many still hoped to end the war with their country reunited. Crowds waved banners "Don't sell out Korea!" and "Down with the Armistice!"

Armistice Signed and Not Signed

Despite Rhee's efforts, the negotiations were not sabotaged. Beijing and Pyongyang while heaping vitriol on Rhee and his "clique," continued with the negotiations. That summer, while they were going on, the Chinese launched two more offensives. On June 10, 1953, some 30,000 Chinese troops attacked two South Korean and one U.S. division along a 13km (8 mile) front. On July 13, the Chinese launched an even larger attack with 80,000 men aimed mainly at South Korean held positions. In both attacks, the Chinese managed to make small advances before being halted by heavy American firepower involving the most intensive use of artillery in the entire war. South Korean troops took heavy losses, but the Chinese suffered far greater casualties with only marginal gains, only reinforcing the futility of continuing the war in the face of American firepower, and the determination of UN forces not to give ground. The armistice was signed on July 27. It was concluded without the signature of the ROK government.

The U.S. and its allies, Beijing and Pyongyang, were relieved to see the war that had become increasingly pointless end. But, of course, it did not end. Rather it entered a new phase that would continue for seven more decades.

Syngman Rhee

Whether or not he was indispensable, there was certainly no one in Korea quite like Syngman Rhee. His extraordinary life began in a village in Hwanghaedo, in what is now North Korea, on February 19, 1875. His family was not wealthy but proudly traced its lineage back to the founder of the Joseon dynasty, thus he claimed to have royal blood. His family moved to Seoul when he was four and he attended a *seodang*, a traditional Confucian school. He studied for the civil service exam but when it was abolished in 1894, he enrolled in Pai Chai an American Methodist mission school. There he learned English, was exposed to modern political ideas, and became involved in the Independence Club. He was arrested for his activities in 1898. While in prison he compiled an English-Korean dictionary and wrote *The Spirit of Independence*.

In 1904 after being released, Rhee went to the United States and met Secretary of State John Hay and Theodore Roosevelt at the Portsmouth Peace talks where he tried to persuade them to support Korean independence. It was a rather futile cause since the Roosevelt administration had no sympathy or concern for Korea. He went on to study further, receiving degrees at George Washington University, Harvard, and a Ph.D. at Princeton. He returned to Korea in 1910, became implicated in the plot to assassinate the Governor-General and fled back to the U.S. He lived in America for over three decades except for a brief interlude in Shanghai where he served for a time as the president of the Korean Provisional Government. He worked tirelessly in keeping the cause of Korean independence alive and in the consciousness of the Americans.

Despite being disliked and distrusted by officials in the State Department he returned to Korea in 1945 in General McArthur's personal plane, a feat he managed to finagle giving the public the false impression he was the U.S.-backed leader. Rhee, however, was nobody's man but his own. Working with conservatives he was elected president in 1948. During the conflict, he worked single-mindedly on one goal—to reunite the country under his leadership. Rhee was so focused on reunification and so aggressive in pursuing it that he was a constant thorn in the side of the Americans. At first, many Americans praised his firm resolve to defend the country in the early days of the war; one declared he "was worth his weight in diamonds" to the UN cause. But later he became the chief obstacle to a truce, insisting that the UN must try again and invade the North and unify the country. Yet he remained to many in Washington a valued ally and had many influential supporters, including publisher Henry Luce who put him on the cover of his influential *TIME* magazine several times. Rhee famously refused to sign the July 27, 1953 armistice agreement. For him the Korean War did not end, the armistice was just a temporary setback to the cause of reunification. He remained implacably anti-Japanese as well as anti-communist and after the Korean War, he refused to sign a peace treaty with Japan. His crusade against communism was well received by the anti-communists in the Americas. In 1954, he became one of the first foreign leaders invited to address both houses of the U.S. Congress. In fluent English, he was an effective speaker, he thanked the Americans for their help but then wondered if they had "the guts" to stand up to the communists. While Rhee remained a hero to some South Koreans, many especially the urban middle class grew hostile to him. His authoritarian rule ended when he was ousted during a student-led uprising in April 1960. He died in exile in Hawaii.

Panmunjom

The armistice was negotiated and signed in the small village of Panmunjom 31 miles (53km) northwest of Seoul. It was a tiny place, no more than ten houses by a small stream, 10 miles (16km) south of Kaesong. Panmunjom, while small, was on the main road that ran from Seoul to Sinuiju on the North Korean-Chinese border. In the summer of 1951, representatives of the Military Armistice Commission set up tents and began truce talks there since it was on the line that marked the boundary between the two sides in the conflict. The advisories worked together to construct a building where the negotiations could take place. In a rare exercise in co-operation, they worked day and night and in just 48 hours put up the building.

North Korea supplied most of the labor and the UN supplied most of the building materials and the generators that powered lights making it possible to work during the night.

After the agreement was signed, a new site was constructed 0.6 miles (1km) east of the village. This became the permanent site for the meetings of the two sides in the endless Korean War. The area is known as the Joint Security Area or JSA. After the armistice, all civilians were removed from the Korean Demilitarized Zone (DMZ) except for two villages near the JSA, one of each size. The JSA is roughly circular and about 2600 feet (800 meters) in width. Until 1976 it was a neutral zone where people could walk freely, but after a border incident, movements had to follow strict protocols. South Korea paid farmers to remain in their village while the North Korean settlement became a Potemkin village, lights went on after dark but there was little or no sign of any activity in the largely deserted village.

At the JSA main building, a North Korean soldier (or soldiers) stands inside the conference room in front of the door that leads to South Korea and a UN soldier (or soldiers) stands on the side that leads to North Korea. In the center is the table. Visitors coming from the South can walk around the table escorted by guards and thus enter North Korea when they are on the north side of it. The guards at the JSA are chosen carefully to represent the fierce determination of their respective countries. South Korean guards had to be at least 5 feet eight inches (172 cm) tall and have a blackbelt in taekwondo. North Korean guards are similarly chosen. Each soldier is armed with a pistol and maintains a stoic expression. About 100,000 tourists visit the JSA every year from the south on carefully escorted tours. A smaller number come from the north also on carefully escorted tours. But it is not an amusement park; the border is heavily armed and often quite tense.

While it is still common to refer to the site as Panmunjom, the actual village of Panmunjom has disappeared. Houses have decayed and there is no longer any obvious trace of the original village. Instead in its place, North Korea has created a Peace Museum on the site where the truce talks were first conducted.

Impact of the Korea War—Did Anyone Win?

Historians simply don't agree on the number of casualties in the Korean War. We have no figures from North Korea or reliable ones from China. It is estimated that the ROK Army suffered 227,000 killed, and civilian deaths including those by disease, exposure, and starvation were at least twice that. This does not include the thousands of South Koreans who were kidnapped and taken to the North never to be seen or heard of again by their families. About 37,000 Americans and 4,000 UN allies were killed. Estimates of Chinese losses vary but perhaps 300,000 died in combat or from disease. North Korean casualties are even more a matter of guesswork but a common estimate is that 200,000 soldiers were killed or died of disease and at least twice as many civilians perished. Considering that North Korea had only ten million people, 600,000 deaths is a high number, six percent of the population, and the real number might be higher. This amounted to one of the highest rates of casualties suffered by any country in modern times.

The Korean War had no real winners. Pyongyang and Seoul both failed in their efforts to unify the country. The Americans stopped South Korea from falling to the communists at a cost of close to 40,000 lives but ended up where they did not want to be—stuck in the peninsula, with the threat of the resumption of war always present. The war did not cost the Soviets much, but they did not gain anything either; it did not divert U.S. attention from Europe as they may have hoped it would. China could claim some success—defending an ally and fighting the Americans to a draw may have enhanced the prestige of the new regime but it came at the cost of perhaps 300,000 Chinese lives. The war also preserved a North Korean ally that would later prove troublesome to China. It strengthened the U.S. military presence near their border, and it cost them Taiwan. Most of all, the Korean people lost—perhaps as many as a million and a half men, women, and children died in the war. The death and destruction were truly horrific, and yet the one thing almost all Koreans wanted—unification—was now farther away than ever.

Especially for the DPRK, the war was a disaster. It suffered horrific loss of life, the cities were in ruins, and much of its industrial infrastructure was destroyed. It was certainly a failure for the regime, since rather than reunifying the country on its terms, it ended up strengthening both the South Korean regime and the U.S. commitment to defend it. The failure of the South Korean people to rise and support the KPA was a demoralizing blow to Kim and his comrades. Even more troubling was the passive response of the North to the occupying ROK forces. The extent of death and destruction was not as great in the South, but still horrible. Seoul was left a jumble of half-standing buildings and rubble. Besides the many killed, tens of thousands of South Koreans—mostly young men but also intellectuals and others of varied ages—were taken to the North and never seen or heard of again. There was another tragic result. Millions of South Koreas were now totally cut off from family members. In most cases, they would never learn what became of their siblings, parents, children, or spouses.

A popular South Korean movie, *Ode to My Father*, made in 2014, is the story of a boy separated from his father when the family was fleeing Wonsan on a U.S. naval vessel. He spent the next half-century operating a small shop in Busan, one his father had owned, hoping for the day his father would return to it. Although a sentimental work of fiction it rang true for many Koreans who for decades waited to be reunited. A small handful were reunited when, many years after the war, North Korea allowed a limited number of family reunions. Kim Kwang-ho participated in one of these. He was 14 years old when he said goodbye to his younger brother who stayed behind with his mother as Kwang-ho fled south with his father and older siblings. His mother and younger brother were supposed to join them days later but never were able to. After sixty-six years the two were finally reunited. Before he met his seventy-eight-year-old sibling he couldn't remember what he looked like.

Not only was the Korean War a bad war for almost all—it didn't end. The agreement in July 1953 was only a ceasefire. It certainly did not end for Kim Il Sung, who never gave up his plans for reunification. Over the next several decades he sought to learn from his mistakes and prepare for a final victory. And what were the lessons? To make sure his country was militarily and industrially strong enough to carry out a war without allied support. To make sure the citizens of the Democratic People's Republic were well indoctrinated so they would give all their efforts and would not cooperate with the enemy. To foster the revolutionary forces in the South until the people were ready to turn against their regime and support the North. To gain international support for his efforts at reunification, and prevent the U.S. from interfering. For decades these were the goals his regime worked to achieve.

The war didn't end for the South, either. It left the republic with one of the world's largest armed forces—600,000 citizens under arms and with a large U.S. military presence in their country. It hardened the attitudes of many in South Korea who were outraged by the North Korean invasion and appalled by the way its occupation had been conducted. An entire generation of South Koreans was now ardently anticommunist and pro-U.S., and even if they were often critical of the government in power, they accepted the legitimacy of the Republic of Korea as the real successor to the historical Korean state. Unlike the leadership of the North, South Korean leaders knew that they could not reunify the country by force, but like their northern counterparts, they believed that they had to create an industrially and militarily strong society that would eventually be able to achieve victory in a renewed conflict. Both Koreas would now engage in an economic development race to better prepare themselves for the next outbreak of fighting, while at the same time demonstrating the superiority of their system to their people and their neighbors across the demilitarized zone.

Divided Countries

From the Korean point of view, the most tragic result of the Korean War was that the country remained divided. Korea was not the only country to be divided in the twentieth century. The case of Korea, however, was unique and this uniqueness helps account for the volatility of the peninsula, and the passions that led to continuous conflict.

India and Palestine were partitioned along ethnic and sectarian lines. There were no sectarian and ethnic differences between North and South Koreans. Germany and Vietnam offer better analogies since they were also divided as a result of Cold War conflicts. East and West Germany, like Korea, were created by the Soviet and the Western powers at the close of World War II and after a brief occupation—four years versus the three years of Korea, two rival regimes were set up. Both were able to draw upon pre-existing ideological divisions. But the parallels end here. East Germany was much smaller than West Germany with one-quarter of the population while North Korea had half the population of the South and was larger in area. Since the North was much more industrialized than the South the disparities in size and economic potential were less pronounced. And East Germany was clearly a Soviet puppet state which never seriously challenged West Germany for the title of the legitimate heir to the prewar German state. Furthermore, the two states were less cut off from each other. East Germany unlike North Korea was not hermetically sealed off. West Germans could visit relatives in East Germany, and many East Germans were able to watch West German television and listen to the radio from the West, even if illegally. This was not true in the North where all communication and contract were terminated. Furthermore, Germany itself was a fairly new nation-state formed only in 1871 when Bismarck unified several German-speaking states. Regional dialects and differences in traditions ran stronger than in Korea. And unlike the Koreans, the Germans themselves bore some measure of responsibility for their situation, and have historically been a menace to their neighbors.

Vietnam might seem a better analogy. It was divided in 1954 into roughly equal halves—also into a communist one in the north and an anti-communist one in the south. It is like the division of Korea reflected ideological divisions. And like Korea, the division was not acceptable, especially to the people of the North. But there were some pronounced differences. Vietnam's divisions reflected a certain historical and geographic logic. Although in each half the overwhelming majority was ethnically Vietnamese, the two population centers of Hanoi in the Hong River Basin in the north and Saigon, now Ho Chi Minh City, in the lower Mekong River basin in the south were separated by a long, narrow coastal plain and rugged highlands. Lifestyles differed in the two regions which were, in reality, two separate states for several centuries before re-unification in 1802. As tragic and unacceptable as its division was, Vietnam simply did not have a comparable history of unity or the same degree of cultural homogeneity, nor was the division so arbitrarily drawn and imposed. And unlike Korea, North Vietnam, and its Viet Cong supporters prevailed after two decades of fighting.

In short, there is no case truly comparable to the division of Korea, to its suddenness, its arbitrariness, and the tragedy it resulted in. For almost all Koreans the division was not just unacceptable but unnatural; a foreign-imposed anomaly in the nation's long history. The border between the two states in 1953 was most tense, most sealed off, and perhaps most unacceptable to those that shared it in the world. This is why the Korean Peninsula became such a volatile, dangerous place.

CHAPTER 6

The Three Revolutionary Forces, 1953–1972

At 11 pm on January 17, 1968, thirty-one specially trained North Korean commandos cut through the fencing of the U.S. Second Infantry Division's sector of the DMZ. During the night they made their way to nearby woods and hid. The next night they made it to Simbong Mountain south of the DMZ on the way to Seoul and set up camp before dawn. A few hours later four woodcutters, all brothers, came upon their camp. According to their training, the commandos were supposed to kill the witnesses immediately, but they didn't. Instead, they deliberated for a while and decided to try to persuade the South Korean woodcutters not to report them to anyone. After all, they were fellow Koreans and the commandos had come to liberate them. This proved to be a mistake. The woodcutters, rather than be persuaded to help their liberators by remaining silent, reported them. However, by the time three battalions of the South Korean 25th Infantry Division arrived and began searching for them, the commandos had moved on closer to Seoul, closer to the target they had been training to attack for the past two years—the South Korean presidential palace and its resident South Korean president Park Chung Hee.

On the night of January 21, they approached the vicinity of the Blue House, as the presidential palace is known. They had practiced for this moment by assaulting a mock-up of the building in North Korea. Now it was for real. They came to within 100 meters of their target before a suspicious guard at a check post drew out his pistol. The commandos shot him but now there was no more surprise and

Korean Demilitarized Zone

Hyesan

Kanggye

Kilju

Pyoktong

Kimchaek

Yalu

Sinuiju

Chongju

Hamhung

Taedong

NORTH KOREA

Pyongsong

Wonsan

Korea Bay

Pyongyang

Sea of Japan

Nampo

Ch'odo Island

Imjin

Bukhan

Sariwon

Military Demarcation Line
Demilitarized Zone

Baengnyeongdo

Haeju

Kaesong

Panmunjom

Chuncheon

Gangneung

Daecheongdo

Sochoengdo

Sunwi-do

Ganghwa Island

Uijeongbu

Yeonpyeongdo

Seoul

Han

Incheon

Bucheon

Seongnam

Wonju

Suwon

Namhan

Deokjeok-myeon

SOUTH KOREA

Cheongju

Andong

Geum

Daejeon

Nakdong

Yellow Sea

Pohang

Gunsan

Joenju

Daegu

Ulsan

Gwangju

Busan

100 km
50 miles

a furious firefight ensued. There were 92 South Korean casualties, some wounded, some dead, including two dozen civilians who just happened to have the misfortune of being on a bus that passed through the line of fire. Some of the commandos were killed but others escaped only to be pursued in a massive manhunt. One was captured but committed suicide.

The incident, fifteen years after the armistice was one of the more dramatic of many that occurred after 1953. The armistice did not bring peace or change the fundamental fact that the division of Korea was unacceptable and both Koreas were determined to reunite it under their leadership. For North Korea, especially, reunification was a central obsession. So, the Korean conflict continued. It did so in the form of occasional violent confrontations and as a competition between the two Koreas for the mantle of legitimacy. North and South competed in rebuilding their societies, in economic development, and in winning over the support of all the people of the peninsula. They also competed for international recognition of their cause. All the while the peninsula remained one of the most dangerous and tense places in the world.

North Korea After the War

For the North Korean leadership in 1953, the armistice was a temporary setback. The war was not over and the main goal—the reunification of the country, remained unchanged. The entire history of the DPRK for the next few decades was aimed at reversing that setback and achieving what they viewed as the inevitable victory. To accomplish this, Kim Il Sung and his comrades consolidated their power, rebuilt the ruined cities, created an industrial-based economy that supported a powerful military, indoctrinated the people, built up the military, and worked toward achieving autonomy from outside control while trying to undermine the regime in the South and weaken the U.S. commitment to its defense. All of this was done with an impressive single-mindedness of purpose.

Kim Il Sung's immediate task was to rebuild what had been destroyed and consolidate his power. He wasted no time in doing both. Rebuilding the country was a formidable task since North Korea was a country in total ruins. Pyongyang and other cities looked like Hiroshima and Nagasaki after the atomic attacks with hardly a major building standing. The last bombing campaign in the spring of 1953 had destroyed much of the irrigation system, disrupting agricultural production and causing food shortages. Hwang Jang Yop, who later became the DPRK's highest-ranking defector to the West came back from his studies in Moscow and was shocked at what he saw. There were hardly any houses in Pyongyang standing and people were living in subterranean dugouts. Beggars lined the streets and thieves roamed them. Even he as a professor at Kim Il Sung University, the country's most prestigious center of learning, was forced to line up in the street for turnip soup and was often hungry.

Faced with this situation Kim Il Sung almost immediately after the ceasefire presented his Soviet allies with a list of aid he needed. Then he traveled to Moscow and Eastern Europe to get it, and he succeeded. The Soviet Union and its allies such as Czechoslovakia, East Germany, and Poland provided considerable material aid. Every member of the Communist block contributed; even Mongolia sent 10,000 horses. Thousands of Soviet and East European technicians and engineers helped in rebuilding the cities and factories, and infrastructure. China provided loans and put its large number of troops still stationed in the country to work on construction projects. Most of the aid came in the form of loans at very generous repayment terms which were never repaid. The whole rebuilding of North Korea from 1953 to 1956 was probably the biggest joint communist enterprise ever undertaken up to that time.

But not all the credit for the recovery can be given to generous help from its friends. Ordinary North Korean people were mobilized by the state for endless reconstruction work. They cleared rubble, repaired dams, rebuilt old buildings, and constructed new ones. It was a national mass mobilization of all available men, women, and youth. As a result, by 1956 the state was able to begin where it left off in 1950 and launch its first Five-year Economic Development Plan to convert the country into an industrial powerhouse. Aid levels quickly dropped off but never ended. The Soviets continued to assist by providing petroleum and other resources, and some capital equipment at "friendship prices" meaning far below real market prices.

Pyongyang

North Korea's biggest reconstruction project was the capital Pyongyang. The term "capital" has to be used with qualification since Seoul was the capital and Pyongyang was the temporary capital or the "base camp" for reunification. Pyongyang is on the impressive Daedong River about 70 miles (110km) upstream from the Yellow Sea on the largest area of non-mountainous land in northern Korea. It is perhaps the oldest city in Northeast Asia, but its true origins are lost to history. Pyongyang was the capital of the Old Joseon state that emerged around 300 BCE. It was taken by the Chinese and became their main administrative center in the peninsula from 108 BCE to the fourth century. It has served as the capital of several early Korean states. After the unification of the peninsula in the seventh century, it remained one of Korea's most important urban centers.

As the most important northern city Pyongyang logically served as the administrative center of the Soviet occupation zone and the capital of the Democratic People's Republic of Korea. But it remained a provincial city. Seoul, capital of Korea since 1394 was the real cultural center of Korea. A Korea without Seoul was like France without Paris. This is why even the 1948 constitution of the DPRK listed Seoul as the capital, and Pyongyang as the temporary administrative center until the liberation of all of Korea.

The city was so destroyed by U.S. bombing that almost all vestiges of its ancient history were gone. This allowed Kim Il Sung to rebuild this "base camp" for the reunification effort into a showpiece. Like North Korea itself, few cities in the world reflect the vision of one person. Kim Il Sung took a personal and direct role in planning the rebuilding and chairing the Pyongyang City Rehabilitation Committee. The city is divided into small self-sufficient neighborhoods with residences, mostly high-rises, each with a food store, a clinic, a library, and other amenities: a barbershop, and a public bathhouse. This follows the patterns of towns and even collective farms in the countryside.

Above all, however, Pyongyang is a display city—a city to symbolize and show off the glory and success of the North Korean Revolution. To this end, it was dominated by monuments to the Revolution and Kim Il Sung himself. The residential areas were hidden behind the wide boulevards and great squares built for military parades, mass rallies, and as massive propaganda. The largest public area is the mammoth Kim Il Sung Square. Among the original monuments of the city built in the 1950s is the Arch of Triumph built in 1972 for Kim Il Sung's 60th birthday, it is modeled on but bigger than the famous *Arc de Triomphe* in Paris. The Tower of Juche, a 557-foot (170 m) granite spire symbolizing the state ideology was completed in 1982. This imposing monument was built with 25,550 granite blocks, one for each day of Kim Il Sung's life at the time, and a bright red flame on the top glows in the mostly dark city at night. The whole city was a celebration of the Great Leader, his revolution, and its inevitable victory.

In 1972, Pyongyang officially became the capital of Korea, not the temporary one according to North Korea. From the 1980s and 1990s history was re-written relegating Seoul to minor importance and making Pyongyang the center of the Korean nation from the earliest times. Its history was then creatively traced back to an ancient five thousand year civilization, the Daedong Society which was the original home of the Korean race and nation. Towering among the monuments was one more symbol—the Ryugyong Hotel. Built to outdo the skyscrapers going up in Seoul, this 330-meter (1,085-foot) 105-story hotel was to be the tallest in the world, with more than 3,000 rooms and multiple revolving restaurants. It was started in 1987 but structural flaws resulted in it never being opened. Instead, the strangely shaped building became a symbol of North Korea's economic problems and its failure to rival its southern counterpart.

Socialization and Consolidation

While cities and infrastructure were being rebuilt, the DPRK carried out the complete socialization of the country. Between 1954 and 1957 the state collectivized agriculture in stages. First farm families were lumped together and required to share tools, draft animals, and other equipment. Then the farms were merged into large state-run enterprises. The process was done cautiously at first to avoid the kind of resistance and starvation that had taken place in the Soviet Union when it carried out its collectivization. And in this Pyongyang succeeded—the process went smoothly with little disruption and minimal if any resistance. As a result, the peasants who so eagerly embraced the regime when they received their land in 1946, lost it a decade later. Rather than tenants for an absentee landlord, they became salaried employees of the state. At the same time, the surviving small businesses, such as shops and restaurants, were closed and replaced by state exchanges and cafeterias. While some communist states such as Poland and Hungary gave a little space for private enterprise, allowing farmers private plots, and permitting some private markets, North Korea opted for a total state-owned, command economy.

When a confident Kim Il Sung launched the Five-Year plan in 1956, he aimed to build an industrial base to prepare his country for war. He emphasized heavy industry: steel; heavy equipment; and vehicles such as trucks and tractors. Some of his comrades raised concerns about this, suggesting such a poor, mostly agricultural society should focus more on basic consumer goods. Kim transferred them from their administrative posts to prison cells. The DPRK was to be the base for reunification, and it was to be an autonomous state free from dependency on capital and manufactured goods from its trading partners. This required building industrial plants. From 1958 influenced by Mao's Great Leap Forward he became more ambitious in his economic goals. He launched the Cheollima or "flying horse" campaign to encourage people to devote themselves to achieving wildly unrealistic economic targets. Workers were told to see the morning stars as they went to work (go in early) and not drink soup (to avoid bathroom breaks), to take one stretch only after a thousand shovels. Economic efforts were waged as military campaigns to "capture the hills" of the production goals. Eventually, even Kim began to understand just how unrealistic some of the goals were and modified them in the subsequent Seven Year Plan 1961 to 1967 and others then followed, but the military-like mass campaigns, exhortations and endless demands on workers to put in voluntary hours continued to be a part of life north of the DMZ.

Meanwhile, Kim Il Sung and his Manchurian comrades were busy consolidating power. Just weeks after the armistice he purged Pak Heonyeong and the domestic communists, blaming the failure to liberate the South on them. In 1956 and 1957 Kim purged the Soviet Koreans and the "Yenan Koreans" who had served with Mao during World War II. The purges widened to include ordinary rank and file Party members whose loyalty was suspected. By 1960 more than 100,000 had been arrested and 2,500 executed. Kim and his comrades took no chances with any kind of opposition. The entire population was classified into three groups: the core, the wavering, and the hostile. The first consisted of citizens with personal and family backgrounds that indicated they were loyal. This included those who had fought against the Japanese or who were simply loyal peasants and workers with no compromising past or ancestors. The hostile group were those from capitalist or landlord backgrounds or had relatives in the South or in some way were deemed less trustworthy. In between were the wavering class. Informally the core members were called "tomatoes," red all the way through, the wavering "apples", red only on the outside, and the hostiles "grapes" not red at all. Members of the hostile class, about a quarter of the population were prohibited from living in Seoul or near the border. Many were relocated to the remote northeast. In the 1960s these groups were subdivided into *songbun* ranked by degree of loyalty. Since these ranks were inherited, North Korea reproduced its own version of the hereditary stratified society that the communists had so proudly claimed to have abolished.

By 1960 almost every top position was held by Kim's Manchurian guerilla comrades and his family members. This meant that the country was totally under the control of the leadership of limited education. Few including Kim had more than a middle school education and some had no formal schooling at all. For the most part, they had no real skills or training other than fighting in the mountains, few had ever been outside Korea or China and most had grown up in the frontier regions of Manchuria, not in the country they ruled. They were crude, an unsophisticated group that approached problems like the rough fighters they were. They remained focused on winning the battle for the reunification of Korea and viewed the country they governed as the base camp for that effort.

Pak Jeongae and Choe Seunghui

There was one member of the ruling elite that differed from the others: Pak Jeongae, the only high-ranking woman. In the macho, male-dominated North Korean leadership Pak was an extraordinary figure. She was the only woman to hold high positions who was not a member of the ruling Kim family. She was born in North Hamgyeong province, home to many Korean communists, and in 1907, the year that as much as any marked the start of armed resistance to the Japanese, and Korea's more than century of war. As a young woman, she went to Moscow State University for her education. This was not unusual; many Koreans sought education abroad and some of them choose to go to Russia; but not many were women. She was recruited by the Soviets as an intelligence agent and in the early 1930s was sent to Korea by Moscow. She was caught and imprisoned by the Japanese, released, and returned to the Soviet Union.

After liberation, Pak was dispatched to Korea again, this time with her husband, a Korean communist. Her spouse was appointed by the Soviets to head the newly formed North Korean branch of the Korean Communist Party. He died several months later of stomach cancer. Although trusted and respected by Moscow, her gender eliminated her as a candidate for Party leadership which went to Kim Il Sung. She was a member of the Party Central Committee and became one of its three secretaries. An early and strong supporter of Kim Il Sung she held many important posts in the Democratic People's Republic, including for a time the Minister of Agriculture.

She remained a favorite of Moscow, was given an international Stalin Prize in 1950, and in 1953 was chosen to head the North Korean delegation at Stalin's funeral. In the mid and late 1950s, Kim Il Sung purged those in the Party with close links to Moscow but not Pak Jeongae. That is, not until 1966 when she was removed from all positions and disappeared. Unlike many of the victims of purges, Pak survived and after being banished to the countryside for two decades reemerged in 1986, and as an octogenarian held minor positions in the government. Her daughter Pak Sunhui became the chairperson of the Korean Democratic Women's League. Just as her gender made her an exception among the leadership, the fact that she was not part of the Manchurian guerilla elite and associated with the Soviet Union but still survived, and her family is prominent in North Korea today is unusual.

In its efforts to prove that it was the legitimate representative of the Korean nation, the North Korean regime welcomed major intellectual and cultural figures that promoted both Korean culture and the DPRK as its sponsor. One of the regime's cultural stars was the dancer Choe Seunghui. Born in a *yangban* family in Seoul at the start of the colonial period Choe graduated from Sookmyung High School at fifteen and became a student of Baku Isshi, a modern dance and ballet teacher, who brought her to Japan to study. Choe returned to Korea and opened her dancing art institute. She married An Pilseung in 1931 but three months after their wedding he was arrested for communist activities. He was later released and they moved to Japan. Choe incorporated Korean folk dances and shamanist ceremonies into her modern dances creating unique Korean art. She traveled to America and Europe where her dance performances were well received; her admirers included John Steinbeck, Charlie Chaplin, Jean Cocteau, and Pablo Picasso. During the second world war, she performed for the Japanese troops.

Despite this act of collaboration, because her husband was a dedicated communist and her leftist sympathies were known she was welcomed in the North. Setting up a studio in Pyongyang she was sent abroad as a cultural ambassador and was performing in Moscow when the Korean War broke out. Things deteriorated as they did for most of the intellectuals and artists who had gone to the North. Her husband was arrested during the purges of the late 1950s, and she was purged and arrested in 1967. She disappeared but a defector reported seeing her in the prison camp where he was serving a sentence. Only in 2003 did the North Korean government announce she had died in 1969. There was little room for a creative independent spirit like Choe Seunghui in the DPRK.

The Four Lines

In the first decade after the armistice, Kim Il Sung was busy rebuilding after the destruction of the war, completing the construction of a command socialist economy, and consolidating power. But North Korea remained a nation at war with the South and the concern for achieving victory in the conflict was never far away. In the late 1950s, he expanded military training but the big refocus on preparing the country for war came in 1962. At the start of the Korean War, the regime set up a Military Committee to supervise the war effort and coordinate the economy with it. In December 1962, this committee was reconstituted in a renewed effort to put the country on a war footing. Membership in the Military Committee which was never publicized consisted of the top leaders and blurred the lines between military affairs and the rest of the government.

The renewed effort to prepare the country for conflict was known as the "four lines" which were: to "arm the whole people," intensify military training, make the entire nation "an impregnable fortress," and provide modern equipment for the armed forces. To carry out the arming of the whole people the state created a Worker-Peasant Red Guards. It built upon a smaller version that had been formed in 1959 to replace the withdrawal of the Chinese People's Volunteers. Now it was expanded to include all able-bodied men between 18 and 45 and all single women between 18 and 35. Participation in it was compulsory. Men and women were assembled after work and on weekends for training in fighting as well as political indoctrination. Farmers trained during the quieter seasons. Hamlets in the countryside and neighborhoods in the city formed squads, while villages formed battalions. These were organized at the county level into regiments and at the provincial levels into corps. Military training for active-duty soldiers was set up and political indoctrination sessions intensified.

A big problem for North Korea was that it had only half the population of the South. All North Korean men served long periods of military service, but in the 1960s the DPRK still had only 400,000 soldiers compared to the 600,000 in the ROK. Kim offset this by expanding the length of compulsory military service. ROK men served three years, but in the North, it was extended to eight. For many, it was longer. By the 1970s it was not uncommon for young men to graduate from school at 16 and to serve until they were 28. Only Eritrea after its independence had anything comparable to this burden. As a result, the DPRK had far more soldiers than its rival. In fact, by 1980 it had nearly a million on active duty while the South's armed forces remained at about 600,000.

The country was made into an "impregnable fortress," literally. Shelters were constructed throughout the land, including the Pyongyang subway which was designed as much as a deep underground shelter as a means of transportation. During the Korean War underground factories and military installations had been constructed all over the country. The elaborate tunnels that hide so much of the country's military activity became permanent characteristics of North Korea, to the dismay of later U.S. intelligence analysts heavily reliant on satellite photos. Of no less importance was the fourth policy of developing modern weapons. The production of military hardware, especially in the 1970s, became a central focus of industrialization targets.

While carrying out "the four lines" Kim Il Sung managed to achieve another of his goals: freedom from outside control. Initially, North Korea was very dependent on the Soviet Union whose ambassador in the late 1940s acted as a kind of proconsul, giving advice that bordered on instruction. During most of the Korean War, the North Korean leadership was sidelined while China took charge of the conflict. These were reminders of the limits of the country's sovereignty. By the late 1950s, he had reduced the influence of both Moscow and Beijing in the country's internal affairs. With the Sino-Soviet split that emerged from 1959 to 1961, Pyongyang was able to achieve a balancing act, supporting both sides at once.

The Three Revolutionary Forces

North Korea gained a reputation for being unpredictable and even irrational, but it always adhered closely to one goal: the reunification of Korea. The entire rationale of the DPRK was that it was the legitimate heir to the premodern state and that it had chosen the correct path to recreate that state in the form of a modern, progressive, strong, and independent nation that could protect the integrity and autonomy of the Korean people and even be a model to the world. Its foreign policy and its domestic policy were both focused on this. For Kim Il Sung the DPRK had to recover and learn from the setback of the Korean War and complete the reunification of the country. He had a clear plan for how to do this. It wasn't a secret plan; it was publicly announced in a speech given to his people, translated into English, and presented to the world.

The speech "Let Us Strengthen in Every Way the Revolutionary Forces for the Realization of the Great Task of Fatherland Unification" was given on February 27, 1964, after he had a decade to think about what went wrong and work out a plan to correct the mistakes the regime had made. Of course, he blamed these mistakes on the people he purged. This speech outlined a three-part plan based on what he called the three revolutionary forces: one at home, one in the South, and one in the world. All had to be utilized and strengthened to carry out the task of unification. The revolutionary forces at home in the DPRK must be strengthened by building up the military, developing the economy, and enhancing the discipline and resolve of the people. By being a strong, economically powerful state, not only would the DPRK be in a better position to win a renewed active conflict, but it would also be a model that naturally drew support from the South. It would be clear to all Koreans that

North Korea had taken the correct path toward modernization.

He also pointed out that the North must be ideologically strengthened. What that meant was the people had to be indoctrinated and committed to the goals of the state, or to put it another way: to be loyal to the regime. The northern leadership was shocked by how little resistance there was by ordinary people to the ROK and UN troops when they had occupied the North in the fall of 1950. Most people had passively accepted the occupation, while a few actively supported it. The conclusion Kim reached was that the people had not been sufficiently revolutionized in their thinking. They needed to develop revolutionary consciousness so they would be dedicated to achieving the goals of the regime.

The second part of the plan was to cultivate the revolutionary sentiments among the people of the South. In other words, to get them to turn against their own government and support the North. This was another great lesson Kim learned from the Korean War. The invasion failed because the great uprising of the people in support of the DPRK and the KPA failed to materialize. South Korean people were often ignorant of their own oppression by their "puppet" government and their subjection by the American imperialists. So, the people of the South would also have to develop revolutionary consciousness and understand the oppressive nature of the foreign-dominated regime they lived under for what it was: a great obstacle to unity and progress. This could be achieved by demonstrating, through its economic and political achievements, that the North was a true leader for all the Korean people. The DRPK was independent, self-reliant, prosperous, and strong. It was the success, the ROK the failure. It also required supporting anti-government sentiment among the people of the South whenever possible and educating them through propaganda.

Strengthening the "international revolutionary forces", the third part of the plan, involved winning international support for the North's cause and pressuring the United States to withdraw from the South. In short, to get the Americans out. Kim, a realist, understood that no renewed conflict (if one had to take place) could succeed as long as U.S. forces were stationed on the peninsula. The best way to accomplish this was through international pressure on the United States to remove its troops from the peninsula.

Kim made it clear that unification would be a long-term process. Building a solid industrial base, creating a powerful military, and indoctrinating the people would take time. Promoting the revolutionary forces in the South would take some time too. For this effort, he created a Department of External Intelligence Inquiries, better known as the 35th Office. It trained agents to work in the South. To assist in this effort there were two other organizations. One was the Liaison Bureau, a department within the Korean Workers party that acted as a channel to communists in the South, as there were still (secret) southern communists. Another, the Department of Culture, later renamed the United Front, was in charge of propaganda. North Korean agents regularly slipped into the South to promote work with anti-government students, intellectuals, and others. In 1964 they organized a Revolutionary Party for Reunification led by Kim Chongtae, a schoolteacher and small shop owner.

However, these efforts were hampered by the fact that Kim had purged the Korean Workers' Party of South Korean communists at the end of the Korean War. In their place, he had put people chosen for their loyalty, not their knowledge of the South. So those in charge of these agencies were now northerners who had no experience or connections in South Korea. Another problem was that the ROK became more efficient at counter-intelligence, and northern agents often had a short shelf life before being arrested. For example, the Revolutionary Party for Reunification was soon penetrated by ROK's Central Intelligence Agency. Kim Chongtae was executed and 158 were arrested. After 1968 it ceased to exist, although North Korea continued to claim it remained active. As a result, for all their efforts Kim's agents and propaganda specialists achieved only modest results. The effort to win global public opinion over to its side and isolate the United States did achieve some results but these came a little later. It was only in the 1970s that the DPRK made some gains on this front. Nonetheless, North Korean leaders looked for any opportunity to undermine the government of the ROK, and there were plenty of opportunities in the politically turbulent South.

The Turbulent South

In the first decade or so after 1953, the outcome of the competition between the two Koreas seemed to favor the North. While the DPRK was laying the foundation for a military-industrial state and appeared to be transforming itself into a Northeast Asian powerhouse, South Korea was struggling. South Korea in the 1950s was hardly a very promising society. Already poor, it had suffered a level of destruction that while not as great as experienced by the North, was still appalling. Millions had been displaced during the war, and thousands of homes and buildings were destroyed. Almost every family had lost someone during the war—either family members had been killed or marched off to the North.

Over this devastation presided the government of President Syngman Rhee. It was authoritarian, corrupt, and seemingly incompetent. Rhee himself, in his late seventies at the end of the Korean War, was energetic, intelligent, and politically shrewd, but primarily interested in maintaining his position as president and lacking any vision of how to pull his nation out of poverty. His Liberal Party was mainly an instrument to keep him and his supporters in power; it had no ideology or program for development. Rhee relied on American aid. The U.S. supplied direct support to his government and Washington funded half the state budget. South Korea produced little, exported almost nothing, and despite massive U.S. infusions of money, achieved only modest growth. The country was isolated. Rhee, deeply suspicious of Tokyo, refused to establish relations with Japan, demanding reparations first. It faced a hostile China and had limited diplomatic relations with the rest of the world. Its military, large and increasingly well-trained, depended on the U.S. for most of its weapons and a good part of its budget.

On paper, the ROK was a liberal democratic society with free elections and opposition parties, but Rhee and his Liberal Party made full use of the government apparatus to intimidate voters and manipulate the election procedures. Rural voters were sometimes simply brought to the polls by local officials and told who to vote for. Still, the party was only able to maintain a bare majority in the National Assembly. It never succeeded in winning over most urban voters or the small but growing middle class. Rhee changed the constitution so he could run for a third term in 1956. His chief opponent died before the election. He easily prevailed over a more left-leaning candidate Cho Bongam, yet had him arrested and executed after the election anyway. He ran again for a fourth term, despite being eighty-five, and this time had no opponent since his opposition candidate again died before the election. This sounds suspicious, and certainly, Rhee had no problem engineering the death of his rivals, but in fact, the candidate Cho Byeongok was an elderly man with bad health who died a natural death. Rhee's immensely unpopular vice president Yi Kibung ran for re-election against the much better regarded Chang Myeon. Yi won in a wildly lopsided landslide that everyone knew was a blatant fraud. When the results were announced student-led protests began, grew ever larger, and were joined by other citizens. Rhee was toppled when the military refused to fire into the crowds. The Americans whisked him off to exile in Hawaii.

A new constitution was written creating a parliamentary system, and an experiment in actual democracy took place from 1960 to 1961 under Prime Minister Chang Myeon. It was a well-meaning attempt but was characterized by labor strikes, student demonstrations, and general disorder. North Korea was quick to take advantage of this and in 1960 Kim Il Sung proposed the two sides meet to discuss a "Confederal Republic." The two Koreas would maintain their systems but form some sort of vague union. It was, of course, North Korea's way of fishing in troubled waters. In 1961 the North made an overture to South Korean students, proposing northern and southern students meet. This was too much for the South Korean military and it carried out a coup in May 1961 led by General Park Chung Hee.

However, it should not be thought that the years of civilian rule before the military took over were lost ones. In the 1950s South Korea finally gave the peasants what they wanted: land. The land reform gave each farm family about 7.5 acres (3 hectares)—enough to support a family and perhaps produce a small surplus for the market. Unlike in the North, the landlords were compensated by

the farmers who had to make payments for years but due to infla-
tion, these payments were not too difficult to pay off. And unlike
the North, the land was not then taken away by the state. Rather,
the state helped turn the country's farmers into small agricultural
entrepreneurs. The most startling achievement was in education;
South Korea achieved universal primary education by 1960 and
greatly expanded schooling at all levels. Along with adult education programs, by the early 1960s South Korea had become a very
literate if still poor country. A steady stream of South Koreans
poured into U.S. universities, some with American aid and others
somehow managing to scrape together the money. As they returned,
they provided large cohorts of highly trained scientists, engineers,
economists, educators, and other specialists. South Korea was developing a large pool of talent. It also experienced the emergence
of some clever and ambitious entrepreneurs.

So, in the 1950s, as poor and chaotic as South Korea was, it
was laying the foundations for its extraordinary economic and
social takeoff. It needed leadership. This was provided by Park
Chung Hee, the head of the new military government. Park was
disturbed by the country's dependence on the U.S. that limited its
sovereignty and by North Korea's progress. Economic growth was
a matter of national security. In many ways, his aims and methods resembled Kim Il Sung's. He sought to develop a prosperous
society that would legitimize the state as the one true Korea and
create a strong military and an industrial base to support it so that
the ROK could defend itself and eventually reunify the country.
Economic growth, therefore, was not just an end in itself but part
of the struggle for legitimacy, survival, and victory in the conflict
with the North. He developed and implemented the first of a series
of five-year plans in 1962. Like the North, they had specific targets,
and like the North, the state directed economic development. But
unlike the DPRK, the ROK set the goals and had private enterprises
implement them. The state which nationalized the banks provided
cheap loans to private firms, subsidized their training and utilities,
and identified markets for them. Enterprises had to compete for
this state aid. The most efficient were generously rewarded and the

others were left on their own to fail. Unlike the North, the South focused on exports and encouraged foreign investments. This made its enterprises more efficient and made technology transfer easier. South Korea's economic model proved to be far more successful, although this was not immediately apparent in the 1960s.

At first, it was not clear to North Korea what the military coup meant. Park once had a communist leaning and was never fond of the Americans. Pyongyang had hopes he might be open to some sort of arrangement with the North. Kim Il Sung sent Hwang Seongtaek to Seoul to meet with the new military leaders and determine how amenable they were to talks and possible cooperation with the DPRK. Hwang was selected since he was a former southern official who had fled to the North in 1946. Park gave Kim his answer: he had Hwang arrested and executed. Park's military-led government turned out to be hardline anti-communist.

South Korea became famous for its "economic miracle." Few countries have ever climbed out of poverty so fast to become an economic powerhouse after such an unpromising start. Park Chung Hee has been given credit (probably too much credit) for inaugurating this "miracle." Economists have praised Park's economic development. He was pragmatic and took advice from the country's talented entrepreneurs and its corps of economic experts and encouraged their input into the state's economic growth. What has not been generally appreciated is the fact that much of the motivation behind that Park's economic policies was military and strategic. Economic development was another front in the conflict between the two Koreas. Park, like Kim Il Sung, was determined to have his Korea outshine the other in the eyes of the Korean people. Also like Kim, he wanted to build an industrial base that could support an armaments industry for his military without being dependent on a foreign power. Therefore, Park's goal was to outperform and ultimately vanquish his rivals in the North, and to secure as much autonomy as possible for his country. But Park had less freedom of action since he relied on American economic support and military protection, and he was also quite pragmatic. So, in the 1960s he focused on the exports of consumer goods such as textiles, footwear, wigs, and electric fans. Then in the 1970s as the economy grew, he focused more on heavy industry, but unlike the North, South Korea continued to devote considerable resources to consumer goods.

Chung Ju-yung

If the conflict between North and South Korea was fought on the economic front as much as on the military, then Chung Ju-yung was one of Korea's greatest generals. Park Chung Hee had a vision of a powerful economy with a heavy industrial base; Chung more than any other individual made it a reality. He was born in what became the North Korean half of Gangwon province in 1915, the eldest of seven children in an impoverished peasant family. He attended a local Confucian school run by his grandfather but otherwise had a very limited education. The one thing Chung seemed to know from an early age was he did not want to be a farmer, and he did not want to remain poor. He ran away from home three times, but his father always found him and brought him back. The third time he stole a cow to pay for a train ticket to Seoul. The fourth time he did not return but found a job at a rice store in Seoul. At only twenty-two, he became the owner, but the business closed when in 1939 the Japanese began restricting rice sales in Korea to ship a greater amount to Japan. Chung then entered the auto repair business, but this too was shut down by the Japanese.

After liberation, Chung Ju-yung began a construction company but then had to flee to Busan during the Korean War. While in Busan he began contract work with the government and the UN. Upon returning to Seoul after the war, his construction business flourished. He completed a bridge over the Han River ahead of schedule, a trademark practice. This impressed Park who began supplying him with more projects. During the Vietnam War, Chung built military facilities for the Koreans and Americans, becoming noted for the speed with which he completed them. Park wanted heavy industry and provided Chung with government loans to establish the Hyundai Motor company, which built trucks for both military and civilian use and the first Korean car in 1967. His Hyundai Heavy Industries built almost every type of heavy equipment imaginable, and Hyundai Shipbuilding became one of the world's largest ship makers. The Hyundai Group, which included construction and in the 1980s, electronics, was the largest of South Korea's *chaebols* (conglomerates). While contributing to the South Korean "economic miracle," Chung never gave up hope for reunification, which he hoped could be accomplished peacefully with reconciliation. In 1998, Chung crossed the DMZ with 1,001 cattle to repay with interest the one he stole as a young man.

The Alliances

The two Koreas depended on their alliances. For North Korea, it was a delicate balancing act since China and the Soviet Union had suffered a falling out beginning around 1960. Kim Il Sung was careful not to take sides in the Sino-Soviet split in the international communist movement. On July 1, 1961, he signed a Treaty of Friendship, Cooperation and Mutual Assistance with Moscow and, the next day, another with Beijing. Of the two powers, Moscow was the most important. Beijing provided mostly moral support; the Soviets, weapons and generous economic aid. But Kim's sympathies were clearly with Beijing. In 1963 he sided with China when it refused to sign the Nuclear Test Ban Treaty. He criticized the Soviet Union for its attack on pro-Beijing Albania, and for the accounts of Korean history published in the Soviet Union which he thought slighted its glorious past. Moscow grew tired of this sniping and sharply reduced economic aid which almost immediately harmed the North Korean economy. Pyongyang dropped its criticism and resumed its policy of evenhandedness toward both powers. This was not always easy. During the Cultural Revolution in China in the late 1960s, Maoist Red Guards denounced Kim Il Sung and began to claim land along the border. But when the Cultural Revolution abated, good relations were restored. Until the unraveling of the Soviet bloc after 1989, Kim relied on Moscow for economic and military support while maintaining cordial relations with its communist rival Beijing.

South Korea was more dependent on the United States than North Korea was on its allies. The Americans kept 60,000 troops in the country, later reduced to 40,000. This included airbases and some nuclear weapons. The U.S. trained the military, provided it with much of its weaponry, and subsidized its economy. From the mid-1960s, as South Korea's economy grew, American aid was gradually reduced but the U.S. was still of key importance. It was South Korea's largest export market by far, the largest source of foreign investment, and the presence of U.S. troops not only protected the nation but reassured foreign investors. The latter was especially important as the country depended on American, Japanese, and European firms for its export economy. They provided the plants, and the technology, and South Korea the cheap, disciplined labor. But most of all the presence of Americans was a kind of tripwire. It meant another invasion from the North was unlikely since it would require killing large numbers of U.S. troops, sitting ducks on the border, and that would assuredly necessitate a swift, massive American response.

However, relations were not always smooth. While most South Koreans liked Americans and were attracted by American culture, they were also intensely nationalistic people with a xenophobic streak. Most felt uncomfortable about the presence of American troops looking so conspicuously out of place in their homogeneous society. Additionally their dependency on the Americans made them uncomfortable. South Korean forces served under the American military commander in Korea, another humiliation for proud Koreans. Successive governments grew weary if not resentful of being lectured to by the well-meaning but often arrogant U.S. government and its representatives in Seoul. And the Americans sometimes became frustrated with the South Koreans. The crude and thuggish behavior of the Park Chung Hee government toward its opponents didn't help relations. Nor did the Tongsun Park scandal of 1975, in which a lobbyist for Seoul was found guilty of bribing US Congressmen. Tongsun Park fled to South Korea which refused to hand him over to American authorities. This was just one of many incidents that troubled relations between Washington and Seoul. Nevertheless, the alliance endured.

Korea's Vietnam War

Both North and South Korea found the Vietnam War an opportunity. In 1965 President Johnson was looking for support for the U.S. involvement in Vietnam. Park was happy to provide it in return for considerable concessions. Park committed the country to supplying 20,000 troops for the U.S. military effort. Over the next several years this number grew. Eventually, 350,000 ROK troops did tours of duty between 1965 and 1973, with troop strength reaching 60,000 at one time. They were the second-largest foreign presence in Vietnam after the Americans. About five thousand were killed in combat. They fought well but gained a reputation for brutality and a high rate of civilian casualties, especially the notorious "Tiger Division." So hated were they by the South Vietnamese that some have argued they drove many villagers to support the Viet Cong. Despite their reputation, involvement in the war brought benefits to South Korea. In return for this help, South Korean firms were given lucrative contracts to supply goods and services to South Vietnamese, American, and Allied forces. South Korean construction companies built many military installations, providing valuable experience that opened a new source of foreign earnings—overseas construction. Vietnam also provided the ROK forces with firsthand combat experience.

The Vietnam conflict was observed closely by Pyongyang. In the early 1960s, North Korea began drawing up plans for armed conflict in the South based on the guerilla campaign waged by the communists in South Vietnam. Although they abandoned these plans, the war still presented an opportunity for them. They hoped the U.S. position in Asia would be weakened by its involvement in Indochina. One slogan in 1968 stated that the Vietnam War was part of a process of "Cutting off the limbs of U.S. Imperialism Everywhere." The Vietnamese were breaking the leg of the American bandit, "we [North Koreans] are breaking the other leg," the slogan went. Most of North Vietnam's support for the Vietnamese Communists was verbal but they did send a few pilots who flew planes.

1968—A Year of Provocations

A belief that the U.S. was getting bogged down in Vietnam may have contributed to North Korea's aggressive behavior. In 1967 North Korea began to take a more provocative stance toward South Korea. North Korea had from time to time caused "incidents." There were frequent seizures of southern fishing boats. Along the DMZ there were little crises ranging from failures to adhere to some agreed-upon protocol, such as having soldiers along the border wear the proper insignia, to exchanges of gunfire. Generally, these were just occasional occurrences. Then in 1967 the number of such incidents increased eleven-fold, keeping the American and South Korean forces in a constant state of tension. By the end of the year, gunfire erupted almost daily across the border. For the first time since the armistice, North Korean fired artillery shells across the DMZ.

Meanwhile, in July 1967 North Korea began training Special Unit 124. These were commandos whose mission was to infiltrate South Korea and launch attacks. One group of 31 commandos made the daring attack on the Blue House. Following several days of manhunting twenty-nine were killed, one was captured and one escaped and fled to North Korea. Between October 30 and November 2, eight infiltration teams each with about fifteen commandos from the same 124th Army Unit, landed on the east coast between Samcheok and Uljin. Villagers were rounded up and forced to hear speeches about the socialist paradise in the North. The commandos must have been better at infiltrating than enlightening because most of the guerillas were quickly reported by locals and killed or captured by ROK security forces. Nonetheless, these actions left 63 southerners dead. On the sea, 115 southern fishing boats were seized by the North that year. South Korea responded by stepping up patrols of the coastline, tightening security, and offering generous rewards for all reports. The efforts were successful enough to make infiltration increasingly difficult.

At the same time as the commandos stormed the presidential palace, North Korea seized the American intelligence ship, the USS Pueblo. The ship was off the DPRK coast, not far from the port of Wonsan. North Korea claimed it was in its territorial waters, a claim the U.S. denied. The 82-member crew was held captive for 11 months before being released that December. The Americans initially responded with a show of force, sending the aircraft carrier, the Enterprise, into the waters off the east coast. However, rather than leading to military retaliation as Kim Il Sung might have feared, Washington negotiated for the release of the crew, issuing an apology and a confession signed by the crew members. Americans were amused by the confession written by the navy men. It contained many puns mocking the DPRK which the North Koreans didn't understand. However, the Pueblo Incident provided a useful lesson for the North. From the failure to militarily respond to the seizure of its ship, Pyongyang learned just how much the U.S. sought to avoid armed confrontation. This was reinforced the following year when, in April 1969, the North shot down a U.S. EC-121 spy plane, again with no serious retaliation from the Americans. This became a repeated pattern in which North Korea would engage in aggressive acts and then seek to negotiate with the Americans, frequently both winning concessions and demonstrating its military prowess to its people.

It is not clear why North Korea launched these provocative and dangerous actions. Most likely the leadership hoped to create instability and stimulate support for their cause in the South. There were signs of discontent in the South that Pyongyang may have misread. In 1965 Park decided to normalize relations with Japan. In exchange for modest reparations, the two countries established diplomatic recognition. This made sense economically since the booming economy of Japan was a much-needed source of foreign investment and the treaty did stimulate economic growth. But for many Koreans, the treaty opened the country to Japanese economic domination and the paltry reparations sum was an outrage. Massive demonstrations followed. The strong nationalist sentiment and the feeling of betrayal by the Park regime, and the fact that Park himself was a former officer in the Japanese military, could only support Pyongyang's argument that it was the real bearer of the Korean nationalist cause.

This and other anti-government demonstrations may have led North Korean leaders to underestimate the loyalty of southerners to the ROK and overestimate pro-DPRK sentiment. Again, as in 1950, Pyongyang interpreted anti-government sentiment in the South as sympathy for the DPRK. There was no enthusiasm for the infiltration teams. The attacks seemed only to have created fear and resentment against the northern regime. For South Korea, that it could be so easily penetrated, the slow response, and the difficulty killing and capturing the commandos were embarrassing. However, it did little to weaken the Park regime, if that was the North's intention. More troubling for South Korean leaders was the unwillingness of the U.S. to retaliate and risk war. In this respect, Pyongyang did gain from these adventures. They helped it measure ROK's military readiness and American willingness for renewed conflict on the peninsula. Overall, however, Kim Il Sung appears to have been disappointed at the results of the mini-invasions carried out in 1968, and as in the Korean War, Kim blamed these failures on others and carried out a purge. The two most prominent were Kim Changbong, his defense minister, and one of his top military commanders, General Heo Bonghak. In the South, President Park responded by trying to tighten his grip on power, strengthening the national security apparatus, and further militarizing society.

A Dramatic Turn: from Confrontation to Conversation

North Korean provocations continued sporadically. On December 11, 1969, North Korean agents hijacked a South Korean civilian airplane with 51 passengers, and on June 22, 1970, they detonated a bomb at South Korea's national cemetery in an attempted assassination of President Park. On January 23, 1971, DPRK agents tried to hijack a Korean Airlines plane, and at a party meeting in April 1971, Kim Il Sung gave an even more militant than usual speech about the need to struggle against American imperialists, Japanese militarists, and their agents in the South.

Then the situation began to change dramatically. First, there was the announcement in 1971 from Washington that the United

States and China had been secretly holding diplomatic meetings and that President Nixon would be visiting Beijing. President Nixon arrived in February 1972, met with Mao Zedong and other Chinese leaders, and started the process toward normalization of relations. All this came as a surprise to Park and Kim. Park was shocked that his chief patron and protector had carried out these negotiations behind his back. It called into question the reliability of the U.S. as an ally. In its desire to pull out of Vietnam would America abandon the peninsula as well? News of a thaw between these two rivals must have been disturbing to Kim Il Sung as well since they suggested that Beijing might cease to be a reliable ally. He reacted to the news of the coming visit by publicly declaring it a victory for the communist cause: "Nixon's visit to China will not be a march of a victor but a trip of the defeated. It fully reflects the destiny of U.S. imperialism which is like a sun sinking in the western sky." Yet he must have worried that it called into question China's future support for his regime.

Following the announcement of a rapprochement between Washington and Beijing, Kim decided to make use of the situation. At an August 6, 1971, rally he announced, "we are ready to establish contact at any time with all political parties, including the Democratic-Republican Party [the ruling party of Park Chung Hee]." This was a sharp reversal of Pyongyang's insistence that talks with Seoul could only take place when the Park regime was removed from power. South Korea countered with a proposal for a joint meeting of the two countries' Red Cross societies. The North immediately agreed and Red Cross officials from the DPRK and ROK met on August 20, 1971.

Later, Lee Hu Rak, director of the powerful KCIA, the Korean Central Intelligence Agency in charge of foreign and domestic intelligence, made a secret midnight trip to Pyongyang to meet Kim Il Sung. North Korea's Vice Premier Pak Seongcheol went to Seoul. This was the first ever high-level exchange of visits. ROK officials brought up the issue of reuniting families separated by the DMZ. This was an emotional issue for the several million South Koreans who had family members or relatives in the North. Hundreds of thousands of siblings were separated from each other, parents from their children, and even spouses. There was no communication or postal service, let alone telephone links between the two countries, so they were entirely ignorant of the fate of their loved ones in the North. Therefore the issue of divided families was a good starting point for any movement toward rapprochement between the two sides. Other talks followed in secret until July 4, 1972, when the two sides issued a joint communiqué stating three fundamental principles of unification. First, that unification must be carried out independently, without outside interference. Second, it must be achieved peacefully. Third, it must be implemented as a show of great national unity based on the homogeneity of the people first, with the differences in thinking, ideologies, and systems worked out later.

The two Koreas formed a North-South Coordinating Committee that held three meetings: one in Seoul from November to December 1972, a second in Pyongyang in March 1973, and a third in Seoul three months later. But little progress was made at the meetings. South Korean officials wanted to proceed with gradual confidence-building measures. Family reunifications, they felt, would be a good first step, and from there they could gradually work on bigger, more complex issues. The North proposed they discuss major issues across the board. DPRK representatives also insisted that South Korea's National Security laws, which gave the government broad power to arrest communists or communist sympathizers, had to be repealed before any family reunions or other humanitarian issues could be pursued. They also insisted on the withdrawal of US troops from South Korea as being a precondition for any further negotiations. South Korea, for its part, insisted that the DPRK end its support of the Revolutionary Party for Reunification. In the face of these demands, the talks became deadlocked. After seven meetings between August 1972 to July 1973, the Red Cross talks came to an end. The North-South Coordinating Committee ceased to meet after mid-1973. Mid-level meetings continued at Panmunjom from December 1973 to March 1975; with little promise of any breakthroughs these too fizzled out. The talks failed because Kim Il

Sung lost interest when he realized that a withdrawal of US troops was not imminent and would not be on the table for serious consideration. He also turned down a proposal by President Park in 1973 for dual admission to the United Nations. This would have meant a de facto mutual recognition of each other's regime. In the mid-1970s Kim returned to the rhetoric of military confrontation with the South. North Korean officials told diplomats from friendly East European countries "Korea cannot be unified in a peaceful way."

The 1972–73 negotiations began a pattern that would be repeated over the next half-century. North Korea would initiate or respond to offers for talks. There would be some diplomatic or even cultural and economic exchanges. In the South, there would be optimism from much of the public and many officials over the prospect of a thaw in relations. Pyongyang would then set conditions that were difficult or unrealistic or that it knew the South would find unacceptable. Seoul would offer small confidence-building measures that would eventually be rejected, with the DPRK insisting that major issues be discussed. Talks would break down and Pyongyang would ratchet up the tension with its rival again. Neither side trusted the other and their goals were incompatible. Each wanted reunification under their leadership, under their system.

CHAPTER 7

Tension, Détente, and Renewed Tension, 1972–1994

On November 20, 1974, a South Korean army patrol near the DMZ saw steam coming from the ground. They thought they had discovered a hot spring but upon closer inspection, it turned out to be a tunnel entrance 2/3 of a mile (1km) inside ROK territory. Before they had much time to study it, North Korean soldiers fired on them, forcing them to leave. Five days later U.S. Navy Commander Robert M. Bellinger and Major Kim Hacheol of the ROK Marine Corps entered to explore the tunnel. They were both killed by a North Korean booby-trapped explosive device. The 3 by 4 ft (.9m by 1.2m) tunnel was reinforced by concrete slabs. It contained weapon storage and sleeping areas, and a narrow-gauge railway to transport troops rapidly into the South. A second tunnel was discovered four months later, on March 19, 1975. Located between 160 and 520 feet (50 and 160 m) below the ground, it was wider than the previous one, 7 by 7 ft (2 by 2 m). It was drilled through granite using specially imported equipment.

A Korean Workers' Party functionary who defected reported that there were up to fifteen tunnels. Later, South Korean intelligence officials came up with an estimate of twenty-two. A search for tunnels began. The U.S. installed 245 seismic devices to detect them. A third was discovered on October 17, 1978. It was one mile (1,600 m) long and 240 feet (73 m) below the ground. A fourth was discovered on March 3, 1990, very similar in construction to the second and third tunnels. No more were discovered but the Americans and ROK troops occasionally heard digging noises, so there were more out there. Later these tunnels became tourist attractions. For a small fee tourists can enter three of them. The "Third Tunnel of Aggression" is the most popular. After passing through a gift shop and wearing a hard hat for protection from low ceilings, visitors enter one of the world's creepiest tourist venues.

The tunnels, through which thousands of troops could pass every hour, were built at great effort and not as tourist attractions. They were part of the continual threats, provocations, and preparations for war that North Korea carried out after the brief thaw in relations in the early 1970s. Despite the negotiations of 1971 to 1973, North and South Korea remained two countries locked in a series of incidents and flare-ups in tensions; two countries always on the brink of war. Most of the incidents were initiated by North Korea. The South focused on economic development and did not want to provoke the North into war, and it could not do so in any case without alienating Washington, on which it was so dependent.

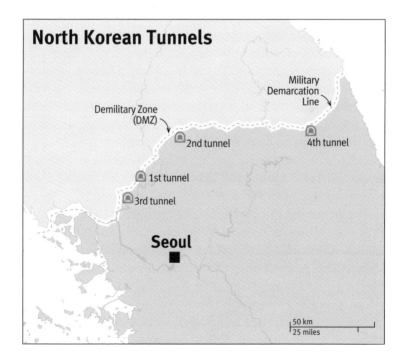

North Korean Tunnels

Military
Demarcation
Line

Demilitary Zone
(DMZ)

2nd tunnel

4th tunnel

1st tunnel

3rd tunnel

Seoul

50 km
25 miles

North Korea lacked such external restraints and was more focused on its three-fold strategy for reunification. As a result, Pyongyang kept the South constantly on edge. South Korean patrols along the coast were always on the lookout for infiltrators, raking the beaches in the evening to check for footprints in the morning. ROK naval vessels tried to protect the country's important fishing fleet but were not always successful. On February 4, 1972, DPRK naval patrols captured five southern fishing boats. They seized another boat on August 30, 1976. Additionally, South Korean security forces were always on the lookout for northern agents. They caught quite a few, but some always slipped by them.

The Attempted Assassination of Park Chung Hee

One of these North Korean agents who slipped by the security forces was Mun Segwang. Mun was born in 1951 in Osaka, a city with a large Korean population. Most had come, voluntarily or not, during the Second World War and stayed afterward. Mun's family, however, had fled there at the start of the Korean War. As a young man, he became an admirer of Mao Zedong and Kim Il Sung. This was not unusual as many of the highly ostracized Korean minority in Japan were sympathetic to the North versus the "former Japanese collaborators" in the South. Mun was recruited by DPRK agents who told him that he was to assassinate Park Chung Hee, an action that would spark an uprising of the people in South Korea.

Mun entered South Korea with a stolen Japanese police pistol hidden in a radio. He checked into a fancy hotel and rented a limousine, tipping the driver to act obsequiously toward him. Posing as a young, wealthy big shot he entered the National Theatre where Park was to give a speech to mark the 29th anniversary of the liberation of Korea. He had planned to assassinate the President in the lobby, but his view was obstructed. Seated at the back of the theater, Mun attempted to get closer to Park as he was giving his speech, but accidentally discharged his revolver, injuring himself. He then ran toward the President firing wildly; all the shots missed Park but the fourth hit First Lady Yuk Youngsu. As security men seized

Mun, a shot fired by Park's security detail accidentally killed a high school student. After his badly-wounded wife was carried out, the iron-willed Park resumed his speech. Yuk Youngsu died later that day. A grainy film of the incident can be viewed on YouTube. Mun claimed he was a prisoner of war and should be treated as such, as after all, the two Koreas were at war. Ignoring this demand, the ROK government tried him as a terrorist and executed him.

Tree Cutting Incident

North Korea's provocations sought to maintain pressure on the South, destabilize it if possible, and keep its troops and people prepared for war. Yet, they did not intend to start a war that Pyongyang knew it couldn't win. North Korea would go to the brink, then back down. The most dramatic example of this took place along the DMZ in 1976.

In the Joint Security Areas near the Bridge of No Return, a 100 ft (30m) poplar tree blocked the line of sight between a United Nations checkpoint and a northern observation post. The Americans insisted on removing the tree, but the North Koreans claimed it had been planted by Kim Il Sung and could not be moved. On August 18, 1976, a group of Korean Service Corps personnel escorted by a UN security team consisting of Captain Arthur Bonifas, his South Korea Army counterpart, Captain Kim the platoon leader, First Lieutenant Mark Barrett, and 11 South Korean and American enlisted personnel, went to the JSA to trim the tree. As the trimming began, they were approached by fifteen North Korean soldiers led by Lieutenant Kim Chul, nicknamed the "Bulldog" by the Americans for his aggressive confrontations. Boniface, a West Pointer who was three days from ending his one-year tour of duty in Korea, ignored Kim's demand that they cease trimming. The North Koreans, reinforced by 28 more soldiers, then attacked the UN team with crowbars and ax handles. Boniface and Barrett were killed and most of the UN troops were wounded.

The Americans responded with a show of force. Naval vessels and an aircraft carrier moved into the area. Kim Il Sung ordered the evacuation of Pyongyang, fearing American bombing. But none took place. Park did not want the situation to escalate into war and neither did President Ford. In Operation Paul Bunyan, named after the legendary lumberjack, a task force of 23 American and South Korean vehicles arrived at the JSA without warning three days later and a crew with chainsaws cut down the tree. Then Kim Il Sung did something highly uncharacteristic: he apologized, sending a message of "regret" for the incident. Nobody wanted a war to break out. Again, as with the Pueblo Incident, the North Koreans found that there were few consequences from the U.S. for their acts of aggression and provocations.

The Two Koreas and the Third World

The Korean War took place on another, more peaceful, front. The two Koreas competed for influence and recognition in the Third World. This, like the many "incidents" on the DMZ and the terrorist attacks, was mostly a North Korean initiative. The DPRK aggressively sought to establish formal relations with the nations of Asia, Africa, and Latin America, gaining support in the developing world. With this support, it hoped to use the United Nations, the Non-Aligned Movement conferences, and other international forums to put pressure on the United States to withdraw from Korea. This was threatening to South Korea as the commitment of the United States to maintain troops in South Korea was key to the ROK's strategy of survival. Seoul worried and Pyongyang hoped that the humiliating American withdrawal from Vietnam in 1975 might result in their withdrawal from the peninsula. While this did not happen, the possibility increased with the election of Jimmy Carter as U.S. president in 1976. Nixon had reduced the number of U.S. troops from 60,000 to 40,000 but made it clear the U.S. would keep its bases in the ROK, and this was reconfirmed by his successor, Ford. Carter, however, was adamant that the U.S. pull its troops out of the peninsula. He ran into resistance from his cabinet who regarded this as a destabilizing move. In 1978, giving in to pressure, he backed down from his pledge to pull out. Yet his statements on the need to withdraw were unnerving to the South Koreans and gave hope to the North. Ultimately, he reduced the number of troops to 37,000 and the number of nuclear weapons in the country from 700 to 250.

This did little to alter the strategic value of the U.S. forces in the South. It was not the absolute size of the U.S. forces in South Korea but their presence in harm's way of any conflict could be the tripwire that would almost certainly result in a massive American response and most likely the destruction of the North Korean regime. Neither the DPRK's allies in Moscow nor Beijing were likely to risk a conflict with the Americans so Pyongyang would be on its own. Therefore, the withdrawal of US troops was a necessary precondition for unification under its leadership. The prospect of this happening was a real one. The Americans did withdraw from South Vietnam and at some point, it appeared they might withdraw from South Korea. To create an international environment that would isolate South Korea, pressure the United States to withdraw its troops, and win the support of progressive nations for its cause, Kim Il Sung began cultivating close relations with the Third Word. "If the small countries jointly dismember him the American bandit will be torn apart," a North Korean propaganda slogan went.

North Korea had other motives for reaching out to the Third World. It helped the DPRK emerge from the shadow of its two patrons, the Soviet Union and China, and announce its presence in the world as an independent state. Kim remembered, and did not want to return to, the time when he needed Stalin's permission to establish diplomatic relations with a country. Furthermore, being a major world leader added to Kim's prestige at home and appealed to his vanity. This was especially true in the 1970s when Kim Il Sung began portraying the DPRK to his people as a shining example of progressive socialism admired around the world. Yet, above all, it was another front in his rivalry with the South. He wanted to demonstrate that the DPRK was the globally-admired Korea not the pathetic American puppet state in the South. As a result, a new competition began between the two Koreas, each seeking to receive more diplomatic recognition than the other.

Before the 1980s this was a front that the North was winning. At the Non-Aligned Movement Conference in Lima in August 1975, it became a full member. A committee of that General Assembly in 1975 passed a pro-North Korean resolution on the Korean Question that year which called for the withdrawal of all foreign troops from the peninsula. Since there were no foreign troops on North Korea's side of the DMZ this meant the withdrawal of U.S. troops. Of course, the U.S. could and did ignore these calls, and it had veto power if it needed to use it. But these resolutions were an embarrassment to the ROK, reminding its people of their dependence on foreign troops. At another Non-Aligned Movement Conference in Colombo in 1976, the member states endorsed Kim's stance on Korean unification. By the early 1980s, the DPRK had established relations with 110 countries, considerably more than the ROK, and its voice was louder at Third World forums. A constant stream of leaders from Africa, Asia, and Latin America visited Pyongyang, where, no matter how small their nation or how little actual strategic or economic importance they might have had, they were sure to receive an enthusiastic welcome from the thousands of North Koreans who dutifully turned out to greet them. To reinforce the impression that these visits represented the global recognition of the great leader and his achievements, a huge museum was built on the slopes of the sacred Myohyang Mountain specifically to house all the gifts Kim received from around the world.

In an outreach effort, North Korea sent performance troupes and exhibitions to many Third World countries. These were given much publicity at home, contributing further to the official line that the DPRK, its culture, its socialist path, and especially its leader were globally admired. Often expensive, these efforts produced little in the way of practical benefits, and the goodwill and influence they developed were often undermined by the clumsy and ill-informed behavior of North Koreans. Much of this problem stemmed from North Koreans' ignorance of the world outside their isolated state as well as the lack of experienced diplomats. Non-Aligned Representatives soon tired of having North Korea use its meetings and forums for pushing its agendas. The crude use of bribery and bluster to try to get their way offended many governments. North Korea's use of terrorism and the illegal activities of its diplomats, several of whom were expelled from countries for engaging in drug smuggling also eroded some support for Pyongyang. North Korea sponsored some 200 pro-Pyongyang organizations in 50 countries, but these never generated much support among the local populations and were dependent on DPRK funds. It is not clear how much North Korea gained from these efforts. They did little to pressure the United States to leave, but they did worry South Korea enough that it responded by stepping up its efforts, especially after 1980, to win support in the Third World.

Industrialization and Militarization in the 1970s

Another key component in its plan for reunification was for North Korea to maintain military superiority over the South. To achieve this, the DPRK in the 1970s and early 1980s reached a level of militarization and regimentation that was remarkable and possibly without equal anywhere. It was a nation designed for war. Kim Il Sung wanted his people to have the will to resist any invasion with a ferocity that had been absent in 1950. The entire nation was in a constant state of alert as if war was always imminent. Most able-bodied men were either in the military or some sort of reserve, as were many women. In the reserves, they engaged in frequent military drilling, and military drills were not just confined to those on active duty or in the reserves, but were practiced by the entire population at all levels. Music, drama, school lessons, and every possible medium were used to promote a militarily ready society. The vocabulary of public announcements on virtually any subject was laced with fierce, militant rhetoric. International events were either interpreted as a sign that the U.S. and its allies were planning an invasion or used as a warning of the need for preparedness.

Military and political indoctrination went together and began in childhood. Even preschoolers at daycare centers were given toy guns and taught songs like "My Heavy Little Machine Gun." Math lessons used problems such as how many American "wolf-bastards" remained after so many had been killed. Children at all levels spent considerable time on carefully-choreographed performances that were very much like military drills. Most movies and revolutionary operas had military themes and often focused on the anti-Japanese guerilla war led by the great leader. The country had few art museums, but many dedicated to Japanese and American atrocities. Then there were the political study sessions that were regularly held after work and devoured much of ordinary people's free time. These emphasized the loyalty to the leader and the heroic struggle to resist imperialist aggression and liberate the South.

In the 1970s and 1980s, military production was given priority over all other forms of industrial output. What the regime referred to as "the second economy" expanded the production of artillery, tanks, military vehicles, and small arms. For a small, still poor country the DPRK was able to produce an impressive array of increasingly sophisticated weaponry. Still, it was never adequate for the demands of its mammoth military armed forces, and the country also imported weapons from the Soviet Union.

South Korea too underwent militarization. However, the government had to make at least some concessions to a more open democratic society to reassure its American allies that it was on their side. Under pressure from the U.S., General Park put on civilian clothes, ran, and was elected as President in 1963. Under his regime, the ROK maintained the façade of democracy with opposition parties and elections. In practice, it was an authoritarian state with a tolerated opposition. Behind the Park regime was the Korean Central Intelligence Agency (KCIA) which ran a vast network of spies and informants used for both combating North Korea's subversion and for rooting out dangerous opposition to the regime. In 1972, Park, tired of dealing with the opposition, declared martial law and created a new constitution that gave him such extensive powers that he was for all practical purposes a dictator. Under this new constitution, the president no longer had to run for re-election in a popular contest but instead was elected by a Unification Board whose members he appointed. In practice, this meant he elected himself. Various presidential decrees made criticizing the president and his constitution a criminal offense. Even criticizing the decrees was a crime.

Park's newly-acquired powers were accompanied by an intense effort to militarize society. Military drills became part of the school curriculum. High school students were enrolled in a student defense corps that instilled military virtue. Every day at 5:00 pm all traffic came to a halt, and everyone was required to stop in their tracks and stand at attention while the national anthem played on loud-speakers. Anti-communist education was intensified in the schools. After completing three years of compulsory military service, men had to spend years in the active and then inactive military reserve. The economy shifted from consumer goods to heavy and chemical industries that could be used to produce military hardware. In other words, South Korea in the 1970s was in some ways becoming more like North Korea. North Korea's periodic terrorist attacks and other provocations served to reinforce the need to focus on military discipline and preparedness.

Yet South Korea was not North Korea; it was still a far freer and more open society. Opposition parties and newspapers, though often harassed and censored, still existed, and military strength was not the all-consuming goal that it was in the DPRK. In fact, by the 1970s South Korean were already enjoying a higher living standard than their northern cousins. Unlike the sterile, empty streets of Pyongyang, Seoul was a noisy chaotic city filled with restaurants, bars, tea houses, and lively nightlife. Stores were stocked with mostly locally-made consumer goods whose abundance and variety would have amazed those in the North. Even Park's oppression failed to create a submissive population. Labor strikes, student protests, and opposition rallies were regular occurrences. There were many reasons for this. The South was more pluralistic, with organizations like churches not controlled by the government. It still claimed to be a liberal democratic society and many of these ideas took root. Furthermore, the South was less independent. The U.S. had an enormous impact, sometimes intervening on behalf of political dissidents and issuing warnings if it thought Park was going too far. But there was more to it than this. South Korea had twice the population of the North and it had the traditional cultural center,

Seoul. By the 1970s it was already richer, linked with the world's most powerful country, and plugged into the global economy in a way North Korea was not. It was simply in a stronger position, less preoccupied with the struggle for unity, and, by the 1970s, growing more confident that history was on its side.

1980: South Korea's Awful, Terrible, No-Good Year

The year 1980 was a terrible one for South Korea. In the fall of 1979, unrest with Park Chung Hee's authoritarian rule was growing. On October 26, when the increasingly isolated president refused to listen to advice that he compromise with his opponents, he was shot and killed by his KCIA chief. The sudden demise of his regime was followed by a "Seoul spring" and an outpouring of demands for a more open and democratic regime. But before a transition to democracy could take place, a military clique led by General Chun Doo Hwan seized power, murdered several military rivals, and began arresting civilian opposition leaders. Among those arrested was the popular dissident politician, Kim Dae Jung. News of his incarceration led to an insurrection in the city of Gwangju in Kim's home province. Chun sent paratroopers into the city and retook it at the cost of hundreds of civilian lives. After imposing a nationwide crackdown on dissent, Chun ran for president unopposed and unsurprisingly won.

The political turmoil, bloody resistance, and oppression of 1980 were accompanied by a sharp economic downturn; the GDP fell six percent. The unrest frightened investors and worried the Americans. Prices for the imported energy South Korea's economy was dependent on were soaring and to further add to the country's troubles, bad weather led to poor rice harvests. Many observers feared that with rising labor costs, South Korea had reached the limits of what could be achieved by its low wage, export-oriented economic model. The immediate prospects in the South did not look promising.

While this was happening south of the DMZ, Kim Il Sung called a Party Congress in the north, the first in a decade. He used it to make it known to the public that he had selected his son Kim Jong Il as his successor and to celebrate the achievements of the regime. And it was looking good for him. While South Korea's economic growth was disconcerting to the North, it looked as if the boom was over. In contrast to the political turmoil of the South, the DPRK was beginning an orderly transition to a new generation of leadership under Kim Jong Il. Unlike the qualms Seoul's patron was feeling, Pyongyang still had the firm support of Moscow, if not Beijing. It had also achieved a bigger role on the world stage, with greater international recognition. In an hour-long speech, he summarized the achievements of his regime and its bright prospects. Just to again fish in troubled waters, he called for the Confederal Republic of the two Koreas, dusting off a proposal he had made during another troubled year in the South, 1960.

There is every reason to believe that Kim felt history was on his side and the people of the South would turn to his regime, the Americans would leave, the military rulers of the South would be weakened and isolated, and victory in the decades-long civil conflict was not far away. But that would not prove to be the case. The troubled year, 1980, proved just a temporary setback for the South; the following year the dynamics in the struggle between the two Koreas began to markedly shift in the South's favor, never again to reverse. In retrospect, 1980 was the last moment when there was a possibility the North could prevail in the struggle for mastery of the peninsula.

Seoul Goes for Olympic Gold

1980 was a bad year for South Korea but the following year, 1981, brought about a beginning of a dramatic change in fortune for the ROK. South Korea's economy roared back, growing by 9 percent in 1981 and continuing to expand in the 1980s, peaking at 12 percent in 1986–1988 when it was the highest in the world. The country shifted from low-skill, low-wage, labor-intensive exports such as textiles, to steel, ships, automobiles, and electronics. Workers still toiled long hours under sometimes appalling conditions, but wages rose and conditions improved. The education system continued to expand, and vast numbers of young people studied abroad, creating a pool of highly trained workers, managers, and professionals. The middle class grew, farmers left for the city, and the ones left behind benefitted from generous price-supported and protected markets. The entire country in the 1980s was looking like a construction project; highways, subways, high-rise apartments appeared everywhere, and gleaming skyscrapers emerged in Seoul and even in provincial cities. The transformation was astonishing.

Nothing better symbolized the rise of South Korea than the Olympics which was awarded to Seoul in 1981. The date of the games—1988—became the target date for the country's big coming-out party. It would be a sign that the nation had arrived, ready to join the first world of advanced societies. Already, the "miracle on the Han" was being noticed by much of the world. South Korea began an aggressive move to win over the Third World from their tilt toward its rival. A steady stream of official visitors from developing countries came. They did not receive the adulation of well-rehearsed crowds, but they did get an opportunity to learn from what appeared to be the formula for successful development, and South Korean firms entered lucrative markets.

Not that everything in the South was going smoothly. Although the Chun regime had hoped to use the Olympics as a way of gaining support, this did not happen. Rather, the rising middle class began to demand a more active role in public affairs, including free and open elections. Spearheaded by university students and labor groups, anti-government demonstrations grew in frequency and scale. In 1987, Chun, as promised, agreed to step down after seven years as president but reneged on his promise for popular elections, instead hand-picking another former general, Roh Tae Woo, as his successor. This announcement was greeted with widespread anger and massive anti-government demonstrations. After several chaotic months, the Chun regime gave in. It abolished most censorship, freed political prisoners, and agreed to freely contest the presidential election that fall. The opposition to the regime fragmented and put up three candidates, all named Kim, and lost to Roh. But the months later they handily won control over the National Assembly which now had real power. In short, after a period of unrest in 1987, South

Korea made a surprisingly swift and smooth transition to democracy.

The democratization of South Korea changed the nature of the Korean War. As the country became a more open, less authoritarian society it became less militaristic and diverged farther from North Korea. It also became more politically stable.

Chun Doo Hwan

The last authoritarian ruler of South Korea was Chun Doo Hwan. Chun was part of the second generation of leaders whose early careers were shaped by the Korean conflict. He was the first South Korean president not to reach adulthood under Japanese rule. Chun was born in 1931 in South Gyeongsan province, the fourth son of poor farmers in a poor farming village. At the age of five, his family moved to Daegu where he attended elementary school. When he was seven his father murdered a Japanese policeman and the family fled to Manchuria. Two years later they returned, and he resumed elementary school. Just fourteen at liberation, he attended a vocational high school and upon graduating in 1951, he attended the Korea Military Academy. He graduated in 1955 in the eleventh class. His classmates would remain close and help him in his rise to power; one, Roh Tae Woo, succeeded him as president. He trained in the U.S. in guerilla tactics and psychological warfare. He also married a Korea Military Academy commandant's daughter, Lee Soonja. Within a relatively short time, he became a trusted advisor whose connections helped him in his rise. While still a young officer, he worked directly under Park Chung Hee in the Supreme Council for National Reconstruction, the governing organization created by the military after it seized power in 1961. He also served in the Korean Central Intelligence Agency and, in 1969, became a senior advisor to the Army Chief of Staff.

When Park was assassinated in 1979, Chun was in a key position within the military as the commander of the Security Command. This body was in charge of internal security within the military, maintaining its loyalty to the regime and watching for signs of subversion. Upon Park's death, his vice president, Choi

Kyuh Ha, became president. Despite being a loyal civil servant, he was not taken seriously as anything but a caretaker while politicians jostled for power. Chun almost immediately took control of all the intelligence organizations. He never wavered from his belief that, considering the dangerous position South Korea was in, the power had to be securely in the hands of the military. On December 12, 1979, Chun, along with others from his eleventh graduating class, seized control of the military command. They took command of the military headquarters and the Ministry of Defense, during which several high-ranking officers fled to the U.S. military compound, and one was killed in an exchange of gunfire. While the "Seoul Spring" was taking place in the streets, Chun was consolidating his power. He promoted himself to Lieutenant General and the head of the KCIA, and on May 17 he expanded martial law. He closed the universities, banned political activities, curtailed the press, and began arresting civilian opposition leaders. When an uprising occurred in Gwangju he had it brutally repressed. He ran unopposed as president.

Chun's administration was, in many ways, similar to Park Chung Hee's. He continued to pursue the same development policies. He was pragmatic and more interested in practical results than ideology. He also shared with Park the same vision of an economically strong country and presided over rapid economic expansion, rising living standards, and the emergence of South Korea as a respected player in international affairs. Yet Chun lacked Park's charisma, and he was despised by much of the rising middle class of the country who resented the way he had seized power and were weary of military rule. His failure to prevent family members from enriching themselves further contributed to his unpopularity. While many South Koreans accepted the argument that dangerous security problems with North Korea called for order, stability, and a strong military, they did not interpret this as military rule. There was a feeling among many that if South Korea was going to join the ranks of advanced countries such as the United States, Japan, and Western Europe it had to move beyond the politics of military coups and strong men to a more representative government, more political freedom and orderly processes. In the face of this unpopularity, Chun stepped down in 1988. He managed to engineer the appointment of his successor—his former classmate, Roh Tae Woo. But he could not prevent the democratic, civilian transition of South Korea, and in the mid-1990s he was tried for corruption, spent a short term in prison, and returned to private life.

Hwarangdae

Chun Doo Hwan was a graduate of South Korea's Military Academy, the Hwarangdae. The Korean Military Academy was founded on May 1, 1946, by the United States Military Government in Korea. It was located on the outskirts of Seoul. South Korea renamed the institution Hwarangdae after the legendary Hwarang from the ancient state of Silla. The name Hwarang means "Flower Boys" and it dates to before the unification of the country in the seventh century. Most of the information about the Hwarang comes from later accounts and historians differ on exactly how the institution functioned. Young aristocratic men, selected for their looks as well as their talents, served the king and were trained as warriors. Whatever, their exact functions, twentieth century Koreans saw the Hwarang as representing the martial spirit and patriotism of ancient Koreans, virtues that they hoped to revive and instill in modern young men.

The Academy produced most of the leading military figures who emerged after 1960. Each graduating class has had strong bonds. The eighth graduating class in 1949 was of particular importance. Shortly after graduating, they fought as officers in the Korean War. Afterward, they emerged in key positions in the ROK Army. The most important member was Kim Jongpil, an intelligence officer, who, along with his classmates, plotted the May 16, 1961, military coup that brought Park Chung Hee to power. Members of that class, including Kim, played key roles in the new military government. Kim Jongpil founded, and for a time headed, the KCIA, Park's powerful intelligence service. The eleventh graduation class led the internal military coup of December 1979 that brought to power the military officers who then took over the government in 1980. This class produced Chun Doo Hwan, president from 1980 to 1988, and his successor Roh Tae Woo, president from 1988 to 1993.

The Hwarangdae officers differed from the older generation of South Korean military leaders. They had not served the Japanese and were too young to have been shaped by the colonial period. They were strongly influenced by U.S. military training. Many embarked on additional training in the United States. They saw themselves as modern professionals, patriotic Koreans, and were, of course, staunch anti-communists. Indeed, the institution created a high degree of professionalism and competence, but the temptation of power resulted in the corruption of many alongside the growing public resentment of military participation in politics. After the transition to democracy in the late 1980s and 1990s, the South Korean military was no longer involved in politics. Its influence in public life diminished. The newer generation of graduates was committed to democratic institutions and saw themselves as military specialists, not as saviors of their nation.

Things Not Going Well for Pyongyang

South Korea's transition to a prosperous, democratic, civilian-led society increasingly connected to the global economy contrasted with North Korea, for which the 1980s did not bring much good news. Its economy stagnated. Kim Il Sung needed current capital and equipment but had trouble getting foreign exchange. He wasted resources on useless, massive projects, such as the world's tallest hotel that was structurally flawed and never opened. The world's longest barrage was built to seal off and drain a bay to create new farmland, but the reclaimed land was too salty for agriculture and the barrage caused the Daedong River and its sewage to back up. The regime built a multi-lane highway from Pyongyang to Kaesong near the border, mainly to show off to foreign visitors. However, it had so little traffic that one could safely take a nap on it. Failed agricultural policies led to food shortages. In 1987, after cutting food rations, it launched a "Let's Eat Two Meals A Day" campaign to

The Bombing of Wonsan, North Korea The U.S. dropped more bombs on North Korea than it did on Japan or Germany during World War II. Bombing was especially intense beginning in 1952.

Signing the Armistice On July 27, 1953, after two years of negotiations, a cease-fire was signed at the truce village of Panmunjom. The United States, China and North Korea signed it; South Korea, unhappy with leaving the country divided, did not.

The Truce Village at Panmunjom When selected as a site for negotiations between North and South during the Korean War, the facility consisted of just a few tents. A permanent structure was later built.

Seoul during the Korean War Captured and recaptured four times in less than a year of heavy fighting from 1950 to 1951, Seoul was left in utter ruins during the war. Busan served as the temporary capital until the conflict was over.

Kim Il Sung The North Korean leader traveled continuously throughout the country during his nearly half century in power. These included official inspections and just meeting the people.

Pak Jeongae was the only woman to hold a high-ranking position in North Korea who was not a member of the ruling Kim family. She was purged in 1966 but given a minor post in 1986.

Park Chung Hee Perhaps no one had a greater impact on transforming South Korea into a modern industrial state than Park Chung Hee. After nearly three decades of increasingly authoritarian rule, Park was assassinated in 1979 by his own security chief.

Chung Ju-yung If Park Chung Hee was the general directing South Korea's industrialization, Chung Ju-yung was his greatest field commander. His activities ranged from construction and ship building to founding the Hyundai Motor Company.

Kim Jong Il The eldest son of Kim Il Sung, Kim Jong Il became his father's designated successor in 1980. His succession to power in 1994 went smoothly since by then he was already effectively administering the country.

The Blue House in Seoul South Korea's executive residence is called the "Blue House." It was the scene of a North Korea commando attack in April 1968.

USS Pueblo After seizing the U.S. intelligence vessel USS *Pueblo* in April 1968, North Korea returned the crew but not the ship. Later it was anchored in the Daedong River in Pyongyang and opened as a tourist attraction.

South Korean Forces in Vietnam with Captured Viet Cong Between 1966 and 1973 almost 300,000 South Korean soldiers served in Vietnam as part of a deal between President Park and the Johnson Administration. They earned a reputation for brutality. *(Manhhai, Flickr)*

Independence Hall in Cheonan, South Korea Opening in 1987, this huge exhibition hall is mainly focused on the independence movement under Japanese colonial rule. Graphic images of the Japanese oppression are included among its many displays.

North Korean Tunnel Tunnel Number 4 (the fourth North Korean tunnel discovered in 1990) crossed the DMZ and ran one kilometer south of the South Korean border at a depth of 145 meters. Many more tunnels are believed to have never been found.

Cadets at Hwarangdae Modeled in part on West Point, Hwarangdae, the Korea Military Academy, is named after an ancient military youth group. It has produced many of South Korea's leading military officers and three of its presidents.

North Korean Factory After 1953, North Korea rapidly developed becoming by 1970 the second most industrialized country in Asia. However, the economic growth stalled in the 1980s and North Korea's factories became outdated with many ceasing to function.

Kim Il Sung and Kim Jong Il All North Koreans and visitors to Pyongyang are expected to pay homage to the Great Leader and his successor son.

Yeonpyeongdo under Fire from North Korea The North Korean shelling of the South Korean island of Yeonpyeongdo on November 23, 2010, killed four and wounded 22. The provocation shocked and angered the South Korean public.

North Korean Guards at Panmunjom North Korean soldiers at Panmunjom observe all activities on the South Korean side of the border, a reminder of the state of tension between the two Koreas.

Summit between Kim Jong Un and President Trump The unprecedented summits between Kim Jong Un and President Trump in 2018 and 2019 brought about a great deal of international attention and excitement but little progress in improving relations. *(Trump White House Archived, Flickr)*

Kim Jong Un and South Korean President Moon Symbolically Cross the DMZ Together Moon Jae-in resumed the earlier efforts by President Kim Dae Jung and Roh Moo-hyun to seek rapprochement with the North but was no more successful than his predecessors.

South Korea's Hyunmoo-3 Missile In the late 2010s South Korea began an arms race with North Korea building its own fighter jets and advanced missiles but chose not to develop nuclear weapons.

Kim Yo Jong Kim Jong Un's younger sister Kim Yo Jong has emerged as the de facto number two person in the regime. It has been rumored that she was being groomed to be his successor.

Kaesong Industrial Complex Opening in 2004 just inside North Korea, Kaesong had, at its height, 50,000 North Korean workers employed by around a hundred South Korean manufacturing firms. While the plan was to gradually integrate the two economies, it proved to be a failed experiment and closed in 2016.

North Korean Missile on Display Despite economic hardships, North Korea continued its military buildup under Kim Jong Un developing larger nuclear weapons and more advanced delivery systems.

우리군대제일주의를철저히구현해나가자!

North Korean Propaganda This poster from 2013 urges support for North Korea's "Military First" policy. Note the futuristic metropolis depicted which is in stark contrast to the reality found in North Korea today.

Ryugyong Hotel Designed to be the world's tallest hotel when construction began in 1987, the Ryugyong Hotel never opened due to structural flaws. It remains a prominent feature on the Pyongyang skyline and a symbol of the country's economic failures.

Park Yeonmi A North Korean refugee who fled to the South and later moved to the U.S., Park Yeonmi has become a best-selling author and YouTube personality who works for international recognition of the plight of North Korean refugees.

Newly Elected South Korean President Yoon Suk-yeol In the country's closest presidential election, the conservative party candidate Yoon won the 2022 election promising a harder line on North Korea and closer cooperation with the United States and its allies.

reduce food consumption.

The DPRK was becoming more isolated. From about 1982 the Non-Aligned Movement stopped endorsing pro-Pyongyang resolutions at the UN. By the end of the decade, Seoul had an increasing number of embassies abroad and much better relations with most of the developing world. The North had lost this front in its struggle with the South. In 1984, Moscow increased economic and military aid but at the same time made it clear it would participate in the Olympics in Seoul and was establishing more contacts with the ROK. So did Beijing, which began to refer to South Korea by its official name "Republic of Korea" and invited some sports and other officials to its country. Few things could have been more disturbing to the leadership in Pyongyang than these developments.

Rangoon (present-day Yangnon, Myanmar)

North Korea still hoped to destabilize the South Korean system. Seeing the chaos that followed the assassination of Park Chung Hee, it sought to assassinate his successor, Chun Doo Hwan. The first attempt was to be carried out during Chun's visit to the African country of Gabon in 1982. Chun, who was annoyed when one African country greeted him by accidentally playing the DPRK national anthem at his arrival, was spared a far worse welcome when, at the last minute, Kim Jong Il called the plot off. The next year the North Koreans plotted to kill him when he visited the Burmese capital of Rangoon on a six-nation visit to Southeast Asia.

The Rangoon plot was a carefully planned operation. Three specially trained KPA officers were involved: Major Zin Bo and two captains, Kang Min-chul and Kim Jin-woo. They entered the country clandestinely by ship with diplomatic passports. Chun's itinerary included a visit to the Martyr's Mausoleum where he, accompanied by other ROK officials, was to lay a wreath to honor the memory of Burma's independence leader, Aung San. North Korean agents planted three bombs on the roof of a platform erected for the occasion. Chun barely escaped assassination. North Korean agent Major Zin Bo prematurely set off the explosion when he mistook one of the arriving vehicles for the one carrying the ROK president, thinking Chun was among the ROK officials entering the platform. According to another account, a bugle mistakenly signaled the arrival of the president. In either case, Chun was delayed in traffic and arrived several minutes after the bombs had been detonated. The powerful blast killed four South Korean cabinet members and fourteen other South Koreans including advisors, journalists, and security officials. Among them was the Foreign Minister Lee Bum-suk who advocated working with Moscow and Beijing to work out a peaceful reconciliation with North Korea. Four Burmese, including three journalists, were killed, and dozens of others were injured.

Captains Kang Min-chul and Kim Jin-woo attempted suicide with a hand grenade, but they were less competent at blowing themselves up than blowing up others. Kang lost an arm and Kim an eye and an arm. Both were arrested. Kang confessed, cooperated with Burmese officials and was imprisoned. Kim, who didn't cooperate, was executed. A manhunt for Major Zin resulted in his being shot dead, but only after he had killed three Burmese soldiers. The Burmese didn't know what to do with Kang. They offered to send him back to North Korea, but he feared he would be executed as a traitor for providing information about the plot. They offered to send him to South Korea, but he feared he would be assassinated by Pyongyang agents there. Twenty-five years later he died in a Burmese prison.

The Rangoon bombing did little to improve North Korea's downward slide in its standing in the global community. It further contributed to its loss of support in the Third World. Burma broke off diplomatic relations with the DPRK. China was appalled and, in a rare development, publicly criticized the DPRK. The bombing contributed later to North Korea's listing by the United States and other countries as a state sponsor of terrorism. Beijing, worried about what else it might do, urged Pyongyang to engage in dialogue with Seoul and offered to act as a facilitator in trilateral talks between the DPRK, South Korea, and the United States, but little came of this.

Scaring the World Away from the Olympics

North Korea rightly saw the coming of the Seoul Olympics as a threat. It undermined its efforts to isolate the South, eroded attempts to claim the mantle as the true leader of the Korean nation, made it harder to portray the ROK as an apathetic, impoverished state to the North Korean people, and was an opportunity for Seoul to court the DRPK's allies, Moscow and Beijing. Pyongyang vigorously protested the award decision by the Olympics committee, citing the South's instability and the tensions on the peninsula. Its propaganda organs warned of an out-of-control AIDS epidemic, although the country had relatively few cases of the disease. In 1985 it switched to a demand to co-host the game. The Olympic Committee considered this and in 1986 offered to hold table tennis, archery, soccer, and cycling events in the DPRK. Pyongyang rejected this. Then it resumed trying to frighten away participants. On October 14, 1986, North Korean agents set off a bomb at Seoul's Kimpo airport. The most dramatic effort was the destruction of Korean Air Flight 858.

In the 1980s, thousands of South Koreans found lucrative work on Korean construction projects in the oil-rich countries of the Middle East. Working long hours and living away from families, these employees were able to make a nice sum of money after a couple of years. On November 29, 1987, a planeload of these hardworking South Koreans never made it home. North Korean agents placed a bomb, made from liquid explosives disguised as a liquor bottle, above their seats on a plane returning to Seoul from Baghdad. They then got off at a stopover in Abu Dhabi. While the plane was flying near the Andaman Islands in the Indian Ocean, on its way to the next stopover in Bangkok, the explosives went off. All 104 passengers and 11 crew members were killed. The two agents were to take a plane from Abu Dhabi to Amman on a circuitous route back home, but complications in their visa forced them to change their route and they flew to Bahrain. In Bahrain, the authorities discovered their passports were forgeries. However, before they could be taken into custody, they took cyanide hidden in cigarettes. The older male agent died but the younger female agent, Kim Hyonghui, survived. She was taken to Seoul for trial. She confessed and her testimony suggested that the incident was planned at the very top.

Meanwhile, Pyongyang began a campaign for an Olympic boycott. However, almost every country including China, the Soviet Union, and its Eastern European allies, indicated their intention to attend. One hundred and sixty nations participated in the games in Seoul in September 1988—a record number. Only Albania, Cuba, Ethiopia, Madagascar, and the Seychelles answered North Korea's call for a boycott. The games, the first in 12 years in which all major countries participated, were a great success, enabling South Korea to show off its economic achievements. That same month, the DPRK was celebrating its 40th anniversary. For a regime that loved to celebrate anniversaries, the symbolism could not have been lost. Isolated and ignored by the world, North Korea hosted the 13th Festival of Youth and Students in 1989 by way of compensation. Some 22,000 young people from 177 countries attended. However, the games were a costly burden that the state could hardly afford and whatever domestic purpose they may have served, they drew little international attention.

The Collapse of Communism and the Two Koreas

From 1988 to 1991 the geopolitical environment around the Korean conflict changed dramatically—almost entirely in Seoul's favor. A cascade of developments, each a blow to Pyongyang, closely followed each other. The Soviet leader Gorbachev, concerned with reforming his country's economy and reducing military commitments, sought to improve relations with its former adversaries. As a result of this change in policy, the Soviet Union established economic ties with South Korea. In 1988, Moscow established direct economic contacts with Seoul through the Soviet chamber of Commerce and Industry. In September 1988, Hungary became the first Communist bloc country to exchange ambassadors and begin to establish full diplomatic ties. In 1989, the Soviet Union and the ROK exchanged trade missions. In September, Presidents

Roh and Gorbachev met and agreed to establish full diplomatic relations. Meanwhile, in 1989 the communist regimes in Eastern Europe starting with Poland were being overturned or dissolved. Their successors had little interest in dealing with North Korea, but all were quick to establish ties with South Korea.

No blow was harder on the North than the changes in the Soviet Union. Moscow no longer viewed North Korea as being of key strategic significance and in 1990 it suspended most aid. The DPRK now had to pay real international market prices for petroleum and other major imports. Military aid virtually ceased. This had severe repercussions for the DRPK. Its faltering economy had been briefly buoyed by generous Soviet aid in the late 1980s. Now this was abruptly reduced and by 1991 had come to a complete end. In December of that year, the Soviet Union itself came to an end. The Russian Republic under Yeltsin was eager for South Korean trade and investment and had little interest in the North.

China was never as important as the USSR to North Korea's economy, but it was culturally and historically closer. That did not stop it from moving toward closer economic and diplomatic relations with the South. As it did so, Chinese officials assured the North Koreans of their continued support. However, the pragmatic Chinese saw the advantage of increasing trade with, and seeking investment from, booming South Korea and continued to improve relations. Meanwhile, Beijing was either unable or unwilling to make up for North Korea's loss of Soviet trade and aid.

For South Korea, these were heady days. The change in the relative position of the two countries happened faster than most had thought possible. South Korean President Roh tried to take advantage of the situation to improve relations with the North and bring the long conflict to an end; what he called his "Nordpolitik." In July 1988 he issued a Six-Point Declaration which defined the DPRK as part of a "single national community" not as an adversary. In subsequent addresses, he called upon both Koreas to work on a Korean Commonwealth. This was not a new idea and resembled the DPRK's call for the Democratic Confederal Republic of Goryeo. Pyongyang did not embrace the idea, and instead proposed interparliamentary talks between the two sides, but set as usual conditions that were not acceptable to Seoul. In 1990 the two sides again began talks that continued throughout 1991. Nothing significant came of these. Roh's policies were not successful in either ending or even changing the tone of the conflict.

Facing the decline in Soviet aid and pressure from China to open itself up to Western trade and investment, Pyongyang made a few token efforts at reform. In 1991 it created the Free Trade and Economic Zone in the Rajin-Seonbong area called Raseon. The UN Development Program provided some seed money. The zone was located in the most remote part of the country, the furthest from Pyongyang. It was near the Chinese and Russian borders but was only connected to them by dirt roads. It was clear this was a token gesture and not a sincere move to emulate China's economic reform policies.

The Nuclear Crisis

Rather than ending the Korean conflict entered a dangerous nuclear phase. Both Koreas had long considered acquiring nuclear weapons. In the South, Park Chung Hee had sought to develop advanced weapons and had created an Agency for Defense Development for that purpose. It was hindered by the United States which did not trust him, just as it had not trusted his predecessor Syngman Rhee, and made sure that the South Korean air force and the military in general, did not have offensive weapons that might tempt him to invade the North. However, his Agency had a secret Weapons Exploitation Committee answerable only to him, even the National Assembly knew nothing about it. After the decision of the Nixon administration to withdraw the Seventh Division from South Korea, Park decided to use the agency to work on nuclear weapons. According to one of his advisors, he sought the capacity to produce nuclear weapons but not necessarily to build one, which would be too provocative a measure.

Creating a Korea Atomic Research Institute Park embarked on an ambitious plan to develop nuclear energy for use in power plants. This was a reasonable move as the country was moving into energy-hungry heavy industry and had to rely on expensive imports of petroleum. This technology came from the United States and the Americans were watching it closely, so he turned to France which was quietly supplying Israel with the technology it needed for an atomic bomb. In 1974 the French helped the Koreans develop the design for a nuclear processing plant. At about the same time, Park began luring American-trained Korean nuclear scientists and engineers to return to their home country and work for him. They were put to work at a newly created science center south of Seoul. However, Washington had intelligence agents watching and they discovered the covert nuclear program. When the U.S. told France to stop helping Park with nuclear technology, the French resisted. In 1975 the U.S. Secretary of Defense told Park directly that a nuclear weapons program would pose a threat to U.S.-ROK relations. Park, while never admitting its existence, canceled the deal with France and ceased the program after a long U.S. campaign of pressure and threats.

Or at least he pretended to end his nuclear program. Secretly, he kept his nuclear team in place, and in 1978 they were again working on developing nuclear fuel rods and other elements of atomic bomb construction. At one point Park may have planned to have a bomb ready by 1981. However, Park's assassination in 1979 brought the effort to a halt. His successor Chun Doo Hwan, seeking American support, tried to avoid a clash over a nuclear weapons program. In 1981 he downsized the Korea Atomic Energy Research Institute and renamed it the Korea Energy Research Institute. Its scientists still conducted small-scale experiments such as extracting minute quantities of plutonium in 1982 but there was no serious effort to build an atomic bomb. In short, South Korea may well have become a nuclear power by the early 1980s, had the U.S. not interfered. South Korea under Park had additionally worked on developing a missile program, also strongly opposed by the United States. This Park had managed to keep secret, taking the Americans by surprise when he successfully tested a guided missile in 1978. Under pressure, this program too was shut down. But it was the atomic bomb that Park wanted most and perhaps came close to getting.

No such restraint stopped North Korea from pursuing its nuclear program. Like the South Koreans, the North saw the possession of atomic weapons as the ultimate insurance policy against an invasion. It was also part of a larger effort to expand every possible weapon in its arsenal. North Korea had started work on chemical and biological weapons perhaps as early as the 1950s. It operated chemical weapons factories that produced chemical agents such as sarin and mustard gas. Its Germ Research Institute developed biological weapons including anthrax, botulism, cholera, hemorrhagic fever, the plague (Yerisnia pestis), yellow fever, and smallpox. The DPRK joined the Biological and Toxin Weapons Convention in 1987 and signed the Geneva Protocol in 1989 banning the use of biochemical weapons, but it remained one of only five countries which had not signed the Chemical Weapons Convention.

These were potentially formidable weapons, but what North Korea was interested in above all was acquiring nuclear ones. This was not surprising since it faced hundreds of nuclear weapons kept by the Americans in the South and wanted its own. In 1959, the Soviets agreed to a North Korean request to develop nuclear energy and constructed a small "furniture factory" near the town of Yongbyon. North Korea sent hundreds of technicians to study at the Nuclear Research Center at Dubna, near Moscow. Yet the Soviets had no intention of helping them develop nuclear weapons. When the Chinese detonated a nuclear device in 1964, the North Koreans asked them for help in developing one, but this request was denied. So, the North Koreans had to work on their own to make an atomic bomb. They focused on expanding the capacity of the small nuclear research reactor at Yongbyon. They made slow but continual progress. In the 1980s the DPRK built a secret facility for reprocessing fuel into weapons-grade material. Under Soviet pressure, Pyongyang signed the Nuclear Non-Proliferation Treaty in 1985 but not the safeguarding agreements. By the later 1980s, the U.S. began to suspect North Korea may be developing an atomic bomb. They noted its work with chemical high explosives used for detonation. Then satellite photos revealed a new structure that appeared to be capable of separating plutonium from nuclear fuel rods. This set up a chain of events that came close to a war between North Korea and the United States.

In the late 1980s, with the transition to democracy, the South Korean government and the public became committed to a nuclear-free peninsula, although South Korea continued to develop a major nuclear energy program. North Korea, playing to these concerns over nuclear weapons, worked out a Joint Declaration with Seoul in December 1991, in which both countries agreed not to test, manufacture, produce, receive, possess, store, deploy or use nuclear weapons. The following month the DPRK signed up to the safeguards with the International Atomic Energy Agency (IAEA). It is not clear that Pyongyang ever took this declaration or the safeguards agreement seriously. It appeared to have continued to work on nuclear weapons development. IAEA inspectors soon complained about the lack of transparency they encountered. North Korea's lack of cooperation only made the international community more suspicious that they were pursuing an atomic bomb. The biggest concern was over fuel that experts believed had been removed from the 5-megawatt reactor when it was shut down for 70–100 days in 1989. This could be enough to make one to three nuclear bombs. North Korea turned down an IAEA request for access to these sites. As tension rose over this dispute, in February 1993 North Korea announced its intention to withdraw from the Nuclear Non-Proliferation Treaty in June of that year. The UN Security Council then passed a resolution calling for the DPRK to reconsider its withdrawal.

The Clinton administration announced that if North Korea reprocessed plutonium it would be crossing a "red line" that could result in military action. North Korea's reaction caused tensions to increase. The U.S. called North Korea's bluff, but Pyongyang didn't back down. Washington considered many options, including a military strike on the main reprocessing facility. Plans were made to begin a massive American military build-up of as many as 400,000 reinforcements. However, this would take time and the DPRK backed in a corner might strike first before enough US forces could move into the peninsula. The prospect was truly frightening. Seoul was within the range of over 8,000 long-range artillery pieces and an estimated 2400 rocket launchers. Massive retaliation by Pyongyang could devastate the city of 10 million. One Pentagon estimate was that as many as one million people would be killed if full-scale war were to resume on the peninsula, including 80,000 to 100,000 Americans.

After years of living with the threat of war and the DPRK's provocations, many Southern Koreans had become almost blasé about the conflict with the north, shrugging it off with a "so they are at it again?" attitude. But in the late spring of 1994, as North Korea's brinkmanship was escalating to dangerous levels and full-scale air raid drills were being carried out, people became genuinely concerned, and many began stocking up on groceries. The U.S. embassy was quietly making plans to evacuate the 80,000 non-military-related Americans in Korea. The arrival of Jimmy Carter in June led to a defusing of the crisis, as the two sides began working out an agreement that was satisfactory to both nations. Carter was officially traveling in a private capacity but with the approval of the Clinton administration. He stopped in Seoul to consult with South Korean President Kim Young Sam then crossed into the DPRK and began talks with Kim Il Sung. Kim Il Sung also agreed not to expel the remaining IAEA inspectors and agreed to an unprecedented summit conference with Kim Young Sam. They were to meet in late July. Then, on July 8, 1994, Kim Il Sung died suddenly of a heart attack. His robust appearance during the negotiations and a rare interview with Western journalists just days earlier made his death all the more unexpected.

The Two Koreas in 1994

In what was to be his last New Year's Day address on January 1, 1994, Kim Il Sung made a rare admission that things were not going well for the DPRK. He pointed to the economic hardships, including food shortages. The public distribution system that provided most people with their basic needs, food, cooking oil, and clothes was not functioning well. Such an admission of economic failure was previously unheard of. But he had little choice but to face the reality of the dire straits the country was in. A severe energy shortage, in part caused by the end of cheap Soviet oil, had resulted in blackouts, constant power cuts, and stalled trains. Tractors were idle and irrigation pumps were not working. The country was more isolated than ever. Foreigners had begun speculating on how much longer the DPRK could survive without collapsing like the countries in Eastern Europe. Its military was still formidable but even its soldiers often did not get enough to eat, and military vehicles were idle for lack of fuel.

South Korea, by contrast, was doing well. Its economy had begun to slow down a little but was still growing at a good pace. Exports were up, as were wages, and millions were entering the middle class. The transition to democracy had gone well. The military was in the barracks and politics were open and free. The 1992 presidential elections went without a problem and without a military man in the race. A former political dissident, Kim Young Sam, defeated another former dissident, Kim Dae Jung. Relations with its ally, the United States, were good, and trade and friendly exchanges with all its neighbors were increasing—except of course for its neighbor on the other side of the DMZ. The nuclear crisis was being peacefully resolved and all seemingly was going well.

In the summer of 1994, the end of the half century long Korean conflict appeared to be in sight. Many foreign experts believed the most likely scenario was that the DPRK would collapse and be peacefully absorbed by the South. Another possibility was that the North would follow China's lead and reform, open up to the global marketplace and make peace with its southern neighbor. But neither of these possibilities happened. The Korean conflict would continue for decades more.

CHAPTER 8

Sunshine and Nukes: the Korean Conflict, 1994–2011

On June 26, 1995, it started to rain in North Korea as it usually does during the rainy season. However, this time ten days of heavy downpours dumped 23 inches. Floods occurred over much of the country inundating rice fields and wiping out much of the crop. It pushed the country over the edge into mass famine. The real cause of famine was years of poor agricultural policies. North Korea did not allow the private plots and markets that helped feed the people in the Soviet Union, Vietnam, or other communist countries but relied entirely on inefficient state farms. Bureaucratic ignorance had led to the deforestation of hillsides (which contributed to flooding), planting crops where they were not suited, planting crops too closely for them to grow properly in a vain attempt to increase output per acre, and other counterproductive practices. As a result, agricultural production had declined for years and much of the population suffered chronic hunger. The rains were only the trigger for mass famine.

The famine was truly horrific. Children were too hungry to attend school. If they attended their teachers were absent due to looking for food or too weak and tired to come to work. Factories and other workplaces ceased to function as their employees joined the men and women foraging the countryside for food. Many sickened and died. People made meals of grass and twigs that made their bowels bleed without providing much nourishment. Cities and towns became eerily quiet as vehicles were not operating, people were not going to work or school and many were silently dying at home rather than out and about. Dogs and cats disappeared. So too did livestock, including work oxen, as people ate whatever they could.

Yet while this nightmarish situation was unfolding, on the other side of the DMZ, the monsoon rains fell on a prosperous society. Restaurants were busy, supermarkets were well-stocked with food from around the world and private gyms were opening for South Koreans worrying about getting overweight. North and South Koreans lived in ever more different worlds. Politically and ideologically they had pulled further apart. Up to the 1980s, for all their differences, North and South Korea had much in common. Both Koreas had authoritarian governments that sought to mobilize their people and resources to achieve state goals focused on developing a strong military and an industrial base to support it. Both engaged in ideological training. Both restricted the movement of their citizens; South Korea did so to a much lesser degree, but until 1988 it was difficult for South Koreans to leave the country for reasons other than business or study. Both had foreign policies that, at least rhetorically, focused on reunification. Both devoted considerable resources to supporting a huge military, although in South Korea with a bigger economy and the presence and support of US troops this absorbed a much smaller proportion of its budget. North and South Korea were less opposites than variants of centralized, militarized, authoritarian states with a shared goal: the creation of a uniform, united, prosperous, and militarily strong Korean nation-state.

In the 1990s the two Koreas diverged far more sharply. The South became more democratic, less militaristic, more cosmopolitan, and somewhat less preoccupied with reunification. The North, if anything, became more militaristic and more isolated, and its ideology warped into an insular, self-centered ultranationalism. The South became rich, and the North sank into extreme poverty. The Korean conflict also became less a mortal struggle to win the contest for reunification. For South Korea, it became more of a patient effort to coax the North into cooperation and to prepare for the inevitable collapse of the DPRK while preventing a catastrophic conflict in the meantime. The North's goal became less about achieving victory and more about surviving.

Becoming almost Normal: the South

In 1992, Kim Young Sam, a former opponent of military rule, was elected and served his five-year term; ROK presidents were limited to one term. In 1998, Kim Dae Jung, another political dissident and one hated by Park and Chun, was elected and served his five-year term. What is so interesting is that by then the transfer of power was routine, and no one could conceive of a military coup. The press was free, and elections for mayors and governors were lively and freely contested. South Koreans accepted the rules of democracy and eagerly embraced them. Labor unions were active and successful in their efforts to raise wages and improve working conditions. The standard of living rose sharply. Restrictions on foreign travel were gone and South Koreans became among the world's most traveled people. Import restrictions also were reduced and the shops were stocked with goods from all over the world. In 1996, the World Bank reclassified the ROK as a developed state. This was followed by a severe financial crisis from 1997 to 1998 but South Korea quickly recovered and in the early 2000s it had become, by most standards, a First World society.

So fast was South Korea changing that someone waking after twenty years of sleep may have thought they had entered the wrong country. Yet, in one basic way it had not changed—it was still a part of a divided nation that was at war with itself. It maintained a large armed force in which all men served, the border with the North was still tense, U.S troops were still stationed on its soil, and the country was still subjected to unpredictable North Korean provocation. Many families still had relatives whom they had no contact with on the other side of the DMZ. Yet South Korean military expenditures took up a more modest part of the greatly enlarged national economy. Military service was reduced from three to two years and the frequent air raid drills had ceased. There were no longer military drills in the schools or anti-communist education. South Korea appeared less and less like a country at war. Life for South Koreans seemed normal and peaceful until the latest North Korean provocation. Although there were still vestiges of the old anti-communist state—most prominently the National Security Law that gave the government broad powers of censorship and detention of any activity that gave aid to the enemy.

South Koreans wanted the conflict to come to an end and the Korean people to be peacefully reunited. Weary of war, and with the traditional Korean disdain for the military returning, they wanted to be prosperous, secure, and able to lead lives without worrying about the renewal of conflict. They wanted to visit family graves north of the DMZ, see the half of their nation that was forbidden to them, contact long-lost relatives, take a train from Seoul to China, and stop being effectively an island not connected by land to the rest of Eurasia. They did not want to see their fellow Koreans suffer in poverty and experience repression worse than they had only recently experienced. They hoped for a change of regime, a change of heart among the northern leaders, an opening of the country to the outside world, and for gradual reform that would make North Korea more like the South and ease the transition to unification. This was the attitude of most South Koreans. There were some, especially older people, who maintained a hostile view of the North, who wanted to see communism destroyed and to bring revenge on its leadership. They made up a minority, yet were still an influential element in the nation's politics.

Meanwhile, the United States continued to be central to the conflict. For the North, their concern had become less that the Americans presented an obstacle to reunification, than that their presence made "regime change" a more viable option for Seoul and Washington. However, while posing a threat it was also useful for domestic propaganda, promoting the line that "we must be always vigilant against the imperialists on our border, and unite under our great leader." South Korea's relations with the United States were complex. Most of the older generation remained pro-U.S., distrustful of the North and cautious about their relations with China. Anti-Americanism was strong among the younger generation but when in 2003 and 2004 the U.S. announced plans to reduce the number of troops in the country by a third, public opinion polls showed that most South Koreans accepted the need for a U.S. alliance and were not enthusiastic about the withdrawals. Economic ties with America were still important, although China was gradually replacing it as the ROK's chief trading partner. The South Korean government supported the U.S. intervention in Afghanistan and in 2004 sent 3400 troops to assist the Americans in their occupation of Iraq.

Both progressives and conservatives accepted the important role of the U.S. alliance in acting as a deterrent to North Korea's aggression. Not that North Korea could win a war. By the 2000s, with its outdated planes and tanks and its undernourished soldiers, Pyongyang was not likely to defeat the ROK with its more updated and sophisticated weaponry. But a reckless action, a miscalculation in its periodic escalation of tensions or a sheer act of desperation posed a threat of enormous, catastrophic loss of life. Seoul, just 25 miles from the border and within range of thousands of well-hidden artilleries, was vulnerable to a surprise attack. Pyongyang had tens of thousands of specially trained paratroopers and commanders ready to create havoc below the DMZ should war start.

Managing to Survive: the North

In contrast to the South, the 1990s was a terrible decade. The economy deteriorated until by 1994 it was truly in crisis. Most of the country's industries were barely functioning, its modest international trade had shriveled, the cities were plunged into darkness at night and the people were hungry. Then in 1995, it got worse—chronic food shortages turned into a massive famine. The country entered what was called by its propaganda organs, "the Arduous March." Kim Jong Il openly called for international assistance. The UN World Food Program responded, as did the UN International Children's Emergency fund, some European countries, Japan, South Korea, the United States, and many private agencies. By 1997 two out of three North Koreans were being fed by the international community. Relief workers complained about being denied access to communities and being able to assess needs and directly feed people. There were suspicions that some food aid was being diverted from the people who needed it most to the military. Frustrated, some countries and agencies pulled out. Most stayed until conditions begin improving. By 2000 the worst of the famine was over. Chronic food shortages remained, just as under-nutrition had been a problem long before the famine. In fact, by the mid-nineties, the average North Korean was at least three inches shorter than their Southern counterpart, and that was before the famine stunted the growth of an entire generation of children.

Yet it was surprising that Kim Jong Il opened the country up to foreigners at all. It could not have been an easy decision to do so and to admit to such a monumental failure. Even more surprising is that he eagerly sought aid from the United States and South Korea. For South Korea, this was an opportunity to exert some leverage over the North but there was concern about aiding and propping up the regime. So, the ROK government offered limited food aid through private agencies. In 1997 it supplied 50,000 tons of food but this was only a modest portion of the aid the DPRK was receiving. However, as reports of mass suffering and starvation came over the media the Korean public began to support more massive relief. Northerners were, after all, their fellow Koreans. Additionally, Kim Dae Jung who became president in 1998 took a more generous approach than his predecessor. Restrictions on food and other aid were lifted, and South Korea became the biggest source of aid for the DPRK. The change was illustrated by the Hyundai founder and CEO Chung Ju-yung when he brought a herd of cattle to the North in June in October 1998. The well-received gesture became a symbol of the South's desire to help the northerners.

North Korea's famine led to speculation over whether the DPRK would collapse like the communist regimes in Eastern Europe or whether it would somehow transform itself into a more globally open, market-based economy like China. It did neither. The North Korean regime survived by modifying its ideology, altering the narrative it told its people, making adjustments to its economy, and keeping the elite who supported the regime happy and invested in it. These steps provided just enough changes to prop up the DPRK and its ruling elite. What did not change was the state of war between the two Koreas. Continuing the conflict became central to keeping the regime in power.

North Korea managed to avoid the fate of its allies such as Romania and Albania in part by adjusting its economy to the realities it faced. The old economic system was a total command economy in which every need of the citizens was met by the state through its public distribution system, where there were almost no markets, and the use of money was minimalized. This was replaced during and after the famine with something harder to describe. It was a sort of improvised system of state enterprises and private markets. This was not a carefully-planned change, and it came about more from below than above. Faced with the failure of the state to provide for them, millions of North Koreans had to fend for themselves. People traded, they began to grow food in their plots, and workers stripped factories of materials and sold them in China. Guards took bribes and looked the other way as people crossed into the PRC. Officials, often also hungry themselves, ceased to enforce regulations in return for food and bribes. Civilian and military units in need of revenue rented out their vehicles or turn them into means of private transportation. Private markets sprang up everywhere. By the early 2000s North Koreans were getting most of their food and necessities from them. The state reluctantly accepted all this. It legalized private markets, and it gave factory managers more independence in buying and selling raw materials and finished goods. In 2002 it switched to a money economy and began charging real prices for rents and other expenditures. Salaries, too, were raised to more realistic levels. The regime encouraged all branches of government to be creative in generating revenue. Some state firms went into the production and export of seafood, others coal and minerals, and others transportation. It was a messy and disorderly system for a state which still called itself socialist, but it worked well enough for North Koreans to muddle through.

The downside for the regime of this new mixed economy was that the state was worried about losing control over society. To prevent this, the regime periodically cracked down on entrepreneurship and set up regulations to reign in the private markets. But this was not done with any consistency. It often had to back off from its efforts in order to keep the economy functioning. An attempt to revive the public distribution system after 2007 was not very successful. There was another downside of this marketization—dependency on China. The economy relied on trade with China. The most important exports were coal, iron and other minerals, and seafood. Tens of thousands of North Koreans were employed in textile mills in Manchuria near the border and even more were employed in North Korea making textiles for Chinese companies. By the 2010s over 80 percent of all the country's external trade was with China or through China. This gave Beijing enormous leverage.

Secondly, the regime modified its ideology. It did this by retreating into ultranationalism. North and South Korea were always intensely nationalistic, it was a passionate patriotism that had driven both the development of the two states and the conflict between them. Yet in the early 1990s, the DPRK began to promote an extreme form of nationalism. Part of it seemed innocent enough, such as the revival of traditional holidays including the lunar new year and the big autumn moon festival called Chuseok. Yet it went far beyond this. In 1993, Kim Il Sung promoted the idea that Korea was the home of an ancient civilization. After complaining about his archaeologists not having discovered it, they did so. Labeled the Daedonggang Civilization it was conveniently centered on what is now Pyongyang. This "proved" that Korean civilization was not derived from China; rather it was a wholly autonomous development older than China, and as old as Egypt and Mesopotamia. They also found the grave of Dangun. Dangun was the mythical first Korean, the product of the union of a celestial deity and a she-bear who founded the first Korean state in 2333 BCE. Taught in both North and South as a myth, he was now a real historical person who had lived five thousand years ago. But Koreans were much older than this; anthropologists discovered Pithecanthropus, a million-year-old hominin, who was the direct ancestor of modern Koreans. Koreans not only had a distinct and fully independent ancient civilization; they were the product of a separate line of human evolution.

North Korean official histories presented an increasingly xenophobic racial-nationalist interpretation of the past. Korea's history was the story of maintaining the country's independence and purity in the face of foreign invaders. In this way, the narrative that the people were taught was that the country was locked in an age-old struggle to maintain its racial and cultural purity. It had been violated by the Japanese but due to the heroic efforts of the people, led by the brilliant Kim Il Sung, they had been driven out. However, half the country remained unliberated. The people of the South were not so poor, the regime tacitly admitted, but they were under the thumb of foreign imperialist oppressors. The people were humiliated, the women were violated by foreigners, and venereal diseases ran rampant. Only in the North were the Korean people still free from foreign imperialists due to the powerful KPA and the wise leadership of the Kim family, or the "Baekdu bloodline" as they were called. The Kims were portrayed as the embodiment of the purity and virtues of the race. Economic hardships were blamed on the imperialists. This argument was lent support by the series of UN sanctions that were imposed after North Korea began testing nuclear weapons. The Korean people were not portrayed as superior in any way but purer and, by implication, more virtuous and special. It was also pointed out, that the Kim family were not supermen, but good, loving leaders, tirelessly devoted to protecting their people.

The modified racial-nationalist, xenophobic narrative, incessantly reinforced by the state propaganda organs, necessitated the need for constant vigilance, endurance of hardship, and military strength. It underlined Kim Jong Il's "military first" strategy. Kim made military strength and vigilance the highest priority. In the revised 1998 constitution the National Defense Commission became the highest organ of the state. Propaganda organs reminded the people that the nation or race was engaged in an existential effort to fend off the imperialists. This interpretation of the Korean conflict served to justify the devotion of scarce resources to the military at a time when the average person struggled to survive. It led to the need for repeated demonstrations of military strength, and efforts to develop new weapons. Above all, it led to creating crises. Bouts of confrontation reinforced the notion the country was always on the brink of war, that the imperialists and the South Korean collaborators were continually making "feverish preparations" for the renewal of fighting.

A third way the North Korean regime maintained its grip on power was to make the elite happy. Ordinary people were not much of a threat. They were too cut off from alternative information to have a clear idea of their plight and the reasons for it. They were too atomized since there were no organizations of any kind other than those controlled by the state, and too busy struggling to get by to pose a threat. On the other hand, the elite of party and government officials, military officers, and scientists who knew the outside world, and had access to the levers of power had to be taken care of. No matter how short of funds, the regime imported luxury goods for them, from cognac to BMWs. They were made aware that their power, status, and privileges depended on maintaining the regime.

Key to the survival of the regime was the continuation of the Cold War with the South and its U.S. ally. The imperialist designs on North Korea were the explanation for hunger and hardship, for the Military First policy, for the populace to be vigilant against foreign and South Korean influence and subversion, and to support and obey the regime like good soldiers. Pyongyang needed conflict, it needed confrontation to support the fiction that Seoul and Washington were planning an invasion at the first opportunity. However, it also needed aid. So, it continued its pattern of creating crises and then calling for reconciliation. It seemed to outsiders irrational and unpredictable. It was neither. It was a pragmatic strategy that kept the regime in power. Aside from Cuba, it made North Korea the only communist regime that neither collapsed nor reformed.

Kim Jong Il

In 1994, North Korea entered the era of Kim Jong Il. Short and pudgy with his elevated shoes and bouffant hairdo, the eldest son of Kim Il Sung and Kim Chongsuk hardly looked the part of a leader. Appearances aside, Kim Jong Il was the unchallenged ruler of North Korea for seventeen years and had been a powerful figure in the regime for two decades before that. Everything about his early life was so embedded in the North Korean myth that it has taken scholars a great deal of hard work to put his real history together.

Officially he was born on February 16, 1942, on Baekdu Mountain at his father's guerilla headquarters. In reality, he was born in the city of Khabarovsk in Siberia in 1941. The dramatic story of entering the world on Korea's most sacred mountain is a better story than being born in a Russian military camp, but it is not clear why the year was changed. He attended the elite First Pyongyang Middle School, the First Pyongyang High School, and the most prestigious institute of higher education, Kim Il Sung University. While a college student, he initiated a campaign to read 10,000 pages a year, setting a standard that was emulated by his admiring fellow students, or so the story goes.

He was always at the center of power, accompanying his father to a Soviet Party Congress as a teenager in 1956. When he graduated from college he worked in the Organization and Guidance Department, the most powerful department in the Korean Workers Party. In the late 1960s, he moved to the wonderfully named Propaganda and Agitation Department where his work was to promote and direct the cult of his father. A person of artistic tastes and interests, he directed the April 15th Literary Promotion Group which produced novels, the Mansudae Art Troupe in charge of theatre production, and the Mansudae Art Studio which supervised the production of paintings. His first love was film, and he directed the country's film industry and even wrote a treatise on cinema. So seriously did he take filming that he kidnapped one of South Korea's best directors and one of its leading actresses and brought them to North Korea to make movies.

From about 1974, at the age of thirty-two, the younger Kim was chosen as his father's successor. But he remained out of the public eye until the Sixth Party Congress in 1980. From then on he was promoted as the successor, quickly rising to number two in the regime. From about 1983 he was referred to in the same reverent tone as his father and they were frequently depicted together. During this time, he acquired control over all the levers of government, the last being the military. He was made a Marshal in 1992 outranking all the generals, except of course his father who was promoted to Grand Marshal (or Generalissimo). His lack of any military experience was a weakness in a country that was perpetually at war. To compensate he was frequently referred to as "General Kim Jong Il" and referred to as a brilliant military strategist. At the same time, he developed a reporting system within the military that enabled him to exercise control of the top ranks. Many think he may have been behind the 1976 ax murders as well as other acts of terrorism committed by North Korea, such as the 1987 KAL bombing or even the Rangoon Incident in 1983, all to create a reputation as a bold, fearless commander. Whatever, the truth is, his seamless ascension to the top position of the country upon the sudden death of his father, testifies to the success of his father in paving the way for his oldest son's succession and Kim Jong Il's own ability at grabbing and holding the levers of power.

O Jin-u

Kim Il Sung's death and his replacement by his son Kim Jong Il was part of the passing of the original guerilla leadership and the rise of their sons (and, rarely, daughters) to power. One year after Kim Il Sung's death the military commander O Jin U died. O was born to a poor peasant family in South Gyeongsang Province in 1917. At the age of sixteen, he moved to Manchuria. There he became involved in anti-Japanese activity, joining the Manchurian communist guerillas and becoming an officer at the age of twenty-one, serving along with Kim Il Sung. After liberation, he served in the Central Security Officer School in the North and as an officer in the newly formed Korean People's Army. During the Korean War, he served as the 43rd Division Commander and led an attack on the Naktong Perimeter. After the war, he rose to top positions in the military. As one of Kim Il Sung's old guerilla comrades, he was a trusted member of the inner circle of the regime. From the 1950s he was a member of the Central Committee of the Korean Workers' Party and in the 1960s became a member of the Politburo, thus was one of both the army's and the Party's highest-ranking members.

He was one of Kim Il Sung's most trusted and loyal officials and became more so when he became an early backer of his son

Kim Jong Il as a successor. He was said to be important in persuading the other ranking military officers to support his succession. He held many positions of power including the vice-chair of the powerful National Defense Commission and he was appointed first Vice Marshal in 1985 and Marshal in 1992, making him the highest-ranking officer in the military below Kim Il Sung and later Kim Jong Il. When Kim Il Sung died, he was the second-ranking member of the funeral committee. O Jin U represented many things. The tight-knit circle of the Manchurian guerilla core of the regime, the integration of the ruling KWP and the military, and the continuity of the regime from the late 1950s when the major purges subsided. Because of the opaque nature of North Korea, we are not sure what role he played as a decision-maker. Was he responsible or did he at least play a role in the provocative actions the North carried out? We cannot be sure. He died in 1995, one year after his patron Kim Il Sung and left behind three sons, all of whom held prominent positions in the regime. Along with Kim Jong Il, they were part of North Korea's second-generation at war.

On the Verge of War and the Verge of Peace then on the Verge of War again

The first concern of the ROK, its allies, and most of the international community was to prevent the conflict from becoming a nuclear one. Kim Il Sung's death did not end the negotiations between the USA and the DPRK that had begun with Carter's visit. The two sides hammered out what was called the "Agreed Framework." This was not a treaty, since the two countries had no official relations and the U.S. policy was not to negotiate formal treaties with North Korea until the Korean War officially ended. Instead, it was a legally non-binding agreement. North Korea would remain a party to the Nuclear Non-Proliferation Treaty and its terms for international inspection. It would place its 5MW nuclear reactor, and two larger reactors it was constructing, under IAEA inspection. Pyongyang would also take seriously the Joint Declaration on Denuclearization of the Korean Peninsula it made with the ROK at the end of 1991 and adhere to it. Its spent nuclear fuel stocks would be stored and eventually disposed of and not reprocessed. Under this agreement then, its capacity to produce weapons-grade plutonium would be eliminated and its existing plutonium would be removed from harm's way. Since North Korea's nuclear reactors were ostensibly to generate electric power, in return for shutting them down two 1,000MW light water reactors were to be built as gifts by the U.S. and other outside parties. These would supply electricity but be incapable of producing weapons-grade material.

Seoul was to pick up most of the costs for the light-water reactors. But the negotiations made the South uncomfortable. Seoul was not involved in the diplomatic negotiations taking place in Geneva, but rather it was U.S. officials directly dealing with the DPRK. For several decades Pyongyang had wanted to carry out direct talks with Washington that excluded Seoul. It hoped to drive a wedge between the two allies and somehow cut a deal that would lead to an exit of U.S. troops. American policy was that the ROK would have to have a seat at the table in any talks. So, these negotiations were a reversal of this policy. President Kim Young Sam was not happy about this and almost backed away from cooperation. It took a lot of careful persuasion and reassurance of the continued commitment of the U.S. to his country's defense to get him on board.

To implement this the United States, South Korea, and Japan created in 1995 the Korean Peninsula Energy Development Organization (KEDO) to construct light-water nuclear reactors. South Korean workers would do the building, and Japan would assist with the finance. The U.S. and Japan ran into difficulties financing the project which had not been greeted with much enthusiasm by the general public in their countries. In the U.S., the Republicans in Congress blocked funding, and as a result, construction of the nuclear power plants did not get started until 2000. Even then it proceeded at a snail's pace. South Korean workers only began pouring concrete in 2002. The tardiness and delays added to Pyongyang's suspicions that Washington was never sincere, but it was using it as a tactic to keep it from getting nuclear weapons.

Kim Dae Jung and the Sunshine Policy

A new promise for eased tensions came with the election of Kim Dae Jung as president of the Republic of Korea in 1997. Kim was hated by much of the military. Both Park and Chun had attempted to murder him; he was saved both times by U.S. intervention. To some conservatives, he was a dangerous radical. Yet his election went smoothly, testifying to the general acceptance of the new democratic system. Despite what his enemies believed, Kim Dae Jung was no radical but a moderate liberal reformer. He did, however, want to break with the past when dealing with North Korea. For him, North Korea was less an existential threat than a problem, a position that was becoming increasingly common in the South. He wanted to solve the problem by what he called his "Sunshine Policy." The name comes from Aesop's fable in which the Wind and the Sun competed to see who could make a person walking along remove his coat. The Wind blew and blew but the man tightened his coat. The Sun shone and warmed the man, and he took off his coat. This then is what Kim sought to do, to make peace by reassuring the North Korean leadership that the South had no ill will toward it; he wanted to extend a hand and help it economically.

The author of this new policy, perhaps the sincerest effort to date to end the conflict, was a remarkable man. Few leaders worked harder to bring about the end of the conflict between the two Koreas than Kim Dae Jung. He lived an extraordinary life with so many near-death experiences that it is remarkable that he survived to become president at the age of 73. Born in rural Jeollanamdo Province in southwestern Korea, the second of seven children, Kim's family moved to the port of Mokpo in the same province so he could finish high school. He graduated from Mokpo Commercial High School in 1943 and worked as a clerk in a Japanese-managed shipping company. During the Korean War, he was captured by the KPA but managed to escape as it retreated. This would not be his last narrow escape.

In the 1950s Kim Dae Jung became involved in politics, running for office unsuccessfully four times before being elected to the National Assembly in 1961. It was a short-lived victory as two days later the military coup that brought Park Chung Hee to power took place and the elections were nullified. However, he won a seat in the elections of 1963 and 1967, gaining a reputation as a talented orator. He was not yet a well-known national figure when he was nominated by the main opposition party to run against Park Chung Hee in 1971. Park had presided over a decade of strong economic growth that was lifting his country out of poverty, and was facing a young, not too experienced opponent. He expected an easy re-election victory, but surprisingly Kim Dae Jung proved to be a dynamic campaigner and the election was close; it is even possible Kim won. A month after the election Kim was injured when a truck ran directly into his car. He survived but the accident left him with a limp for the rest of his life. It was suspected to be, and most likely was, an assassination attempt.

In August 1973, while in exile, he was kidnapped from a Tokyo hotel room by KCIA agents. They took him out to sea in a boat with weights tied to his legs. His life was spared at the last minute when the U.S. intervened and pressured Park to release him. He was imprisoned, which was reduced to house arrest and then with Park's assassination he emerged as a major presidential candidate, only to be arrested again. Chun Doo Hwan intended to execute Kim Dae Jung but again U.S. intervention saved him and he was allowed to go to the U.S. where he was given a position at Harvard.

Returning to Korea in 1985, he ran unsuccessfully for president in 1987 and 1992 but won on his fourth run for office in 1997. A long-time advocate for democracy, Kim Dae Jung was also an advocate for peace. Now as president he inaugurated his Sunshine Policy. After his one five-year term allotted by the South Korean constitution ended, his Sunshine policy was pursued by his friend and successor, Roh Moo-hyun. Kim died in 2009 but his political legacy lived on. One of his admirers, Moon Jae-in, became president in 2017. He saw Kim Dae Jung's attempts to create a more just democratic society at home and to end the Korean War through peaceful reconciliation as inspiration for his own efforts.

Sunshine and Clouds

In March 2000, Kim Dae Jung gave his "Berlin Declaration" in which he offered North Korea security guarantees, economic assistance, and help in supporting the DPRK internationally. The next month he announced that he would meet with Kim Jong Il for the first summit conference between the two Koreas. In June President Kim traveled to Pyongyang with an entourage of South Korean reporters. Kim Jong Il greeted him warmly and the two soon agreed to reunion visits for separated families, as well as economic, social, and cultural exchanges. Late that summer North and South Korean athletes at the Sydney Olympics marched together. South Koreans were excited; a breakthrough in relations seemed at hand. Kim Dae Jung won the Nobel Peace Prize that fall. Few knew at the time that he had offered Kim Jong Il a bribe of $500 million to hold the summit. The money came from a secret fund, raised by Chung Ju-yung, the Hyundai CEO. Even before this was revealed there were troubling signs that the summit did not herald a new tone in relations. One of the agreements was to open a rail link between the two countries. But when ROK officials came to the ceremonies to inaugurate its construction in the autumn of 2000, no North Koreans showed up. Nor did Kim Jong Il visit Seoul as he had promised.

Still, there were some other promising signs that a peaceful resolution to the Korean conflict was possible. The U.S. Secretary of State visited Pyongyang in the fall of 2000, as did Russian President Putin, and a host of EU and Chinese officials. The DPRK seemed to be opening up to the world. Relations with the U.S. were slowly improving. Then in the autumn of 2002 everything went wrong. During a visit in September 2002 by Japanese Prime Minister Koizumi, Kim Jong Il causally admitted to his government's kidnapping of Japanese citizens to use them to train their spies. This had long been suspected; now it had been admitted. When asked if they could contact the missing persons, the North Koreans explained to the Japanese that the kidnapped people were dead. When the Japanese asked if they could visit their graves, they were told that the graves had washed away in floods. The Japanese public was outraged and relations with Tokyo deteriorated. Meanwhile, the Americans found evidence that the DPRK was violating the Agreed Framework by constructing an enriched uranium plant. When U.S. envoy James Kelly, on a visit to the DPRK in October 2002, confronted North Koreans with the evidence, they casually admitted it, infuriating the Americans. The Agreed Framework was suspended. Pyongyang announced it was lifting its freeze of nuclear weapons and ordered the IAEA inspectors to leave. In January 2003 the North Koreans declared their intention of withdrawing from the Non-Proliferation of Nuclear Weapons Treaty for a second time.

Meanwhile, the Sunshine policy divided South Koreans. It was embraced by many but looked at with suspicion by others. It was a major issue in the 2002 election. North Korea hardly helped its proponents. The DPRK's continued provocations, reports that it was secretly working on nuclear weapons, its often, harsh anti-ROK rhetoric, and its poor human rights records bothered many Southerners. There were still some South Koreans who were sympathetic to the North's socialist experiment, saw Kim Il Sung as an anti-Japanese national hero, and shared the North's anti-Americanism, but their numbers were dwindling. South Koreans were well-aware that the North was no paradise. They could see the satellite photo images of the DRPK's extensive "Gulag." The reports of defectors, who began increasing in number, spoke of a regime of incredible brutality and indifference to the suffering of its people. Meanwhile, the South Korean government created a Truth and Reconciliation Committee to deal with the mass murders during the Korean War. The commission uncovered more than 1,000 executions, including 200 committed by U.S. troops. The investigations into the recent past extended far beyond the Korean War to the harsh repression of Park Chung Hee. These were, in part, signs of a maturing democracy confident enough to look at the dark spots of its past. While this demonstrated the ROK had a bloody history, and was certainly no paragon of democratic virtue, it also both reflected, and contributed to, greater outrage over the political oppression in the North. In short, South Koreans were no longer much interested in the anti-communist propaganda of the past, but they were much more sensitive to human rights abuses among their fellow Koreans in the North.

By the time Kim Dae Jung left office in early 2003, his Sunshine Policy appeared in tatters. But then North Korea agreed to join the US, South Korea, China, Japan, and Russia in a series of Six-Party Talks. Kim's successor Roh Moo-hyun, a former labor and human rights lawyer continued with the Sunshine Policy. He patiently made every effort to encourage exchanges between the two Koreas and lower the tensions but not without neglecting the country's military preparedness or its alliance with the U.S. There was some progress. The South offered food aid and free fertilizer. It conducted a very limited trade with the North. The two countries negotiated agreements on two interesting South Korean ventures: the Kaesong Industrial Complex, where South Korean businesses could build plants in North Korea and take advantage of cheap labor, and the Kumgang Mountain Resort. Roh increased aid and investment in North Korea despite receiving only mixed results for his effort.

When North Korea detonated a small nuclear device in 2006 most Southerners were frightened and angry by this blatant breach of the 1991 joint declaration to keep the peninsula nuclear-free. The pressure was also strong on Roh to insist that the DPRK allow family visits, give up its atomic weapons program, and reduce its military build-up on the border. Much of the public also wanted to make any aid or cooperation dependent on improvement in human rights. Pyongyang showed no real signs that it was willing to do any of these things. Still, Roh pressed ahead anyway and held a second summit conference with Kim Jong Il in October 2007. The two agreed on the construction of two shipyards in the North, and South Korean aid to improve the DPRK's railways with the intention of all rail traffic between the ROK and the rest of Asia passing through. The latter was attractive to the South since it would give it a direct rail link with China. They also agreed to more joint representations at international events. But little came of these agreements.

The following year Roh was succeeded by the more conservative Lee Myungbak who took a harder line. Lee represented the conservative opposition party (whose name changed so often that it is simpler just to call it the conservative party) which was supported by old-time anti-communist Cold War warriors, South Koreans of northern origin who still longed for the liberation of their home areas, and others who were skeptical and distrustful of the North. Older South Koreans, the ones who participated in or remembered the Korean War, gravitated toward the conservative party while the progressives had solid support from younger voters born after the Korean War.

Lee Myungbak, however, was not an old-time anti-communist crusader but had a sort of "Sunshine Policy" of his own. Lee was critical of the large but poorly-monitored aid his country was supplying and the DPRK's lack of significant political, economic, and social reform. Like many in the South, he wondered if the ROK's generous aid was simply propping up the northern regime and disincentivizing it to reform. In the spring of 2008, Lee's administration began insisting on the same monitoring procedures that the UN World Food Program required. North Korea responded angrily, canceling military agreements and ratcheting up tensions along the peninsula. It threatened to shut down the complex at Kaesong even though this would hurt the North more than the South, and it began ordering South Korean businessmen to leave the country. However, Lee countered with a plan of his own he called "Vision 3000" aimed at developing the North Korean economy and helping it achieve a growth rate of 10 percent a year for a decade, so that it would reach a GDP per capita of $3,000. This would be done by targeting aid toward industrial, infrastructure, and educational development, and carrying out financial reforms which would be financed by an international aid fund. Aid from this fund would be tied to political and economic reforms. At the minimum, Lee insisted that North Korea adhere to its 1991 agreement with the ROK for a denuclearized peninsula. In other words, aid would be on the condition of the DPRK abandoning its nuclear program.

Kumgang Mountain Resort

On July 11, 2008, the same day as Lee made his proposal before the South Korean National Assembly, a South Korean woman was shot at the Kumgang Mountain Resort. The Kumgang Mountain Tourist Resort was one of the symbols of the Sunshine Policy. The Kumgang ("Diamond") Mountains have long been famed among Koreans as one of their country's great places of beauty. Joseon artists loved to paint them. They lie along the east coast just north of the DMZ. In 1998 North Korea, as an experiment, allowed a few foreign tourists, including some South Koreans, to visit them. This was the first time any South Korean tourists had ever been allowed in the DPRK. In 2002 the area was made a 200 square mile (500 square km) special tourist zone. Chung Ju-yung's Hyundai Asan company was given a 30-year contract to develop a resort in the region. A road was built through the DMZ so that South Korean tourists could take buses, although some came by boat. The resort was enormously popular with South Koreans. In 2007 it had 1.7 million visitors almost all from the ROK. It was a rare opportunity to visit the North and see one of the country's most beautiful areas.

It was not a place to mingle with the North Korean people. The area was strictly cordoned off from the rest of the country with armed guards making sure no one strayed far from the resort. Many of the staff were South Koreans working for Hyundai Asan. There was little interaction between Northerners and Southerners. On July 11, 2008, a 53-year-old South Korean tourist, Park Wang-ja wandered a bit too far into the military restricted area. She was shot and killed by North Korean security personnel. North Koreans claimed she had been running and refused to heed warnings to stop. However, South Korean forensic experts said she was either standing still or moving very slowly when shot. Seoul requested an inquiry into the incident which the North refused. Pyongyang's unapologetic stance, its contradictory reports of the incident, and refusal to cooperate infuriated the South Korean government which suspended tours to the resort. In August 2008 North Korea began expelling South Korean workers. The resort closed; a sad testament to the difficulty of overcoming the suspicions and hostility between the two Koreas.

North Korea and the Politics of Survival

By the early 2000s, the Korean conflict had increasingly been centered on the problem of what to do about the belligerent regime in North Korea. But for South Korea and its allies, the difficulty was that while emerging from the famine, North Korea's actions seemed more contradictory than ever. This was because the leaders in Pyongyang faced a dilemma. The regime needed the assistance that South Korea, the U.S., Japan, and their allies could offer. This involved not just food but ways to earn foreign exchange through tourism and trade, and to acquire modern technology. Yet it needed to maintain the information cordon, since too much exposure to the outside world, and especially to South Korea, could cause the regime to unravel. What if the people of North Korea found out just how miserable they were compared to the South? They also needed conflict, to maintain the air of constant military preparedness and the periodical crises to maintain the fiction that the country's problems were caused by aggressive imperialists and South Korean collaborators and that only the leadership and its armed forces were keeping them at bay. Hence the seemingly contradictory actions: periods of talks of exchange and cooperation, followed by sudden reversals to harsher rhetoric and manufactured crisis. Then there were the occasional terrorist attacks that measured the American and South Korean responses to provocation. Internal politics within the regime played a role in these acts of belligerency with Kim Jong Il, and later his son and successor Kim Jong Un, needing to demonstrate to their generals and other members of the elite their military prowess, their toughness, and courage.

Pyongyang's survival tactics included receiving as much aid from South Korea and the United States as possible. This meant making gestures at reconciliation. Pyongyang also needed the support of China without getting so close that its sovereignty would be threatened. So, while it seemed irrational and erratic, the regime's behavior was rational and consistent within its logic of survival, even if crudely and often clumsily executed. Therefore, North Korea continued its provocations. In 1998 a North Korean mini-submarine retrieving an infiltration team got tangled in the net of a South Korean trawler; the body of an infiltrator washed up later. On June 7, 1999, a naval clash took place when North Korean naval vessels escorted a fleet of fishing vessels into South Korean waters. One North Korean ship was destroyed. North Korea posed a dilemma for Seoul and its allies. No one wanted to start a war but the problem of containing the threat from North Korea remained. To work together to combat Pyongyang's belligerence, the U.S., South Korea, and Japan created the trilateral Coordination and Oversight Group in 1999. They could share intelligence and coordinate efforts to deal with North Korea, but Seoul, Washington, and Tokyo never came up with an effective strategy to actually deal with Pyongyang.

As part of its survival tactics, North Korea became an outlaw state, a criminal enterprise. Always chronically short of foreign exchange, the regime looked for any means to create it. It needed foreign exchange to purchase machines and weapons parts it couldn't make, and to buy luxury goods to keep the elite happy but produced little that anyone wanted to buy. It tried to solve this problem partly through criminal activity. In the late 1970s, it created Office 39 to find ways of earning income. This included producing and export-ing opioids and amphetamines, counterfeiting US dollars, as well as cigarettes and other products. It included sex trafficking, defrauding Lloyds of London out of hundreds of millions of dollars in false claims, and cyber theft. It is hard to think of a single illegal activ-ity that the regime was not engaged in. The DPRK had become a country that did not play by international norms.

One of the reasons Pyongyang needed foreign exchange was to import items that were needed for another key part of its survival tactics: developing nuclear weapons. Kim Jong Il became convinced that nuclear weapons were essential to the security of the DPRK. The American invasion of Iraq in 2003 only reinforced this. Despite all its agreements and promises, it worked continuously to devel-op nuclear weapons. In addition to its work on nuclear weapons, North Korea worked on missiles that could someday deliver them. In May 1993 it tested a Rodong-1 missile. The Rodong-1 was a sin-gle-stage rocket fashioned from the Soviet SS-1 (popularly called the "Scud") missile. North Korea had long sought to acquire these, but as the Soviet Union did not oblige, it managed to buy some from Egypt and reverse engineered its own copy. It had a range of 1,000–1300km—enough to reach anywhere in South Korea, and could carry a payload of up to 750kg. It was too inaccurate to be much used as a tactical weapon, so the worry in Seoul and Washing-ton is that it could be used to deliver biological, chemical, or small nuclear weapons, as well as simply to spread terror. The Japanese too were alarmed, especially when a missile was test-fired into the Sea of Japan (or East Sea as the Koreans call it) in the direction of the Japanese main island of Honshu. North Korea test-fired seven of these missiles on July 4, 1999. It is unlikely that this being the U.S. Independence Day was a coincidence.

Missiles also became lucrative export items. The DPRK sold them to Libya, Syria, Iran, and Pakistan. They became the basis of Pakistan's Ghauri and Iran's Shahab-3 missiles. In August 1998 the DPRK test-fired a Taepodong 1 medium-range missile that flew over Japan and crashed into the Pacific Ocean 1,500km away. It might have been a failed attempt to launch a satellite. Whether it was or not, the implication was clear, North Korea now could threaten not only South Korea but also Japan. The provocative trajectory emphasized that point. As Seoul and Washington expected, Pyongyang had no intention of stopping its development of missiles until it could develop a long-range rocket capable of reaching the American mainland.

But it was nuclear weapons that kept South Korean, American, and Japanese policymakers up at night. The U.S. had repeatedly warned Pyongyang it would not accept DPRK as a nuclear power. It could not tolerate such an opaque regime, with its aggressive rhetoric of reunification, its disregard for international norms of behavior, and its history of violent and unexpected provocations having nuclear weapons. Officials feared it could set off a nuclear arms race in the region and even the thought that this endless conflict on the Peninsula could become a nuclear one was worth preventing the North from developing weapons. Then there was the fear that Pyongyang could sell its weapons or weapons-making technology to Iran, Libya Syria, or anyone that would pay hard currency, just as it was doing with its missiles. This was a real possibility confirmed by a nuclear facility the North Koreans were helping Syria construct until it was destroyed by an Israeli airstrike in September 2007.

President Clinton warned Pyongyang against developing A-bombs stating that testing a nuclear weapon would be "crossing a red line." On October 9, 2006, the DPRK crossed it when it tested one. This was a very small explosion, suggesting that it might have misfired. Nonetheless, it had the intended effect of making the country a nuclear power. The test violated its 1991 agreement with South Korea, and it outraged China and much of the international community. Foreigners were puzzled at how a country that could not feed its people could have so callously devoted resources to this project. Yet Pyongyang faced no real serious repercussions. Instead of retaliation, the U.S. along with South Korea, China, Japan, and Russia continued the Six-Party talks. During these talks, the U.S.

showed more willingness to meet the DPRK bilaterally, which is what the DPRK had always preferred: one-on-one talks with Washington. South Korea's President Roh Moo-hyun responded by coming to Pyongyang to meet with Kim Jong Il and making various agreements, including a continual flow of aid. North Korea suffered no ill consequences.

North Korea then shifted to a more conciliatory tack, agreeing to shut down the nuclear reactor at Yongbyon and to permit IAEA inspectors to return. Pyongyang also agreed to "disable" all nuclear facilities and give a full account of all its nuclear programs. Washington agreed to unfreeze assets held by the Banco Delta Asia in Macau through which the regime laundered money gained from illicit activities. It also agreed to supply heavy fuel oil and to move toward normalization. In the fall of 2007, North Korea promised not to transfer nuclear materials, weapons, or weapons-making knowledge. In turn, the U.S. hinted at taking the country off the state sponsors of terrorism list. Pyongyang allowed IAEA inspectors to return, and in 2008 the main nuclear cooling tower was destroyed.

All this was a façade; Pyongyang clandestinely continued to work on developing weapons of mass destruction. On April 5, 2009, North Korea sent a multi-stage rocket over Japan before it crashed into the sea. The next month, on May 25, it detonated another much larger nuclear bomb, although still smaller than that of Hiroshima or Nagasaki. This time the international reaction was much stronger. China and Russia joined South Korea, the U.S., and Japan in strongly condemning the nuclear test. On June 12, 2009, the UN Security Council passed Resolution 1874. This imposed serious economic and commercial sanctions on the DPRK. It also authorized UN members to stop, search and destroy, on the land, sea, and in the air, any transport suspected of supplying or aiding the DPRK's nuclear program.

The UN sanctions, supported by the South Korean government now headed by skeptics of the Sunshine policy, were rather toothless. They were designed to make it difficult for North Korea to import materials needed for its nuclear and missile programs followed by further restrictions on the import of luxury items for the elite. However, more than three-quarters of the country's imports came through China, which paid lip-service to the sanctions but did not enforce them. China feared the collapse of North Korea if the economic sanctions were too severe, a scenario that would mean chaos on its border and a wave of desperate refugees flooding its northeast provinces, and it did not like the prospect of a unified democratic Korea allied with the U.S. and Japan on its border. As a result, the UN actions did little to deter the North Koreans from continuing with their development of weapons of mass destruction.

In 2009 an incident occurred that revealed something of North Korea and the state of the conflict on the peninsula. In March of that year two American journalists, who had allegedly crossed into the DPRK when making a documentary about the trafficking of North Korean women, were arrested and tried as spies. Pyongyang was, in effect, holding them hostage. Former President Bill Clinton came to secure their release. He met Kim Jong Il in Pyongyang. Although Washington denied it, the North Korean officials claimed he was bringing an official message to Kim. Following the meeting, Kim Jong Il granted a pardon to the two journalists. What was significant about the incident was the photo Pyongyang released. It showed a proud Kim Jong Il seated next to Clinton. In the background was a huge painting of stormy waves crashing against a rock. It was a symbol, easy for Korean audiences in North and South to decode—the defiant resistance of the DPRK in the face of imperialist aggressors. Pyongyang was making clear to its people that it had stood up to the imperialist aggressors and signaling its fellow Koreans in the South that it was strong, proud, and would not bend under pressure.

During 2008 and 2009 North and South relations reached a low not seen since the 1990s famine. North Korean rhetoric was especially strident. In late 2009 Kim Jong Il began to move toward improving relations. Talks in Singapore hinted at a third summit conference. There were also discussions of the return of South Korean abductees from the Korean War and captured ROK soldiers, in exchange for cash payments or aid. Lee Myungbak, however, lost interest in a third summit that did not promise much in the way of benefits and could subject him to criticisms from conservatives. South Korea was now a supporter of sanctions, but Seoul still held out some hope of friendly, or at least less hostile, relations. It was the conviction of most Southerners that economic reform might lead to political reform. But North Korea was not showing much inclination for either. Nonetheless, some in Seoul still thought there could be some dialogue and continued efforts could nudge North Korea toward economic reform and more openness. Then in 2010, two provocative developments led to anger and impatience with the North. On March 26 the South Korean ship Cheonan was sunk, and 46 ROK sailors were killed. A subsequent investigation indicated that it was most likely to have been destroyed by a North Korean torpedo. As the evidence of this emerged, the public in the ROK was outraged at such reckless action. Then on November 23, the North Koreans carried out an even more dangerous provocation— the shelling of the South Korean island of Yeonpyeongdo.

Yeonpyeongdo

Fifty miles (80km) west of Incheon is a group of islands known as Yeonpyeongdo, in the Yellow Sea. Only 7.5 miles (12km) from the coast of Hwanghaedo province, they are much closer to North Korea than to mainland South Korea. The tiny group of islands consists of Big Yeonpyeongdo which is about 2.7 square miles (7 square km) and six smaller islets. About 1,300 people live on Yeonpyeongdo. Most of the permanent population is there because of the rich fisheries that surround the islands, especially its crab fishery.

The islands lie just below the Northern Limit Line (NLL). This was created by the U.S. in 1953 to delineate the maritime boundaries between the two Koreas. It has no standing in international law and was never recognized by the DPRK, but for decades it had been generally respected by both sides. However, from 1973 North Korea began challenging this by sending fishing vessels over it, where they would be chased back by ROK patrol boats. Later North Korea became more strident in its criticisms of the NLL and insisted that Yeonpyeongdo, was in its territory. On Jun 7, 1999, a fleet of fishing vessels sailed toward Yeonpyeongdo, escorted by North Korean naval ships. Eight days later this led to a naval clash in which one North Korean naval ship was destroyed and several others damaged.

Eleven years later Yeonpyeongdo again became the scene of a military clash, this one even more dangerous. In November 2010 South Korea announced that it would be carrying out an artillery exercise. North Korea warned of a "resolute physical counter-strike" if the South did not cancel it, but the threat was not taken seriously. The exercise took place as planned on November 23. In the mid-afternoon, not long after it ended, North Korea began firing howitzers. About 170 shells landed on the main island over the next hour. Two South Korean marines and two civilians who had been working at the military posts were killed. Several marines and some civilians were injured. A black cloud of smoke could be seen rising from the island from a long distance away. All but 100 residents were evacuated by ferry to Incheon. Not since the Korean War had North Korea rained artillery fire on a South Korean settlement. A second exercise was carried out by the ROK the next month but North Korea did not retaliate.

Yeonpyeongdo was different from other similar provocations. It was not an attack of stealth such as the Cheonan incident or most other provocations, but a brazen attack on a civilian population. The South Korean public was outraged in a way that hadn't been seen in years. Resisting pressure from many sectors of society, the government acted with restraint, although it did consider a strike on North Korean territory. As for the residents of Yeonpyeongdo, some 80 percent returned, and the crab fishing continued. Most islanders expressed the determination to stay on the island no matter what. Living in a country that had endured the constant threats of war and bouts of terrible violence, they were still willing to take that risk.

CHAPTER 9

The Third Generation

By the 2010s the third generation in the Korean conflict was coming to dominate North and South Korea. The first Korean conflict generation was shaped by the Japanese colonial rule, and the second by the 1950–1953 "hot" Korean War and its aftermath. The third generation, with no memory of either, now took power. There was hope that this new generation could bring the Korean conflict, which began before they were born, to an end. Unfortunately, that did not happen.

The Third Generation in North Korea

In 2008 Kim Jong Il fell ill. Nothing was officially announced. He merely disappeared for a while and reappeared looking much thinner, weaker, and displaying signs of someone who had suffered a stroke. The "Dear Leader" of North Korea began grooming a successor. His entire state had been built around the cult of the Kim Il Sung family, so it was only natural that the leadership stay within the family. Kim Jong Il's eldest son Kim Jong Nam, whose mother was the actress Song Hye Rim, would have been the logical choice. However, the fun-loving Jong Nam was not leadership material. He had, among other things, embarrassed his father when he was caught trying to sneak into Japan to visit Tokyo Disneyland with a false passport. Kim Jong Il's second son, born to the dancer Ko Yong Hee, was more interested in music than politics and judged by his father as too soft to lead the nation. His youngest son by the same dancer, Kim Jong Un, however, was the favorite. His father saw him as tough, ruthless, and capable. The problem was he was very young—just in his mid-twenties with little experience.

Nonetheless, Kim Jong Il began preparing the way for his youngest to be his successor. In 2009, schoolchildren were taught to sing the praises of the "young marshal" who was never named. The following year Kim Jong Un began appearing in public with his father. In the summer of 2010, he was given a series of promotions: he was appointed vice-chair of the National Defense Commission, became a high-ranking member of the Korean Workers' Party, and was made a four-star general. The media began referring to him as the "brilliant comrade." All this was not a moment too soon because in December 2011, Kim Jong Il suffered a fatal stroke.

The ascension of Kim Jong Un held the promise of a final solution to the Korean conflict. The young leader was Western-educated, having attended secondary school in Switzerland. He was young, of a new generation, not shaped by the trauma of the division, the Korean War, or the Cold War. He moved away from his father's military-first policy, appointed fewer military men to key positions, and promoted more officials with technical expertise to top ranks. He was different from his predecessors; certainly from his dour, semi-reclusive father. He was outgoing, and affable, and appeared in public with his wife, a fashionably-dressed singer. They were shown acting affectionately, something no previous leader would have permitted. He attended, and applauded at, pop concerts, and clowned around at amusement parks and other venues. In July 2012 Kim Jong Un appeared on television at a concert with characters such as Mickey Mouse and Winnie-the-Pooh, dancing on the stage before them. Women were given permission to wear shorter skirts and the elite in Pyongyang began dressing more fashionably. The first films were released that contained no overt propaganda but were just romances. Kim Jong Un implemented some economic reforms such as giving farmers sizeable family plots, allowing them to sell a larger share of the collective farm's output on the private markets and permitting factory managers more freedom to buy and sell materials and finished goods. These reforms helped the economy somewhat and were cause for early hopes by outsiders that North Korea would finally undertake the market reforms seen in China and Vietnam years earlier. However, this did not happen.

It didn't take too long for Kim to show the ruthlessness that had won his father's heart. In 2012 and 2013 he began removing high-ranking officials left over from his father's regime. In December 2013 he had his uncle, Chang Taek Sang, who was married to his father's sister, publicly arrested, and shown on television being dragged out of a meeting. A few days later, Chang was executed by an anti-aircraft gun that blew his body to bits. The account was further embellished by rumors of dogs eating the scraps that were left of him. This was a break from the past. Kim Il Sung and Kim Jong Il did not execute members of their own families and no high-ranking official had been publicly arrested or humiliated since the show trials of the 1950s.

Even more shocking was the incident at the Kuala Lumpur airport on February 13, 2017. Kim Jong Un's older half-brother Kim Jong Nam lived in self-imposed exile in China, not out of protest but just to be out of the family business. He spent a lot of his time at the gambling tables in Macau. His interests besides gambling were wine, women, and song. He was traveling to the Malaysian resort island of Langkawi when, at the Kuala Lumpur airport, two attractive-looking women, an Indonesian and a Vietnamese, came up to him and placed a poison-soaked cloth over his face. It was the internationally banned, highly toxic nerve agent VX. They later claimed they thought it was just a prank for TV, and they might have been telling the truth. If so, they were unaware they were being used by North Korean agents to carry out an assassination. Kim died within a few minutes. Since Kim Jong Nam was Kim Jong Un's older brother and thought to be apolitical, it was puzzling. A few years later it was revealed that Kim Jong Nam was providing information to the CIA in exchange for cash. That Kim Jong Un murdered a close blood relative (something that had never happened before), someone who was protected by China, and that he would do it so publicly was shocking. It sent a chilling message: that no one among the elite who fell out with the regime or threatened it in any way was safe.

Furthermore, rather than loosening government restrictions on North Korean citizens, Kim Jong Un tightened security. He carried out a crackdown on illegal crossings into China, dispatching thousands of troops to the border until the small flow of refugees nearly dried up. He carried out another crackdown on South Korean videos, CDs, and DVDs that were regularly smuggled into the country. Under his leadership, instead of opening up to the world as many in the South had hoped, the DPRK became even more closed. Most tragically for those who hoped for an end to the Korean conflict, rather than ease tensions, Kim Jong Un worked hard to create them and perpetuate the state of war that justified the regime's tight control over society and served to insulate the people from knowledge of the outside world and influences from the South.

Generational Shifts in the South

If 2011–12 marked a generational shift in leadership in North Korea, it marked a generational split in South Korea. As President Lee Myungbaek was finishing his five-year term in 2012, his conservative Grand National Party nominated Park Geun-hye as their candidate. Park was the daughter of the former authoritarian president Park Chung Hee. She had an unusual history. Born in 1952 during the Korean War she was sent to Europe for schooling. Park Geun-hye returned to South Korea when her mother was shot and killed in the 1974 assassination attempt on her father. For five years she played a first lady-like role and had won the sympathy of most South Koreans. Then, when her father was assassinated by his intelligence chief, she withdrew from the public. Never married, Miss Park entered politics years later when elected to the National Assembly. In 2007 she unsuccessfully sought to become her party's candidate, but succeeded five years later. More than three decades after her father's death, many older Koreans looked back on his era with nostalgia, a time when the economy was booming. The opposition Minju (Democratic) Party nominated Moon Jae-in, a former civil rights lawyer and the late President Roh Moo-hyun's chief of staff. Moon was born in 1953, just months before the end of the war, a son of North Korean refugees. Moon's father had been an official in the agricultural department of the DPRK. During the Korean War, his family fled the port of Hungnam on a U.S. naval vessel, moving to Busan. The younger Moon became an anti-government student activist during the Park era and an anti-government lawyer during the Chun era, working with the future president Roh Moo-hyun.

Among Park Geun-hye's supporters, anti-communism was still strong. North Korea was still the enemy, no longer feared as a competitor but still an ever-present threat to national security and the obstacle to national reunification. They took a hard line on Korea and saw the Sunshine Policy as a dangerous failure. Moon and his supporters, on the other hand, saw anti-communist rhetoric as an excuse for internal suppression of human rights, and hardline policies toward the North as counterproductive. Moon himself believed in engaging with North Korea not confronting it. There was little age difference, Park was sixty and Moon fifty-nine, and they were both offspring of fathers who had opposed the communists and whose lives were profoundly shaped by the Korean War. But their followers represented different generations. Park's support came from voters over the age of fifty that overwhelmingly supported her and distrusted the "appeasement" policies of the liberal party. Moon's support came mainly from those under forty. With those in their forties more evenly divided but favoring Moon, Park narrowly won the election.

The 2012 election made clear the generational split over how to deal with North Korea. But the main concern of voters and the newly elected president was not the ongoing conflict, but economic and social issues. South Koreans were concerned about the slowing rate of economic growth, an almost inevitable result of a country that was entering the stage of a mature developed nation, and with issues such as creating a social safety net, gender equity, and the cost of housing. For Southerners, North Korea was something of an intractable problem. And for all the divisions over how to deal with the North, there still was a consensus on many aspects of foreign policy. Most South Koreans supported the U.S. alliance and accepted the need for the continual presence of U.S. troops as a deterrent to Northern aggression and a sign of American commitment to the country's defense. They supported maintaining good, if cautious, relations with China which had replaced the U.S. as the country's largest trading partner, and they remained suspicious and resentful of Japan. Tokyo and Seoul were uneasy allies. Most South Koreans accepted the necessity of military conscription although the terms had been shortened slightly and every government maintained the National Security Law that could still jail those who were deemed as aiding the enemy. The presence of North Korean spies and the threat of terrorist attacks kept tensions alive, and although some South Koreans wished the conflict and perhaps the DPRK itself would go away, they had to deal with its reality.

Renewed Confrontation: 2013

While the international community and many in the South hoped the new leadership in the North would bring about a change in foreign policy, what they soon found was continuity. Quiet negotiations in Beijing between U.S. and DPRK officials that began toward the end of Kim Jong Il's rule continued. On February 29, 2012, a breakthrough was announced. Under the "leap year agreement" North Korea would halt its nuclear program, open its nuclear facilities to international inspections, refrain from missile tests and agree to return to the six-party talks. The conservative Yi Myungbak administration remained distrustful of any agreement with the North but there was hope in Washington. In return, the Obama administration promised to supply the DPRK with 240,000 tons of nutritionally rich foodstuffs such as biscuits. These special foods would alleviate the food shortage and would avoid the problem of monitoring where the food aid went since there was little market value for these foods and they would not be coveted by the elite as rice would be. The agreement was a verbal one, subject to somewhat different interpretations by the two sides. Still, it was considered a promising turning point, at least by the Americans. Seoul was more cautious. While ostensibly relations between Seoul and Washington were smooth, there were underlying differences between the Yi Myungbak and Obama administrations with Obama more open to diplomacy and Yi more concerned with seeing real change in the North first than with negotiations.

Almost immediately Pyongyang violated the "leap year agreement." Hellbent on celebrating the centennial of Kim Il Sung's birth on April 15, 2012, Pyongyang planned to launch a satellite from a multi-stage rocket built for the occasion and called "Brilliant Star"—one of the names for Kim Jong Un's grandfather. Billed as a demonstration of the DPRK's technical achievements for civilian purposes, the fact that it could have a range that reached parts of the U.S. was an obvious point. And in an unprecedented move, Kim invited journalists from the U.S., Japan, Britain, France, South Africa, and Brazil to witness this achievement. The missile was, for unknown reasons, launched two days before the birthday on Friday, April 13. It proved to be an unlucky day for Pyongyang when the rocket disintegrated 90 seconds after takeoff. Seoul seemed to have been proven right: the new leader could not be trusted.

The following year, Kim Jong Un decided to create another crisis to continue the siege mentality that had long served the regime well. On February 12, North Korea conducted its third nuclear test. This was just a prelude to the crisis of the following month. In March of 2013, ROK and U.S. forces began one of their joint military exercises. Both militaries considered these essential to the carrying out of a coordinated response. They were regularly scheduled, routine, and announced in advance. Every year Pyongyang protested in a sort of pro forma way. This time Pyongyang heated the rhetoric to new levels, threatening to launch a preemptive attack if they were carried out. The exercises went ahead. Then the North canceled a non-aggression pact it had signed with the South, although this was not taken very seriously. North Korea closed its border to the tiny amount of traffic between the two countries, which mainly consisted of South Korean managers going to the Kaesong Industrial Complex. It then announced that was it unilaterally canceling the 1953 Armistice. It cut the hotline with Seoul, and on March 30 North Korea publicly announced it was in "a state of war" with South Korea. Its propaganda organs went beyond the routine provocative statements of the past, declaring it might "exercise the right to launch a preemptive nuclear strike to destroy strongholds of the aggressors." Propaganda videos showing its missiles destroying American cities and Obama in flames became internet hits. It also closed the Kaesong Industrial Complex. Even veteran Pyongyang watchers were startled by the viciousness of the propaganda and some of the extreme actions that were being taken. Even blasé South Koreans used to hearing the "crazy" regime to the north banging its war drums began to get nervous. Yet it was a wholly manufactured deceptive crisis. ROK and American intelligence officials detected no sign of troop movements or war preparations. Foreigners in Pyongyang reported seeing some soldiers in the city but they were planting flowers in preparation for Kim Il Sung's birthday celebrations.

On May 18 and 19 Pyongyang fired four short-range rockets into the waters off its coast. Then it switched gears. In June, dialogue between the North and South began, and in September the Kaesong Industrial Complex reopened and things returned to normal, or what was now accepted as normal on the peninsula.

2017—Crisis Yet Again

In May 2016, Kim Jong Il held the Seventh Congress of the Korean Workers' Party. It was the first party congress since 1980, the one where his father Kim Jong Il had made his public debut. Observers waited to see what this interesting development meant—would it signal a move away from confrontation toward economic reform and peaceful trade? There were a few promising signs. The National Defense Commission, the state's highest administrative body, was renamed the Commission for State Affairs. A new Five-Year Economic Development Plan, the first in decades, was announced. Significantly the Military First Policy, which had in practice been abandoned, was replaced by a revival of Kim Il Sung's "Equal Emphasis Policy." This meant that the regime was giving equal priority to economic and military development. All signs suggested that Kim was shifting focus toward improving his country's economy. However, if those in Seoul were hoping for more openness they were disheartened when Kim Jong Un denounced the "filthy wind of bourgeois liberty and 'reform' and 'openness,'" declaring, "we will advance according to the path of socialism that we have chosen." Furthermore, in the following year, it appeared that if the new policy was "equal emphasis" military development was more equal than economic development.

Weapons development was pursued with new vigor. North Korea had never stopped its nuclear weapons program. In January 2016, it conducted its fourth nuclear test at Punggye-ri in the rugged northeast. It claimed it was a hydrogen bomb, but no one believed that it was; the yield was too small and there were doubts by foreign experts that the DPRK had reached that level of technological sophistication. In September it detonated a fifth weapon. Both were denounced by the South and the international community and were followed by new UN sanctions that did little to deter Pyongyang. Then missile development took a quantum leap with a successful test of an intercontinental ballistic missile capable of reaching Alaska, launched provocatively on July 4, 2017. A second successful test of a missile capable of reaching most of the continental USA took place three weeks later on July 28. These two missiles brought the Korean conflict back to the forefront of American national security concerns and the attention of the world. Maps appeared in Western newspapers showing the reach of these missiles across North America and Europe. On August 29 and September 15, 2017, it became Japan's turn to be threatened when Pyongyang fired two missiles across that country.

The use these missiles could be put to was demonstrated on September 9, 2017, when another atomic bomb was tested. This was a far more powerful explosion than previous ones, so powerful it could be felt in parts of China and Siberia. It actually moved Mount Muntap, which partly caved in from the force of the detonation in a tunnel at its base. These tests were accompanied by an extraordinary exchange of public insults between Kim Jong Un and American president Donald Trump. Trump threatened to counter these

The Range of North Korea's Missiles

North Korea is developing ICMBs
with the potential to reach
the U.S. East Coast

SOURCE : The James Martin Center
for Nonproliferation Studies

TROY GRIGGS/ THE NEW YORK TIMES

provocations with "fire and fury" to "totally destroy" the DPRK. Kim called Trump a "dotard," and remained defiant. In a television address to his people, he responded to the threat of annihilation from the American president by stating he too had a button to press if necessary to protect the nation. The world watched nervously as the two volatile and unpredictable leaders threatened each other.

2018: Peace at Last?

Meanwhile, dramatic events were happening in the South. Park Geun-hye could have been celebrated as the first woman to hold the powerful office of president, a milestone in the still male-dominated society, but instead, she became a national embarrassment. In 2014 when a horrific ferry accident led to the deaths of over 200 school children, she not only did not respond but did not even appear in public. Then came the scandals. She trusted few people, but one she did trust was Choi Soon-il, the daughter of a shamanistic cult leader Choi Tae-min. His was one of the many strange religious cults that arose during the unsettling years after 1945. Choi declared himself a Buddha at one point, then appropriated the trappings of Christianity, but was best characterized as a charlatan who took advantage of Park Geun-hye by providing her with solace in the days after her mother's assassination. His daughter Choi Soon-il became Park's closest confidant and advisor. The corrupt and un-qualified Choi was given access to classified documents and used her influence over the president for personal gain. She created two foundations that were massive influence-peddling schemes. Almost every major business had to contribute to gain access to the presi-dent. Gradually the press began to reveal the extent of corruption while Park remained remote, isolated, and did nothing. It was clear to the vast majority of South Koreans that she was unfit for the job. Her own party began to dissociate itself from her. Massive daily candlelit protests calling for Park's resignation took place and her approval ratings fell to single digits and then to almost zero. The National Assembly voted to impeach and remove her from office; special elections were held in early May.

With the conservatives in disarray, Moon Jae-in won the presidency handily. The "Sunshine Policy" faction was now back in power after a decade and the geopolitical landscape shifted once more. It was bad timing for Moon since Kim Jong Un was busy alienating the international community, including all of Seoul's allies. Undeterred, the new president was determined to be the South Korean leader to bring the conflict to an end. However, public opinion in the ROK was becoming increasingly impatient and hostile to the North. The hopes for change were diminishing. Moon had little choice but to emphasize his country's military preparedness while hoping for an opportunity to restart talks. In fact, in 2017, public opinion in South Korea was shifting so much that one poll showed that 60 percent wanted the ROK to develop its own nuclear weapons, and 70 percent wanted the U.S. to redeploy its tactical nuclear weapons in the country. This was a dramatic reversal from the previous aversion to nuclear weapons. South Korea was in a good position to become a nuclear power. It had twenty-four nuclear reactors and a large stockpile of nuclear material, enough by some estimates for several thousand bombs and the technical expertise to build them. But Moon remained adamantly against going nuclear.

Winter-Warming: from the Pyeongchang Olympics to Summitry

In 2011 Seoul was selected by the International Olympic Commission to host the Olympics again—this time the 2018 Winter Games at the resort of Pyeongchang. South Korea had changed a lot since it had hosted a summer Olympics three decades earlier. It was now a fully-fledged First World country, a thriving democracy, and unlike, the 1980s when few were wealthy enough to go skiing, winter sports were now popular. But one thing that had not changed was the concerns about hosting the games on the volatile peninsula. As in 1988, there were worries that North Korea would try to disrupt the event. Pyongyang's nuclear tests and missile tests, and the threat of conflict between the U.S. and the DPRK were a major cause of concern, and some countries including France, Germany, and Austria even threatened to pull out in late 2017. Even the U.S. ambassador to the UN, Nikki Haley, suggested that her country might have to reconsider participation. Then on January 1, 2018, Kim Jong Un in his annual New Year's televised address to the nation announced that he wished South Korea well with the Winter Olympics it was hosting and proposed talks on the DPRK's participation. For President Moon, this was the opportunity he was seeking. A possible breakthrough to end the Cold War with the North. On January 17, 2018, the two sides agreed to field a unified Korean women's ice hockey team and to enter together under a Korean Unification Flag during the opening ceremony.

For Moon, the Olympic organizers, and for the more liberal South Koreans, this was an exciting development. But not everyone in the South was happy. Conservatives feared that this would ease pressure on North Korea, and they feared an overly-eager Moon would give concessions to the North with little in the way of progress toward denuclearization and improvement on human rights to show for it. Critics called it the "Pyongyang Olympics." Tokyo shared similar concerns, as did the Trump administration. The games took place from February 9 to February 25, 2018. When Vice President Mike Pence went to Pyeongchang to attend the games, he met with the father of Otto Warmbier, a University of Virginia student who was arrested while on a tour of the DPRK, and who died shortly after his release, from injuries inflicted by his captors. Pence also met with North Korean defectors, but not the North Koreans. Moon, however, warmly shook the hand of Kim Yo Jong, younger sister of Kim Jong Un, who led the North Korean delegation. At the opening ceremony, Kim sat near Mike Pence who studiously ignored her. The presence of General Kim Yong-chol at the closing ceremony infuriated some South Koreans since he was considered responsible for the Cheonan sinking.

Negotiations between Seoul and Pyongyang continued after the games. On March 8 a representative of President Moon Jae-in arrived at the White House with a letter from Kim Jong Un to President Trump. Excited White House officials surprised the unprepared South Korean official by asking him to announce the letter to hastily assembled reporters. Kim wanted to have a summit meeting with Trump. The U.S. president, excited about the opportunity, began the long negotiations for the conditions of meeting. He was enthusiastic about the prospect of achieving a foreign policy triumph by establishing peace on the peninsula. Crowds of supporters cheered him on shouting "Nobel, Nobel," the prize he would surely receive. The negotiations were not smooth, as could be expected where the Korean conflict was concerned. In mid-May, the North cut off talks with South Korea, citing the joint military exercises between the ROK and the U.S., the perennial excuse for mischief. They also complained about U.S. national security advisor John Bolton's remarks about following the "Libyan model" of disarmament first and compensation later. But this was probably just a negotiating tactic as Kim Jong Un seemed at least as eager to hold the summit as Trump. Sitting down, one on one, with the U.S. president raised his stature as a great world leader and offered an opportunity to win major concessions.

Moon met with Kim Jong Un three times in 2018, in April, May, and September. On April 27 the two met at the Joint Security Area. Kim Jong Un symbolically stepped over the line that separated the two countries and entered the Republic of Korea. It was a matter of meters but it was still unprecedented. The two engaged in long discussions as the press viewed from afar. In the seventy-year history of the two Korean states, it was only the third summit conference. There were shockingly and dangerously few formal channels for dialogue between them. The two sides made all kinds of promising agreements. They pledged to work toward the denuclearization of the peninsula, convert the Korean Armistice Agreement into a fully-fledged peace treaty, end "hostile activities," cease propaganda broadcasts and allow family reunions. All this would mean the seven-decade conflict would be at an end. Further, it was agreed that Moon would visit the North.

The next inter-Korean summit took place only a month later. Moon was anxious to get the U.S.–DPRK summit back on track. On May 22 he visited President Trump in the U.S. Shortly after he returned to Korea, Moon met with Kim again in the JSA. This was not announced beforehand and focused on Kim Jong Un's upcoming meeting with the U.S. president. Each president was accompanied by his intelligence chief and Kim was accompanied by his sister Kim Yo Jong as well. It was held out of sight of journalists; Moon released details of the meeting only the next day. Before meeting with Trump, Kim went to China for the first time since he had come to power. It was the first known time he had left the country since coming to power over six years earlier. Arriving in Beijing on a specially outfitted luxury train he met with President Xi Jinping. Kim and Xi met a second time on May 7 in the Chinese port city of Dalian. China supported the summit and lent the North Korean leader an Air China plane, of the kind that the leadership in Beijing used. The Singapore summit between Kim and Trump was held on June 12. For Kim Jong Un who rarely traveled, this was an exciting opportunity to play the great world statesman. He seemed to relish the global headlines. In addition to his Air China plane, he was accompanied by a Koryo cargo plane carrying his favorite food. A third plane landed with his sister Kim Yo Jong aboard. Trump and Kim had a long meeting followed by a joint statement agreeing to security guarantees, new peaceful relations, the denuclearization of the Korean Peninsula, the return of soldiers' remains, and follow-up talks between officials. As a gift to Kim, Trump agreed to end the U.S.–ROK joint military exercise, a demand the North Koreans had been making for years. This last agreement seemed to have taken even Trump's close advisors by surprise.

Following the successful summit in Singapore, Moon Jae-in went to Pyongyang for his third summit in five months on September 18. Arriving at the Sunan International Airport he received an elaborate ceremonial welcome accompanied by the Central Military Band of the Korean People's Army. The two leaders rode in the same car together to the meeting place, waving to the crowds. The entire meeting was upbeat, South Korean media was invited along to record live all the public events. Interestingly their microphones picked up a private conversation between the two first ladies about watching their husbands' diets and health. It is unlikely the North Koreans would want any hint of worry about Kim Jong Un's obesity. The next day they signed the Pyongyang Joint Declaration of

September 2018 which called for an end to the conflict, cooperation in many areas, and denuclearization. The defense ministers of the two countries signed an agreement on non-aggression and measures to reduce military tensions. These included the removal of landmines, guard posts, weapons, and personnel from the Joint Security Area and the creation of joint military buffer zones. The DPRK agreed to dismantle its nuclear complex in the presence of international experts if the U.S. took correlative measures. The next day the two leaders took a trip to Baekdu Mountain, the sacred birthplace of the Korean nation. It made for great photo opportunities. It was announced Kim Jong Un would visit Seoul in December.

But like the one Kim Jong Il had promised, the visit to Seoul never took place. Instead, problems arose with the whole process. American newspapers reported that despite the pledges to the contrary, North Korea was continuing to make nuclear fuel and build weapons. Many in South Korea and the United States were skeptical about the value or likely success of the summits. Nonetheless, a second summit between President Trump and "Chairman" Kim as he was now referred to, took place in Hanoi on February 27 and 28. It ended early when no agreement was reached. North Korea pushed for the lifting of UN sanctions but offered only vague and unverifiable promises of a halt to its weapons program. Trump ended it early since Kim was unwilling to make a deal that would halt the missile program and prevent new nuclear tests.

The Situation Worsens

On June 30, 2019, Moon and Kim met again at the DMZ joined by President Trump. However, despite smiles little was accomplished and relations between the two Koreas and between the DPRK and the U.S. worsened. North Korea fired several short-range missiles and experimented with other new weapons. South Korea and the U.S. militaries carried out joint drills and Pyongyang responded angrily, calling them "grave provocations." Trump began to lose interest in this effort at a breakthrough with the North, and Moon ratcheted up military spending. As had so often happened in the past, the period of warmer relations was followed by the renewal of tensions and confrontations. On June 9, 2020, North Korea began cutting off communication lines with the South. Citing South Korea's failure to stop North Korean defectors from sending balloons, it blew up the joint North-South liaison office in Kaesong, a dramatic gesture punctuating another turn for the worse in relations. Moon did not abandon hopes of continuing the peace process. In December 2020, the ROK National Assembly passed a law to criminalize sending propaganda balloons. South Korea, in another gesture, dropped the term "enemy" to describe the DPRK in the military's white paper. But these gestures did little to alter the more hostile attitude coming from the North.

One reason the peace offensive of 2018 failed was that expectations on all sides were unrealistic. South Korea and the United States wanted North Korea to give up its nuclear weapons and stop developing delivery systems. Pyongyang had no intention of surrendering its biggest bargaining chip. Ever since the invasion of Iraq, the lesson for the North was clear, it needed nuclear weapons to protect itself from outside intervention. This was not just intervention by the U.S. but by a future hardline conservative government in Seoul bent on regime change, and perhaps by China. Nuclear weapons not only provided the regime with its security blanket, but they also provided the DPRK with an influence on events beyond what a small, impoverished state merited. And they served to impress its population. North Korea could no longer call itself a vanguard of economic progress, but it could demonstrate its ability to defend itself. It was highly unlikely that the regime would unilaterally disarm.

Pyongyang wanted, as it had for decades, to weaken the Seoul–Washington alliance and force the U.S. to withdraw from the South. More urgently, it wanted to ease the UN sanctions. Early resolutions by the UN Security Council prohibited the export of some military items and luxury goods to North Korea. Resolutions passed in 2009 and 2013 strengthened these by encouraging UN members to inspect ships and destroy any cargoes related to the nuclear program. In 2013, following North Korea's third nuclear test, sanctions were imposed on money transfers shutting the country out of the inter-

Military Build-Up 2017

+ Pyongyang

Injin Rive
Hwanggang Dam

United Nations drew
Northern Limit Line
NNL 1953

Haeju (port)
+

PANMUNJOM
1st tunne

KAESONG 37° 58' 0" N, 126° 33' 0" E   +
[Kaesong Industrial Region opened 2003]

3rd tunnel

X

X

X

X

X

Disputed Territory

North Korea-declared "Inter-Korean MOL" 1999 border

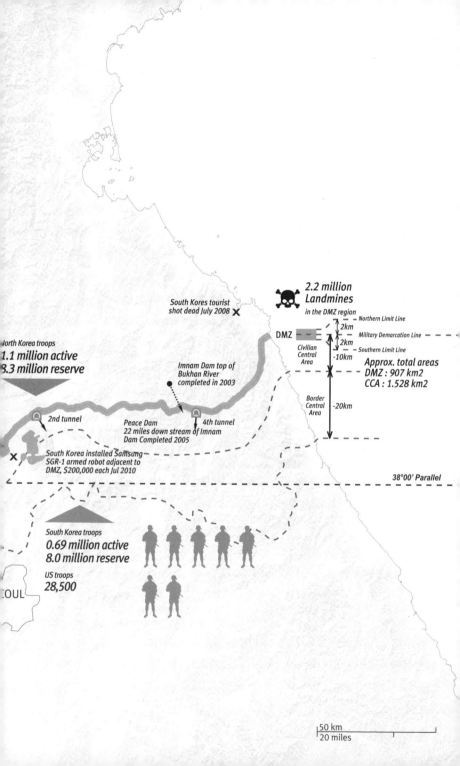

2.2 million Landmines
in the DMZ region

South Kores tourist shot dead July 2008 ✗

North Korea troops
1.1 million active
3.3 million reserve

Imnam Dam top of Bukhan River completed in 2003

Peace Dam
22 miles down stream of Imnam Dam Completed 2005

2nd tunnel

4th tunnel

✗

South Korea installed Samsung SGR-1 armed robot adjacent to DMZ, $200,000 each Jul 2010

DMZ

Civilian Central Area

Border Central Area

Northern Limit Line
2km
Military Demarcation Line
2km
Southern Limit Line
-10km

Approx. total areas
DMZ : 907 km2
CCA : 1.528 km2

-20km

38°00' Parallel

South Korea troops
0.69 million active
8.0 million reserve

US troops
28,500

OUL

50 km
20 miles

national financial system. Particularly painful was a resolution in 2016 banning all exports of gold, vanadium, titanium, and rare earth and severely restricting exports of coal and iron. Then when in 2017 North Korea defiantly tested another nuclear weapon the UN banned all exports of coal, iron, and seafood; its three largest exports. North Korea could export virtually nothing legally. Although China did not fully enforce the bans and Pyongyang found ways to transfer items to third-party ships, the sanctions were hindering the country's efforts to improve its economy. Even the elite was being affected by them. But the South Koreans and Americans wanted to see some concrete steps before recommending the sanctions be lifted, not the deceptive, cosmetic ones Pyongyang offered.

Instead of peace, what transpired was a heated-up arms race. Moon increased defense expenditure. The annual increase of 7 percent was more than the 4 percent of his two conservative predecessors. He sought to develop South Korea's arms program. In April 2021 South Korea's first supersonic fighter jet, the KF-21, took to the air. The country's old ambition to develop its own missiles had been long blocked by the U.S. In 2012 it partially lifted its restriction and in 2017 it gave a green light to further development. The Biden administration in 2021 further lifted restrictions. As a result, in 2021 the ROK unveiled the Hyunmoo-4 missile with a 500-mile (800 km) range and the capacity to carry a two-ton payload. It was intended to deliver bunker-busting bombs that could destroy the North's underground defense facilities. What it could not make it purchased, such as American stealth bombers. The North continued with its own weapons development. It developed solid-fuel short-range missiles that were easier to load, more accurate, and more maneuverable than its old Scud and Rodong missiles. In 2021 it tested one that could carry a 2½ ton payload. Its new missiles were aimed at the South, some flying low enough to evade radar. It developed mobile rocket launchers and tested a submarine-launched missile. In January 2021 Kim Jong Un announced his military was working on a solid-state intercontinental ballistic missile that would not take hours to fuel and would be more difficult to destroy. This was aimed at the U.S. Another development was worrisome to South Koreans.

Trump and his supporters, while no longer in office had quarreled with Seoul over the cost of stationing troops and made it clear they were less interested in defending South Korea. While the abandonment of the ROK was not a widely shared view in America, South Korean officials wondered if the U.S. would be as likely to intervene if it were directly threatened by a North Korean nuclear attack.

Kim Yo Jong

Kim Jong Un's obesity, his noticeable shortness of breath, and his occasional disappearances (for health reasons) led to speculation as to who would succeed him. One candidate was his younger sister Kim Yo Jong. So secret is North Korea that it is not entirely certain when she was born; most reports are on September 26, 1987, and some believe she was born two years later. Kim Yo Jong was the youngest child of Kim Jong Il and his consort Ko Yong Hee. She spent most of her childhood at her mother's residence in Pyongyang along with her siblings. Between 1996 and 2000 she studied alongside her older brother Kim Jong Un at Liebefeld-Steinhölzli school in Bern, Switzerland, under the assumed name of Pak Mihyang. It was during this time that the two are believed to have forged close bonds. Returning to the DPRK, she completed secondary school and received a degree in computer science from Kim Il Sung University. After graduation, she worked with her father on the campaign to promote Kim Jong Un as his successor and at the National Defense Commission.

She made an early public appearance at her father's funeral when she was seen along with Kim Jong Un. However, the first public mention of her was three years later in 2014 when she appeared in state media accompanying her brother; even then she was identified simply as a "senior official of the Korean Workers Party." Behind the scenes, she worked in the same Propaganda and Agitation Department that her father had as a young man. There she directed the efforts to exalt her brother, much as Kim Jong Il had done to promote the cult of his father Kim Il Sung. In 2017 she was made an alternative member of the Politburo, the first woman since Pak Jeongae, decades earlier. Kim Yo Jong came to the world's attention when in February 2018 she headed the North Korean delegation to the Pyeongchang Winter Olympics, the first member of the "royal Kim" family to visit South Korea.

Young and educated abroad, many observers saw in her the promise for a new generation of North Koreans willing to engage with the South and move past the animosity between the two Koreas. Kim Yo Jong married Choe Song, a son of the leader Choe Ryong Hae who, in turn, was the son of one of Kim Il Sung's close Manchurian guerilla comrades, Choe Hyeon. Thus the couple represents the third generation of the North Korean leadership. That she was emerging as the de facto number two in the regime made this an especially hopeful prospect. However, in 2020, when the seesawing North-South relations were tilted in a hostile direction again, she launched vitriolic attacks on the South. In June she ordered the destruction of the Liaison Office in Kaesong. Could she be the next great leader? Her gender might work against that. Yet some thought Kim Jong Un's age would prevent him from being an effective leader, and they were wrong.

Korea at War 2022—China

One fundamental change in the Korean conflict after 2000 was the role of China. The PRC was in an unusual position. By 2005 it had become South Korea's as well as North Korea's largest trading partner. Most South Koreans initially greeted the rise of China as a great economic power positively. Bilateral trade boomed, passing the $200 billion mark by 2012. Unlike most of China's trading partners, the ROK maintained a favorable balance of trade. Many South Korean firms moved production to China with its lower labor costs. South Korean companies were the biggest foreign investors in nearby Shandong Province. By the 2010s several million Chinese tourists a year were going to resorts, shopping, and spending freely. China was a major market for South Korean movies, TV dramas, and pop videos which were all very popular. But there were some disturbing signs. The People's Republic of China too had a third generation of leaders who were not afraid to assert China's power in the region as well as globally.

In 2013 Xi Jinping, China's new authoritarian leader declared an air defense identification zone that required all planes flying over a large area of the sea to identify themselves, a move that was in violation of international law and was ignored by Seoul. Still, relations were friendly; in 2014 Xi visited the ROK the first Chinese leader to do so. However, in July 2016, American and South Korean military officials agreed to deploy Terminal High Altitude Area Defense (THAAD) missiles in the country. THAAD missiles were developed during the Gulf War to protect against Iraq's Scud missiles. They were intended to protect the ROK from North Korean missiles, but Beijing claimed they were to be deployed to track missiles from China and warned South Korea against installing them. When, in 2017, Seoul decided to go ahead with the deployment in the wake of the North Korean missile tests, China retaliated by banning tour groups from entering the country as well as placing restrictions on South Korean businesses such as the Lotte Department Store chain in operating in its country. Tensions eased later, but as relations between China and the U.S. deteriorated, it added a complication to Seoul's geopolitical strategy. It needed the alliance with the U.S., but not only did it need China's trade, it also needed China's influence to restrain the North.

North Korea was far more dependent on China, its only significant trading partner. By 2010 over 80 percent of its foreign trade was with China or went through it. That number rose closer to 90 percent by 2020. China was the main purchaser of its biggest exports: coal, iron, and seafood. Additionally, the UN sanctions with their ability to stop and search North Korean vessels meant that it was almost totally reliant on the cross-border trade to get items in and out. China at any point could easily paralyze the economy. Thus, the DPRK found itself in a position of dependency that it had worked so hard to avoid. Its survival now was based on China's willingness to put up with the regime. For China, as troublesome as North Korea was, it still did not put too much pressure on the DPRK, fearing its collapse would bring chaos and refugees across its border. Furthermore, at the time of the Korean War, North Korea was a useful buffer between the U.S.-led Pacific alliance partners. Another factor may have been the embarrassment of having a long-time ally fall—especially if it led to a pro-Western democratic society, which could influence the Chinese people. Therefore, China still had reasons to support North Korea. The leaders in Pyongyang, of course, were aware of this.

Still, the rise of China was a threat to both Koreas since it endangered the project of creating a unified, autonomous Korean nation that both shared. A warning sign appeared in China's history projects. China created the Northeast Borderlands and Chain of Events Research Project called the Northeast Project for short, whose task was to investigate the ancient history of the border regions. What was "found" was deeply disturbing to all Koreans. The main purpose was to rewrite history to show that the Manchurian region was not, as most historians had found, a frontier area not part of China until the seventeenth century, but a region that had always been culturally or politically part of a greater China. What was so troubling was it claimed the ancient Koguryo kingdom that ruled southern Manchuria and all of what is now North Korea until the seventh century, was somehow a Chinese state. Not only was this offensive to the people of the peninsula who regarded Koguryo as a Korean state (the name Korea is derived from it) but it implied that what is now North Korea was originally part of China. This lent support to South Koreans who were concerned that North Korea would become the "fourth province" of Manchuria. It troubled other South Koreans who feared that half their nation could be absorbed by China someday as part of its policy to tighten control over its periphery, just as it was doing with Hong Kong, Tibet, disputed territories with India, and the South China Sea islands. The same worries most probably haunted Pyongyang.

Rethinking Reunification

China's rise and greater assertiveness was a new development in the Korean conflict. Another was the change in South Korean attitudes toward unification. For decades most were passionate about reunification. They viewed division as an enduring tragedy that had to somehow be overcome. But enthusiasm for reunification began to wane especially among younger people. A significant influence was the reunification of Germany in 1990. The collapse of East Germany and its absorption into West Germany happened unexpectedly and swiftly. At first, this rekindled hope that North Korea too could be absorbed and that it could happen as suddenly and unexpectedly. But as the problems and cost of German reunification became apparent, it caused South Koreans to pause. If a very rich country like West Germany had problems, so too could South Korea. The growing gap in income and the widening gap in culture and lifestyles between the two societies made the process and costs of absorbing the North and its 25 million people even more daunting. Whereas East Germany's per capita income was more than one-third that of West Germany at the time of reunification, it was estimated that North Korea had only one-fifteenth to one-twentieth of the GDP per capita of the South in 2020. In 2014, North Korea's total foreign trade was $10 billion versus South Korea's $1.1 trillion. The total power generation of the DPRK was only one percent of that of the ROK. This shocking disparity would be enormously costly to overcome. Some estimates were that the cost of integrating the two Koreas and bringing the infrastructure of the North up to the levels of the South would cost, at a minimum, $1 trillion. A staggering amount even for a prosperous South, and other estimates were much higher.

But this was not the only problem, and perhaps not the greatest one. In the twenty-first century, the areas of the former East Germany were characterized by high unemployment and political unrest, and many extremist groups found fertile ground there. Cultural integration was not always easy. The cultural gap between North and South Korea was far greater. How could South Korea absorb all the people who had lived so long in isolation and lacked the skills of a modern high-tech society? All this meant the task of integrating the two Koreas would be a formidable one.

Changing attitudes toward reunification in South Korea were, in part, a generational development. Many older Koreans had relatives in the North, so reunification of the country was also reunification of their family. But as these older Koreans died younger Koreans, those of the third generation or the fourth, did not have and did not feel these ties. Younger Koreans in the twenty-first century, while still regarding Korea as one nation and regarding unity as an ideal, were less passionately attached to the idea. South Korea was for them, not just a temporary state, a half-nation waiting for its completion, but their home. They didn't call themselves South Koreans but just *han'guksaram* (Korean) but in a way South Korea was Korea. North Korea was a strange other place, the people there were different, backward, pathetic, and a bit alien. They were more comfortable living with the Korea they knew and saw reunification as a distant, and not an especially urgent goal.

Kaesong Industrial Region

Just how difficult cooperation between the two Koreas is can be illustrated by the Kaesong Industrial Region. Following the modest thaw in relations between the two Koreas that began with Kim Dae Jung's summit meeting with Kim Jong Il in 2000, measures were taken to establish trade and contact between the two sides. Perhaps the most ambitious was the opening of the Kaesong Industrial Region. This was to be a special economic zone, a few miles above the DMZ where South Korean firms would build factories and employ North Korean laborers. Southern businesses would get cheap, Korean-speaking labor and the North would receive a precious foreign exchange. Perhaps most importantly, from Seoul's viewpoint, it would be one step toward establishing economic ties that would bind the two countries together and replace the conflict with cooperation.

The special administrative region was formed in 2002. Construction started the next year. Hyundai Asan, the South Korean construction company, was hired by North Korea to build it. The industrial park opened in December of 2004. Fifteen South Korean companies began to build facilities, the first three opening in March 2005. The original plan was that it would expand into a sprawling

85 square kilometer complex, the size of Manhattan, that would employ over half a million people and include residences, shopping centers, and even a theme park. It might even be a tourist destination.

Run by a committee of South Koreans who had a 50-year lease, it was initially successful but fell short of its full expectations. Eventually, it had 124 South Korean firms employing about 54,000 North Korean workers, impressive enough but far short of the hopes of its planners. Most of the factories were labor-intensive, low-skilled operations of the type that were being offshored to China and Southeast Asia, such as textile and electronic assembly plants. There were many obstacles. These included U.S. economic sanctions that prohibited exports of many items that had North Korean components. Quarrels over wages were another. North Korean workers were paid only a fifth of what their Southern counterparts, made, yet these were very high by local standards. A large chunk was taken by the North Korean government but there was still enough left over to make it a desirable place to work. North Korea pressured the companies to pay more, so it could collect more not to benefit the workers, however, there was a point where manufacturing was no longer profitable.

North Korea began to use the Kaesong Industrial Region as a bargaining chip in relations. In April 2013, at a time when tensions between the Koreas rose, it began to deny South Koreans access to it and that May it was shut down. It reopened in September. But in 2016, South Korea cut off electricity and closed it in protest at North Korean missile tests. It was not reopened. Later a Korean Liaison Office was opened at the site, but on June 16, 2020, this was destroyed by Pyongyang in protest over North Korean refugees in South Korea sending balloons with illegal videos and propaganda to the North. There was talk of reopening the site, its promise of helping with the economic integration of Korea, and making the DPRK a little less dependent on China made it still seem worth pursuing to some in Seoul. Yet in 2022 it remained abandoned. Rather than a symbol and instrument of cooperation and integration, the Kaesong Industrial Region became another sad episode of dashed hopes in Korea's endless conflict.

North Koreans in South Korea

South Korean defectors to North Korea were rare but thousands of North Koreans fled to South Korea. Crossing the open, highly fortified DMZ was almost suicidal, although between 1953 and 2020 twenty people did so and survived, despite some injuries from North Korean gunfire. A few diplomats and officials traveling abroad defected, but the great majority of defectors or refugees crossed the Yalu or Tumen Rivers and entered China. The number was very small until the famine of the 1990s when several hundred thousand North Koreas left for China to find work, food, and sell items. Most of them returned but about 200,000 stayed in China, sometimes getting caught and sent back. North Korean refugees in China often became the victims of exploitation, including sexual workers and women forced into marriages with Chinese men. Many intended to return as soon as they had acquired enough money, but some left China hoping to get to South Korea. It was a precarious existence since, if caught by Chinese police, they would be sent back to North Korea and suffer imprisonment and sometimes execution. Defecting to the South Korean embassy or one of its heavily guarded consulates was risky so most went to Mongolia or Thailand via Laos. Once there, they could ask for asylum and be flown to South Korea.

In 1962, South Korea issued a law in which defectors were to be given an aid package and a government allowance. Additional rewards payable in gold were given to defectors who provided valuable information. Defectors were often given apartments and, if they wanted an education, could enter the university of their choice. Military people who defected could join the ROK military at the same rank. They became, almost automatically, ROK citizens. The numbers were small. But with the famine, they began to increase. A record 800 came in 1998 and then 3,000 by 2009. As the numbers grew, the aid package became less generous and the process of integrating them, more elaborate. After initial interrogation to determine if they were actual refugees and not spies, they were sent to Hanawon, a government resettlement center in the countryside south of Seoul. At Hanawon they received a 12-week crash course on living in South Korea. They learned the political system, information on finding employment, and such basic skills as how to drive a car, use a computer and open a bank account. They received some assistance afterward in housing, health insurance, and finding jobs. North Korean workers did not always have the proper skills for the workforce and employers were reluctant to hire them, so the government gave businesses financial incentives to do so.

By 2020 there were over 30,000 North Koreans living in the South and their experience suggested many problems for integration. Besides lacking skills, they had trouble adjusting to South Korea's highly competitive society and were not used to having to make so many individual decisions. They also faced prejudice. South Koreans saw them as "backward," lacking initiative, and poor workers. Most sought to lose their accents to avoid discrimination. Landlords did not want to rent to them fearing they might be spies or the victims of North Korean agents. The latter fear was the result of several isolated incidents of DPRK agents murdering defectors. Their smaller stature, the result of malnutrition, and general lack of sophistication added to their sense of being inferior. And, of course, many were suffering from trauma which the South Korean government was slow to treat through its national health system. Some refugees became so miserable and so worried about family members left behind that they returned to the North. Some paid agents to try and bring out family members. This was often successful but left them in debt. All this boded ill for the prospect of integrating the two peoples. If South Korea had so much trouble with just a small number of North Koreans who have settled there, what would it do with the possible millions that might come if North Korea were to collapse? This prospect gave officials nightmares.

Most of the defectors, two-thirds, were women. It was easier for women to cross into China, and they had less to lose than men. They were seeking a better life and were more economic than political refugees. But some refugees who were more politically motivated formed small defector groups that sought to bring down the northern regimes in various ways. One was to send balloons over to the North with treats and with South Korean dramas and movies as well as propaganda. These balloons infuriated Pyongyang suggesting they were not totally ineffective. After 1945, thousands fled the North where they formed an influential anti-communist element in the army, government, and society of South Korea. The refugees who started coming in the 1990s were a smaller group, and they were far less influential but still, the more politically active refugees from the DPRK performed a similar function of aggravating tensions between the two Koreas.

Park Yeonmi

For many in the outside world, Park Yeonmi became the face of North Korea's refugees. Park was born in Hyesan, a city on the Yalu River, across from China. It was so close to the border that she recalls as a child shouting to Chinese children on the other side of the river. It was hard to keep people in such a place within the information cordon that seals them off from all but government-filtered knowledge of the outside world. Many locals, including her father, engaged in smuggling. When her father was imprisoned and her family was facing starvation, her mother went to China to seek work. The 14-year-old Park Yeonmi followed her. There, both became victims of human traffickers. Her mother was sold to a local farmer unable to find a wife, a common problem among Chinese farmers. Yeonmi, among other jobs, worked in a brothel.

Eventually, after some horrific experiences, Park was able to escape first to Mongolia and then to South Korea. Her arrival in South Korea in 2009 was like entering another world, modern, rich, and highly competitive. Many North Koreans have found the adjustment overwhelmingly difficult. They also find themselves the victims of discrimination among South Koreas who regard their northern cousins as backward, their manners crude. But Park Yeonmi, still a teen was able to adapt and flourish.

She appeared on a South Korean TV program that tried to humanize North Korean refugees, showing them singing and talking, acting as ordinary and charming people. She left for the U.S. in 2014. The same year she delivered a speech at the One Young World summit in Dublin, an annual meeting that draws young people from around the world to discuss global problems. Her speech was widely viewed on Youtube. The following year she published a memoir titled *In Order to Live*, which was an international best-seller. Park Yeonmi worked to raise awareness of North Korean refugees and to encourage sympathy and concern for the suffering North Korean people. This was important work, since the North Korean people had few English speakers or well-known representatives, and their plight was generally not taken up as a cause by Hollywood or international celebrities. While she helped fill that role, it is not clear how much impact she had on overcoming South Korean prejudices or bridging the gap between the two Koreas.

Conclusion: Is there an End to the Endless War?

On March 9, 2022, South Korea carried out a presidential election. Yoon Suk-yeol of the conservative People's Power Party narrowly defeated the liberal Democratic Party candidate, Lee Jae-myung. Lee had promised to continue President Moon Jae-in's foreign policy based on finding ways of reaching a rapprochement with North Korea. Yoon regarded Moon's efforts as a failure and took a hard-line stance toward the North, promising to work more closely with the United States and Japan as well as other democratic countries to counter the threat of North Korea and its patron, China. Upon being elected he referred to North Korea as "the main enemy" and announced plans for a "three-axis defense system" that included preemptively striking down any North Korean missiles, an establishment of a locally-made Korea Air and Missile Defense System, and a "Korea Massive Punishment and Retaliation" capacity that would target the DPRK's leadership in a preemptive decapitation strike. These were some of the harshest anti-North measures by a South Korean leader in decades. Although Yoon did not advocate nuclear ambitions, a public opinion poll found a record high of seventy percent in support of such a move. Meanwhile, in the very week of the election, North Korea was busy testing new missiles and planning for the launch of a reconnaissance satellite. Rumors were also spreading that Kim Jong Un was planning to test another nuclear bomb and an ICBM.

It was clear in the spring of 2022 that the war on the Korean Peninsula, waged for three-quarters of a century, had not ended and prospects that it would anytime soon seemed bleak. How could the war end? North Korea had painted itself into a corner. It needed to economically develop, but it could not do so without opening up and exposing its people to the outside world. Conversely, it could not open up its country to the world without the regime being undermined and the political system it had built unraveling or crashing down. It needed peace but the regime required tension, confrontation, and brinkmanship to maintain the lies that justified the hardships its people suffered and kept the elite in power. Out of weakness, the regime in Pyongyang continued to build an ever more destructive set of weapons that made the consequences of full-scale war unimaginably horrific. South Korea had no solution to deal with this, and neither did the United States, China, or the wider international community. Reform seemed unlikely, perhaps impossible, for the North Korean regime, and military intervention was far too dangerous to contemplate. There was the alternative of putting on enough economic pressure to cause the undermining of the DPRK regime. The prospect of the regime's collapse, however, was also a potential nightmare with the possibility of nuclear war and millions of refugees pouring into China, and overwhelming South Korea. So, the conflict continued with everyone in Seoul, Washington, Beijing, Tokyo, Moscow, and elsewhere hoping for some kind of change in the situation, although no one seemed to know what kind of change was possible.

Korea's endless war originated with competing visions of a modern Korean nation during the struggle to regain independence. From 1948 it was war between the two halves of that nation that formed these competing visions. For decades, the two Koreas, the ROK and the DPRK, each sought to create a unified nation under their own political and economic systems. They competed in economic and social modernization like two athletes seeking the gold medal for successful development; they competed militarily, diplomatically, and sometimes violently. And they dragged the great powers, who were partly to blame for it, into their conflict.

During the three generations it was waged, the conflict gradually evolved from one between equals to one between a dynamic, economically powerful South and a weak, inward-looking North. While reunification remained aspirational for both, the more immediate goal for the North became survival. For the South it became finding a way to deal with a dangerous neighbor that could start a holocaust on the peninsula out of desperation or miscalculation or that could become the world's first nuclear-armed failed state.

Korea's war with itself was a conflict unlike any other in modern history. Not just that it was the longest between two sovereign states, not just because of its ability to draw the involvement of all the major powers, not just because it was the only major conflict between a people that were so ethnically and historically united, but because of how it contributed to the creation of two of the world's most unusual countries. North Korea had become the world's most isolated, totalitarian, and weirdest anomaly, a strange cultlike society that was capable of menacing the world with nuclear weapons and intercontinental ballistic missiles while being incapable of meeting the most basic needs of its people. South Korea in two generations had gone from among the world's poorest, least promising countries, one that had often been written off by most foreign experts as a near hopeless case into a wealthy, technologically advanced, democratic society, and a global center of pop culture all while constantly facing the threat of catastrophic war with its neighbor.

Yet the strange trajectories of the two halves of the Korean nation held out hope. The Korean conflict and the Koreans themselves had evolved in unpredictable ways, ways that few in the past had foreseen. Perhaps the war between the Koreans could end in an unforeseen way as well: a peaceful way.

Bibliography

There is a large number of books on the Korean War in English, most of which focus on the role of the American forces. This bibliography includes several of these but also includes works that provide a broader understanding of the generations-long conflict on the Korean Peninsula. All have provided information and insights that have been incorporated into this book and are recommended for further reading on the subject.

Armstrong, Charles K. *The North Korean Revolution, 1945–1950.* Ithaca, NY: Cornell University Press, 2003.

Brazinsky, Gregg. *Nation Building in South Korea: Koreans, Americans, and the Making of Democracy.* Chapel Hill: University of North Carolina Press, 2007.

Buzo, Adrian. *The Politics and Leadership in North Korea: Guerilla Dynasty.* London: Routledge, 2017.

Chae, Grace J. "The Korean War and its Politics" in Michael J. Seth, editor, *The Routledge Handbook of Modern Korean History.* London: Routledge, 2016.

Cumings, Bruce. *Korea's Place in the Sun: A Modern History.* Updated edition. New York: W.W. Norton and Company, 2005.

_____. *The Korean War: A History.* New York: Modern Library, 2011.

_____. *The Origins of the Korean War.* Vol. 1, *Liberation and the Emergence of Separate Regimes, 1945–1947.* Princeton, NJ: Princeton University Press, 1981.

_____. *The Origins of the Korean War.* Vol. 2, *The Roaring of the Cataract, 1947–1950.* Princeton, NJ: Princeton University Press, 1990.

Duus, Peter. *The Abacus and the Sword: The Japanese Penetration of Korea, 1895–1910.* Berkeley: University of California Press, 1998.

Eckert, Carter. *Park Chung Hee and Modern Korea: The Roots of Militarism, 1866–1945.* Cambridge. MA: Harvard University Press, 2016.

Hanley, Charles J. *Ghost Flames: Life and Death in a Hidden War, Korea 1950–1953.* New York: Hachette, 2020.

Heo, Uk, and Terrence Roehig. *South Korea's Rise: Economic Development, Power and Foreign Relations.* Cambridge, UK: Cambridge University Press, 2014.

Hwang, Kyung Moon. *A History of Korea.* New York: Palgrave Macmillan, 2010.

Jaeger, Sheila Miyoshi. *Brothers at War: The Unending Conflict in Korea.* New York: W.W. Norton, 2013.

Kang, Chol-Hwan. *The Aquariums of Pyongyang: Ten Years in the North Korean Gulag.* Yair Reiner, trans. New York: Basic Books, 2001.

Kim, Alexander Joungwon. *Divided Korea: The Politics of Development 1945–1972.* Cambridge, MA: East Asian Research Center, Harvard University Press, 1975.

Kim, Byung-Kook, Ezra Vogel, and Jorge I. Dominguez, eds. *The Park Chung Hee Era: The Transformation of South Korea.*

Cambridge, MA: Harvard University Press, 2011.

Kim, Hun Joon. *The Massacres at Mt Halla: Sixty Years of Truth Seeking in South Korea.* Ithaca, NY: Cornell University Press, 2014.

Kim, Key-hiuk. *The Last Phase of the East Asian World Order: Korea, Japan, and the Chinese Empire, 1860–1882.* Berkeley: University of California Press, 1980.

Kim Ku. *Paekpom Ilgi: The Autobiography of Kim Ku.* Jongsoo Lee, translator, and annotator. Lamham, MD: University Press of America, 2000.

Kim, Richard. *Lost Names: Scenes from a Korean Boyhood.* New York: Praeger, 1970.

Lankov, Andrei. *The Real North Korea: Life and Politics in the Failed Stalinist Utopia.* Oxford: Oxford University Press, 2013.

Larsen, Kirk W. *Tradition. Treaties, and Trade: Qing Imperialism and Chosŏn Korea, 1850–1910.* Cambridge, MA: Harvard University Press, 2008.

Lee, Chung-shik. *Park Chung-Hee: From Poverty to Power.* Palos Verdes, CA: KHU Press, 2012.

Lee, Helie. *Still Life with Rice.* New York: Scribner, 1996.

Lee, Injae, Owen Miller, Jinhoon Park, Yi Hyun-Hae and Michael D. Shin, eds. *Korean History in Maps: From Prehistory to the Twenty-first Century.* Cambridge, UK: Cambridge University Press, 2014.

Lie, John. *Han Unbound: The Political Economy of South Korea.* Stanford, CA: Stanford University Press, 1998.

McKenzie, Frederick Arthur. *Korea's Fight for Freedom.* Kansas City, MO: Revell Co., 1920.

Millett, Allan R. *The War for Korea, 1945–1950: A House Burning.* Lawrence: University of Kansas Press, 2005.

———. *The War for Korea, 1950–1951: They Came from the North.* Lawrence: University of Kansas Press, 2021.

Myers, Brian. *The Cleanest Race: How North Koreans See Themselves—And Why It Matters.* Brooklyn, NY: Melville House, 2010.

Oberdorfer, Don, and Robert Carlin. *The Two Koreas: A Contemporary History.* Third Edition. New York: Basic Books, 2014.

Park, Yeomi. *In Order to Live.* New York: Penguin, 2015.

Palmer, Brandon. *Fighting for the Enemy: Korean in Japan's War, 1937–1945.* Seattle: University of Washington Press, 2013.

Peters, Richard, and Xiaobing Li. *Voices of the Korean War.* Lexington: University of Kentucky Press, 2004.

Robinson, Michael E. *Cultural Nationalism in Colonial Korea, 1920–1925.* Seattle: University of Washington Press, 1988.

Schmid, Andre. *Korea Between Empires, 1895–1919.* New York: Columbia University Press, 2002.

Shin, Gi-Wook. *Ethnic Nationalism in Korea: Genealogy, Politics, and Legacy.* Stanford, CA: Stanford University Press, 2006.

Snyder, Scott. *South Korea at a Crossroads: Autonomy and Alliance in an Era of Rival Alliances.* New York: Columbia University Press, 2020.

Soh, C. Sarah. *The Comfort Women: Sexual Violence and Postcolonial Memory in Korea and Japan.* Chicago: University of Chicago Press, 2008.

Suh, Dae-sook. *Kim Il Sung: A Biography.* Honolulu: University of Hawaii Press, 1989.

Suh, Jae-Jung, ed. *Truth and Reconciliation in South Korea: Between the Present and Future of the Korean Wars.* London: Routledge, 2014.

Tudor, Daniel. *Korea, the Impossible Country: South Korea's Amazing Rise from the Ashes.* Rutland. VT: Tuttle, 2018.

Tudor, Daniel, and James Pearson. *North Korea Confidential: Private Markets, Fashion Trends, Prison Camps, Dissenters, and Defectors.* Rutland, VT: Tuttle, 2015.

Wada Haruki. *The Korean War: An International History.* Lanham, MD: Rowman & Littlefield, 2014.

Zhang, Shu Guang. *Mao's Military Romanticism: China and the Korean War, 1950–1953.* Lawrence: University of Kansas Press, 1995.

Index